DATE DUE

DEMCO 38-296

EUROPEAN HISTORICAL DICTIONARIES
Edited by Jon Woronoff

Historical Dictionary of Iceland

Guðmundur Hálfdanarson

European Historical Dictionaries, No. 24

The Scarecrow Press, Inc.
Lanham, Md., & London
1997

SCARECROW PRESS, INC.

Published in the United States of America
by Scarecrow Press, Inc.
4720 Boston Way
Lanham, Maryland 20706

4 Pleydell Gardens, Folkestone
Kent CT20 2DN, England

British Library Cataloguing in Publication Information Available

Library of Congress Cataloging-in-Publication Data

Guðmundur Hálfdanarson, 1956–
    Historical dictionary of Iceland / Guðmundur Hálfdanarson.
        p.   cm. — (European historical dictionaries ; no. 24)
    Includes bibliographical references.
    ISBN 0-8108-3352-2 (alk. paper)
    1. Iceland—History—Dictionaries. I. Title. II. Series.
    DL338.G82   1997
    949.12'003—dc21   97-12399

ISBN 0–8108–3352–2 (cloth : alk. paper)

CONTENTS

EDITOR'S FOREWORD

Iceland bears little resemblance to its fellow European countries: its unique geographic features, physical remoteness, and sparse population set this young nation-state apart. Yet, its political system, economic structure, and social concerns show only slight variations from those of the mainland countries. Iceland has perhaps the greatest communality with Scandinavia, having been discovered and populated by Norwegians and then ruled by Danes. Its language, literature, and culture have also been shaped by this heritage.

Iceland remains somewhat of a European anomaly. Its movement toward European unity and integration has been slow. This may explain why it is hardly familiar to many Europeans and even less known further afield. It is a beautiful and intriguing country whose people have repeatedly had to adjust to difficult circumstances and yet created a successful nation. This book shows how the country was formed, how it evolved, and what it is at present. Entries on significant persons, past and present, explain what the Icelanders are like, and others on institutions and events show how they have organized and acted. Those relating to literature and culture reveal a bit of their collective nature. Historical trends are succinctly summed up in a chronology. The bibliography makes many suggestions for further research.

The author of this book, Guðmundur Hálfdanarson, was born, grew up, and studied in Iceland. He teaches at the Department of History of the University of Iceland and was the director of its Institute of History for two years. He has also lived, studied, and lectured abroad. That is why he has developed a talent for explaining this very special country to outsiders. Both aspects, inside knowledge and the ability to convey it, are essential in producing a useful guide. This *Historical Dictionary of Iceland* will doubtlessly serve that purpose for numerous readers.

Jon Woronoff
Series Editor

v

ACKNOWLEDGMENTS

A book like this is, by the nature of things, a collective effort, although its author bears all responsibility for the final outcome. Thus, a number of colleagues and fellow historians have assisted me in the writing of the dictionary, and I want to express my gratitude for their support. Dr. Guðmundur Jónsson wrote, for example, the first version of 26 entries on economic history in the dictionary, all of which are marked with his initials (G. J.). Anna Agnarsdóttir, Gísli Gunnarsson, Gunnar Karlsson, Ingi Sigurðsson, and Þór Whitehead, colleagues of mine at the Department of History at the University of Iceland, and Dr. Már Jónsson read over entries pertaining to their respective fields of expertise, giving informed and friendly advice and correcting my mistakes when necessary. My students Ragnheiður Kristjánsdóttir and Haraldur Dean Nelson assisted in the making of the bibliography and on the collection of information for some of the most difficult entries. Various historical and biographical dictionaries have been an invaluable source of information, and Einar Laxness's *Íslandssaga a–ö* (1995) and Páll E. Ólason's *Íslenzkar æviskrár* (1948 –76) in particular. Finally, I would like to thank the Icelandic Science Council, the Student's Innovation Fund, and Science Fund of the University of Iceland for their financial support of this project.

NOTE ON THE ICELANDIC LANGUAGE

This dictionary uses the Icelandic alphabet consistently for all Icelandic words. The main deviations from the English alphabet are threefold:

1) A diacritical mark (´) over a vowel indicates a change in pronunciation. The vowel *a* is, for example, usually pronounced either as a short *a* in English (as in *act*) or as a long *a* (as in *father*), while the normal pronunciation of *á* is close to *ow* in *now* or *ou* in *mouse*.

2) Like Danish, Icelandic uses the diphthong symbol *æ*, but unlike Danish it is pronounced similar to the English *i* in the words *ice* and *bite*. Like German and Swedish, Icelandic uses also the letter *ö*, which in Icelandic is pronounced as the English sound *i* in *fir* or *e* in *her*.

3) In addition, Icelandic uses one letter that is no longer found in any other Latin-based alphabet, that is, the letter *þ* (*Þ*), and another one that is only found in Faroese, that is, the letter *ð* (*Ð*). These two letters correspond to the two *th* sounds in English; *ð* is pronounced as *th* in the word *this* (voiced) and *þ* as the *th* in *thin* (unvoiced).

Following Icelandic custom, the letter *þ* is arranged after the letter *z* in the alphabetical order in this dictionary, while the letters *æ* and *ö* are arranged as *ae* and *o* respectively (this is contrary to the normal Icelandic practice where these two letters follow the *þ* to conclude the alphabet). Moreover, this dictionary does neither distinguish between vowels with and without diacritical marks, nor between *ð* and *d* when words are arranged in alphabetical order.

Finally, it should be noted that Icelandic retains the old Germanic custom of using patronymics, but family names are rare. This means that a child carries the first name of his or her father in genitive as his or her last name, with the addition of *dóttir* (daughter) or *son* (son) depending on the gender of the child. Thus the daughter of Jón is Jónsdóttir while his son would be Jónsson. In accordance with this system, first names—or the given names—are of much greater importance than surnames in Iceland, and people are, therefore, never called by their last names only. For this reason, Icelanders arrange persons by their first names in telephone directories, library catalogues, and other such directories. To avoid unnecessary confusion, however, this dictionary uses the English practice of listing people in alphabetical order by their last names.

ACRONYMS AND ABBREVIATIONS

ASÍ   Alþýðusamband Íslands (Icelandic Federation of Labor, *see* IFL)

CBI   Central Bank of Iceland (Seðlabanki Íslands)
CIE   Confederation of Icelandic Employers (Vinnuveitendasamband Ísland, *see* VSÍ)
CP   Conservative Party (Íhaldsflokkurinn)
CPI   Communist Party of Iceland (Kommúnistaflokkur Íslands)

DV   *Dagblaðið Vísir* (*Vísir Daily*)

EEA   European Economic Area
EEC   European Economic Community
EFTA   European Free Trade Association
EU   European Union

FIYA   Federation of Icelandic Youth Associations (Ungmennafélag Íslands, *see* UMFÍ)

GATT   General Agreement on Tariffs and Trade
GDP   Gross Domestic Product
G. J. Guðmundur Jónsson (*see* acknowledgments)
GNP   Gross National Product
GIA   Government Import Authority (Landsverslun)

HÍ   Háskóli Íslands (University of Iceland)
HÍB   Hið íslenska bókmenntafélag (The Icelandic Literary Society, *see* ILS)
HRP   Home Rule Party (Heimastjórnarflokkur)

IFL   Icelandic Federation of Labor (Alþýðusamband Íslands, *see* ASÍ)
IHA   Icelandic Historical Association (Sögufélag)
ILS   Icelandic Literary Society (Hið íslenska bókmenntafélag, *see* HÍB)
IOGT   International Order of Good Templars
IP   Independence Party (Sjálfstæðisflokkur)

xi

ÍSAL   Íslenska álfélagið (Icelandic Aluminum Company)
ISBS   Icelandic State Broadcasting Service (Ríkisútvarpið, *see* RÚV)
ISC   Icelandic Steamship Company (Eimskipafélag Íslands)
ISK   Íslensk króna (Icelandic Króna, the Icelandic monetary unit, *see* Kr.)
ISWR   Icelandic Society for Women's Rights (Kvenréttindafélag Íslands)
IWC   International Whaling Commission

KHÍ   Kennaraháskóli Íslands (The Icelandic University College of Education)
Kr   Króna (*see* ISK)

Lbs   Landsbókasafn Íslands (National and University Library of Iceland)

Mbl   *Morgunblaðið* (*Morgunblaðið Daily*)
MR   Menntaskólinn í Reykjavík (The Secondary School in Reykjavík)
MRI   Marine Research Institute (Hafrannsóknarstofnun)

NAI   National Archives of Iceland (Þjóðskjalasafn Íslands, *see* ÞÍ)
NATO   North Atlantic Treaty Organization
NBI   National Bank of Iceland (Landsbanki Íslands)
NEI   National Economic Institute (Þjóðhagsstofnun)
NPCI   National Power Company of Iceland (Landsvirkjun)
NPPI   National Preservation Party of Iceland (Þjóðvarnarflokkur Íslands)

OECD   Organization for European Cooperation and Development
OEEC   Organization for European Economic Cooperation

PA   People's Alliance (Alþýðubandalag)
PP   Progressive Party (Framsóknarflokkur)

RDH   Reykjavík District Heating (Hitaveita Reykjavíkur)
RÚV   Ríkisútvarpið (Icelandic State Broadcasting Service, *see* ISBS)

SBI   Statistical Bureau of Iceland (Hagstofa Íslands)
SDA   Social Democratic Alliance (Bandalag jafnaðarmanna)
SDP   Social Democratic Party (Alþýðuflokkur)
SÍS   Samband íslenskra samvinnufélaga (Federation of Icelandic Cooperatives)

SUP   Socialist Unity Party (Sameiningarflokkur alþýðu-Sósíalista-flokkurinn)

SÞ   Sameinuðu þjóðirnar (United Nations)

ULL   Union of Liberals and Leftists (Samtök frjálslyndra og vinstri manna)

UMFÍ   Ungmennafélag Íslands (Federation of Icelandic Youth Associations, *see* FIYA)

VSÍ   Vinnuveitendasamband Íslands (Confederation of Icelandic Employers, *see* CIE)

WA   Women's Alliance (Kvennalistinn)

WTO   World Trade Organization

ÞÍ   Þjóðskjalasafn Íslands (The National Archives of Iceland, *see* NAI)

CHRONOLOGY OF ICELANDIC HISTORY

ca. 870	The first settlers come to Iceland from Norway.
930	A general assembly, Alþingi, convenes at Þingvellir.
930–1262	The Commonwealth period.
999 or 1000	Conversion to Christianity.
1056	The ordination of Ísleifur Gissurarson, the first bishop of Iceland.
1096	Icelanders agree to tithe to the church.
1104	A large eruption in Mt. Hekla destroys the settlement in Þjórsár Valley.
1106	Jón Ögmundsson, the first bishop of Hólar Diocese, ordained.
ca. 1220–1262	The "Age of the Sturlungs."
Sept. 23, 1241	Snorri Sturluson slain in Reykholt.
1262–64	Iceland enters union with Norway.
1380	Norway and Denmark unite under one king — Iceland comes under the authority of the Danish king.
1402 and 1494	Two plague epidemics devastate Iceland.
Early 15th century	English fishermen begin to frequent Icelandic waters—the beginning of the "English Age."

1540	An Icelandic translation of the New Testament published in Denmark.
Nov. 7, 1550	Lutheran Reformation completed in Iceland with the execution of Bishop Jón Arason.
1584	Guðbrandsbiblía, the first Icelandic translation of the Bible, published in Hólar.
April 20, 1602	A Danish trade monopoly established in Iceland with a royal decree.
July 26, 1662	Icelanders accept Danish absolutism.
1703	The first census taken in Iceland.
1707–09	Between 20 and 30 percent of the Icelandic population dies in a smallpox epidemic.
1751	Innréttingarnar, state supported textile factories, founded in Reykjavík.
June 8, 1783–Feb. 1784	The Laki Eruption.
1784–1785	Around 20 percent of the Icelandic population killed by diseases and hunger in the so-called Famine of the Mist.
1785	The Skálholt bishop's seat moved to Reykjavík.
Aug. 18, 1786	Reykjavík receives a royal charter.
June 13, 1787	The king issues a decree giving all his subjects the right to trade in Iceland.
1795	Icelanders demand freedom of trade in a public petition to the king.
July 20, 1798	Alþingi meets for the last time at Þingvellir.
June 6, 1800	Alþingi abolished by a royal decree.
July 11, 1800	Foundation of the High Court in Reykjavík.

1801	Iceland becomes a single diocese under the bishop of Reykjavík.
June 25–Aug. 22, 1809	The "Icelandic Revolution."
June 17, 1811	Jón Sigurðsson, the leader of the Icelandic nationalist movement, born in northwestern Iceland.
March 8, 1843	Foundation of a new assembly named Alþingi.
July 1, 1845	Alþingi convenes for the first time as a democratically elected assembly.
July 5–Aug. 9, 1851	Constituent assembly meets in Reykjavík.
Jan. 2, 1871	The Danish king ratifies the "Status Laws," regulating Iceland's place in the monarchy.
Jan. 5, 1874	The Danish king ratifies the first Icelandic constitution.
Aug. 5–8, 1874	The 1,000th anniversary of the Icelandic settlement celebrated at Þingvellir. Danish king visits Iceland for the first time.
Dec. 7, 1879	Jón Sigurðsson dies in Copenhagen.
May 12, 1882	Women receive limited right to vote in communal elections.
Aug. 27, 1885	Alþingi passes the first bill, amending Constitution of 1874.
July 1, 1886	The National Bank of Iceland opens its first office.
1902	The first motor put into an Icelandic fishing boat.
Feb. 20, 1902	Founding of the Federation of Icelandic Cooperative Societies.
Oct. 3, 1903	The Danish king ratifies constitutional

	amendments, giving Iceland a home rule government.
Feb. 1, 1904	Hannes Hafstein becomes the first minister of the Icelandic home rule.
June 7, 1904	The Bank of Iceland opens in Reykjavík.
Sept. 28, 1904	Foundation of the first Icelandic trawler company.
March 6, 1905	*Coot*, the first Icelandic trawler, comes to Hafnarfjörður.
Aug. 25, 1906	A telegraphic cable connecting Iceland with the rest of Europe completed.
Sept. 12, 1907	Alþingi passes laws stipulating compulsory schooling for children.
Jan. 24, 1908	The first women elected to Reykjavík's city council.
Sept. 10, 1908	Opponents of the "Draft" win majority in Alþingi.
June 17, 1911	The official date of the foundation of the University of Iceland.
Jan. 17, 1914	The Icelandic Steamship Company founded in Reykjavík.
June 19, 1915	A new constitution gives women the right to vote in parliamentary elections.
March 12, 1916	The Federation of Icelandic Labor and the Social Democratic Party are founded in Reykjavík.
Dec. 16, 1916	Foundation of the Progressive Party.
Jan. 4, 1917	The number of ministers in the Icelandic cabinet increased from one to three.

Dec. 1, 1918	Iceland becomes a sovereign state in a union with Denmark.
Feb. 16, 1920	The Icelandic Supreme Court meets for the first time.
July 8, 1922	Ingibjörg H. Bjarnadóttir is the first woman to be elected to Alþingi.
Feb. 24, 1924	Foundation of the Conservative Party.
May 25, 1929	The Independence Party founded as the Conservative Party and the Liberal Party merge.
June 26–28, 1930	Icelanders celebrate the 1,000th anniversary of Alþingi on Þingvellir.
Nov. 29–Dec. 3, 1930	Founding of the Communist Party of Iceland.
Nov. 9, 1932	Gúttóslagurinn, a confrontation between workers and police, in Reykjavík.
July 29, 1934	Formation of the "Government of the Laboring Classes."
April 1, 1936	The first comprehensive welfare legislation in Iceland comes into effect.
Oct. 24–27, 1938	Foundation of the Socialist Unity Party of Iceland.
May 10, 1940	Iceland occupied by British military forces.
May 15, 1941	Sveinn Björnsson selected governor of Iceland.
July 7, 1941	The U.S. military replaces the British occupying forces in Iceland.
July 10, 1941	Alþingi ratifies a defense treaty between the governments of Iceland and the United States.
May 20–23, 1944	The Republic of Iceland accepted in a general referendum.

June 17, 1944   Foundation of the Republic of Iceland at
                     Þingvellir. Sveinn Björnsson elected its first
                     president.

Oct. 21, 1944   The "Modernization Government" formed.

Sept. 19, 1946   The Keflavík Treaty between Iceland and the
                     United States passed in Alþingi.

Nov. 9, 1946   Iceland enters the United Nations.

April 5, 1948   Laws on the scientific conservation of the Ice-
                     landic continental shelf fisheries passed.

March 30, 1949   Iceland becomes a founding member of NATO.

May 5, 1951   The governments of Iceland and the United
                     States sign a defensive treaty.

May 8, 1951   The United States Army takes over the Keflavík
                     military base.

May 15, 1952   The Icelandic government extends the Ice-
                     landic fishing limits to four nautical miles.

June 29, 1952   Ásgeir Ásgeirsson elected the second president
                     of the Republic of Iceland.

Feb. 14, 1953   Opening of the first meeting of the Nordic
                     Council in Copenhagen.

Oct. 28, 1955   Halldór Laxness awarded the Nobel Prize for
                     literature.

March 29, 1956   Alþingi demands the closing of the NATO
                     base in Keflavík.

July 24, 1956   The first "Leftist Government" comes to power.

Sept. 1, 1958   The Icelandic fishing limits extended to 12
                     nautical miles.

Nov. 21, 1959   The "Reconstruction Government" formed.

March 11, 1961	Britain accepts the extension of the Icelandic fishing limits to 12 nautical miles.
Nov. 14, 1963	Underwater eruption begins south of the Vestmanna Islands. Surtsey is formed.
June 28, 1966	ÍSAL, the Icelandic Aluminum Company founded.
June 30, 1968	Dr. Kristján Eldjárn elected the third president of the Republic of Iceland.
March 1, 1970	Iceland joins EFTA.
May 5, 1970	The Búrfell power station formally opened.
April 21, 1971	The first Old Norse manuscripts returned to Iceland from Denmark.
July 13, 1971	The second "Leftist Government" formed.
July 2–Sept. 5, 1972	World Chess Championship between Spassky and Fischer held in Reykjavík.
Sept. 1, 1972	The Icelandic fishing limits extended to 50 nautical miles.
Jan. 23, 1973	Eruption begins in Heimaey, Vestmanna Islands.
May 20, 1973	A British squadron enters the Icelandic fishing zone to protect British trawlers.
Aug. 1, 1973	Icelandair is formed through a merger of two leading Icelandic airlines.
July 29, 1974	Commemoration of the 1,100th anniversary of the Icelandic settlement at Þingvellir.
Oct. 15, 1975	Icelandic fishing limits extended to 200 nautical miles.
Oct. 24, 1975	A meeting of 25,000 women in Reykjavík demands equal rights for women.

Feb. 19, 1976	Iceland cuts its diplomatic ties with Britain because of the fishing disputes.
June 1, 1976	Britain and Iceland sign a treaty ending their fishing disputes.
Feb. 8, 1980	Gunnar Thoroddsen, vice-chairman of the Independence Party, forms a government.
June 29, 1980	Vigdís Finnbogadóttir elected the fourth president of the Republic of Iceland.
Jan. 1, 1981	New currency, New Króna, replaces the old Króna.
Feb. 1, 1982	Organization for Women's Candidacy—The Women's List—founded in Reykjavík.
Jan. 17, 1983	The Social Democratic Union is established.
Feb. 3, 1983	Alþingi decides not to protest the whaling moratorium of the International Whaling Commission.
Aug. 18, 1986	Reykjavík celebrates its bicentennial as a chartered town.
Oct. 11–12, 1986	Mikhail Gorbachev and Ronald Reagan hold a summit in Reykjavík.
Nov. 9, 1986	Members of the organization Sea Shepherd sink two whaling boats in Reykjavík harbor.
June 26, 1988	Vigdís Finnbogadóttir wins a landslide victory in a reelection bid for the precidency.
Oct. 11, 1988	Salóme Þorkelsdóttir is the first woman to be elected president of Alþingi.
June 3–4, 1989	Pope John Paul II visits Iceland.
July 20, 1989	The last whale brought to land at the whaling station in Hvalfjörður.

Feb. 2, 1990	Employers, labor unions, and the government sign an agreement to end chronic hyper-inflation in Iceland.
April 20, 1991	The Independence Party victor in parliamentary elections.
April 30, 1991	Davíð Oddsson becomes prime minister.
Aug. 26, 1991	Iceland is the first country in the world to establish full diplomatic relations with the three Baltic countries.
Oct. 21, 1991	The EEA treaty between the EU and EFTA finalized.
May 2, 1992	Iceland, with other EFTA countries, signs the EEA treaty with the EU.
June 30, 1992	Iceland leaves the International Whaling Commission.
Jan. 12, 1993	Alþingi ratifies the EEA treaty.
June 27, 1993	The government announces drastic reductions in the allowed catches of cod.
Aug. 1993	Icelandic trawlers begin fishing in the Barents Sea, launching a fishery dispute with Norway and Russia.
Jan. 4, 1994	The governments of Iceland and the United States come to an agreement on the military base in Keflavík.
April 28, 1994	The united left wins majority in the City Council of Reykjavík.
June 17, 1994	Icelanders commemorate the 50th anniversary of the Republic of Iceland.
Jan. 17, 1995	17 people die in an avalanche in the village of Súðavík, Ísafjörður County.

April 23, 1995   Davíð Oddsson forms his second government.

Oct. 26, 1995   An avalance strikes the village of Flateyri in Ísafjörður County, killing 20 people.

June 29, 1996   Ólafur Ragnar Grímsson elected fifth president of the Republic of Iceland.

INTRODUCTION

Habitat

Iceland is an island situated just to the south of the Polar Circle in the mid-North Atlantic. With a surface of 103,000 square km (39,000 square miles), Iceland is similar in size to the state of Kentucky. It was formed through volcanic eruptions at the place where the Mid-Atlantic Ridge and a ridge extending from Scotland to Greenland cross, rising above sea level around 20 million years ago. Compared to other parts of Europe, Iceland has a short geological history, and its formative process is still far from over. The eastern and western halves of the country are slowly drifting apart, with volcanoes filling the fissures with fresh lava. Fire is not the only element that characterizes the Icelandic environment, because, as the name of the country indicates, ice also is a dominant factor. There are four major glaciers in the country, including the largest glacier in Europe, Vatnajökull, which is around 8,300 square km (3,200 square miles) in size.

A mountainous country, with three-quarters of its surface area more than 200 m (656 ft.) above sea level, Iceland is sharply divided into an uninhabitable interior of rugged plateaus and mountains and coastal valleys and plains. Narrow fjords characterize the coastline in the eastern and northwestern parts of the country with wider fjords and bays in the northern and western parts, while beaches of black sand dominate the landscape of the southern coast. Most of the Icelandic coastline, except for the southern part of the country, is endowed with natural harbors.

The Icelandic climate can best be described as temperate, at least in view of the northerly location of the country. Thus, summers in Iceland are cool but the winters relatively mild. In the period 1961–90, the mean temperature in Reykjavík during the coldest month (January) was –0.5° C (31.1° F), while it was 10.6° C (51.1° F) on the average during the warmest summer month (July). The figures for northern Iceland are similar, or –2.2° C (28.0° F) and 10.5° C (50.9° F) respectively for the town of Akureyri. The weather in Iceland is rarely extremely cold, and never very hot, as the Gulf Stream of the Atlantic Ocean balances its climatic fluctuations. The average annual precipitation in Iceland ranges from around 1,700 mm (432 in) in the south and southeastern coastal

1

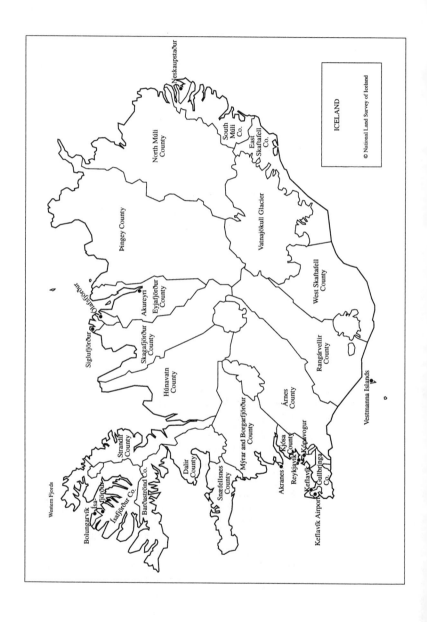

areas to just below 500 mm (127 in) in the North. It is fairly evenly spread throughout the year, although the summer is usually the driest season.

The ecological system sets strict limits on the Icelandic plant life. Today, the country is almost totally void of trees and bushes, and large tracts, especially in the highlands, have become virtual deserts through incessant soil erosion. According to medieval sources, shrubs and birch trees covered the country at the time of the first settlement in the ninth century, but the fragile arboreal vegetation did not withstand prolonged human exploitation. In recent years, different government agencies have tried to reverse this trend, without much success.

Human and Natural Resources

The history of the Icelandic nation reflects its harsh ecological conditions in various ways. Although Iceland is not well suited for agriculture because the short summers render commercial grain-growing very difficult, animal husbandry remained the main occupation of its population for the first millennium of its history. Sheep and cattle were the most important domestic animals; the former raised for their milk, wool, and meat, the latter primarily for their milk. Horses were used for transportation, but a total absence of roads made the use of wagons almost impossible in Iceland. Icelandic farming took the form of sedentary pastoralism, meaning that extensive pastures were crucial for the feeding of the animals during the summer, and, to certain extent, also for the winter, when farmers used hay from meadows as fodder for their livestock.

In congruence with these economic patterns, the rural population in Iceland was dispersed over the whole inhabitable area. Each farm needed a relatively large tract of land to be economically viable, a fact that made a concentration into peasant villages impractical. Rather, the whole countryside was divided between separate farming households living on individual farms. The only common lands were the mountain pastures, which were usually separated from the inhabited lowland. For this reason, there were no hamlets or villages in Iceland to speak of until the end of the 19th and beginning of the 20th centuries.

One of the paradoxes of Icelandic history is that until the late 19th century most people regarded the natural resources that form the basis for the modern economy in Iceland as secondary to the use of land, or saw them as a nuisance at best. Thus fishing, although important for people in many parts of the country, served as a subsidiary occupation to farming, performed during the slack season in the rural areas. Moreover, rivers and hot springs, which are now the main sources of energy in Iceland, were of little use to Icelanders until they gained the technological prowess to exploit these resources in the early 20th century.

The Icelandic waters are ideal for the development of marine life, as the country is situated where cold currents emanating from the Arctic Ocean and warm ocean currents originating in the South Atlantic meet. Primitive life forms, such as the so-called phytoplankton, or microscopic floating plants, are abundant in the top layers of the sea around Iceland, and they serve as food for small floating animals called zooplankton. The latter constitute the main source of nutrition for many types of fish and most fish larva, in addition to the largest mammals in the sea, the baleen whales. At the bottom of the sea, species of invertebrates, such as mollusks, crustaceans, and polychacte worms, provide an ample source of food for various types of bottom-feeding fish, including some of the most important species for the Icelandic fishing industry—species like cod and haddock.

During the late Middle Ages, foreign fishermen began to frequent Icelandic waters, but it was only during the 20th century that full use was made of the fishing grounds around the country. In that period, the Icelandic fishing industry developed rapidly, but increased mechanization and rapid technological development have led to a serious overexploitation of many stocks in Icelandic waters. It is for this reason that the government of Iceland has extended its fishing limits in successive steps to the current 200 nautical miles, in part to have a better control over the amount of fish caught around the country, and to give the Icelandic fishing industry a monopoly over this natural resource.

For the Icelandic fisheries, cod has always been the most important species. It spawns outside the southwestern coast of Iceland in late winter, but for the rest of the year it is spread around most of the island. Since the Second World War, the annual catch of Icelandic ships has fluctuated between around 200 and 460 thousand metric tons, but based on the suggestions of marine scientists, the Icelandic government has recently lowered the fishing quotas to around 150,000 tons a year. For decades, herring was the other main stock caught by the Icelandic fishing fleet, but overexploitation and changes in the natural ecosystem led to a collapse in the Norwegian-Icelandic herring stock during the late 1960s. Because of rigorous preventionist policies the stock is, however, beginning to return to Icelandic waters. To compensate for the decline in catches from traditional stocks, the Icelandic fleet has sought new species in recent years, such as capelin, and Icelandic fishermen have had to seek new fishing grounds outside the 200-mile fishing limits.

The industrialization of the fisheries at the beginning of the 20th century led to revolutionary changes in the Icelandic economy and society. First, farming lost its dominant status in the economy, as it could not compete with fisheries at a time of rapidly rising labor cost. Second, exodus from the countryside to towns and villages by the coast totally transformed the pattern of settlement in few decades. Third, rapid increase in the Icelandic GNP pushed living standards in the country upward, moving the nation in few decades from one of the poorest and most backward in Europe into one of the most technologically advanced nations in the world.

These transformations in Iceland happened in part because the circumstances called for a radical change in the Icelandic economic system. In the late 19th century, rapid and persistent population growth put an increasing pressure on the traditional occupations in Iceland, creating the need for new economic opportunities. Therefore, all attempts to preserve the old Icelandic social and economic system failed, and urbanization and industrialization relegated farming to a secondary position in society.

At the present, Iceland stands again at crossroads regarding its use of natural resources. The traditional primary occupations, fisheries and farming, have both reached their limits of expansion, and Icelanders must find new sources to sustain their high living standards in the future. Rich energy resources seem to provide the most promising opportunities in this respect; at the present, for example, Icelanders use less than 10 percent of the exploitable hydroelectric power in the country (4,500 GWh p.a. out of 45,000 GWh p.a.). This source will hardly be used without considerable foreign investment, however, because large amounts of capital are needed to construct power plants and to build the industries to convert the energy into marketable products. Attempts to attract foreign capital to Iceland has only been moderately successful so far, although scarcity of fossil fuels in the world and ecological concerns may enhance the profitability of hydroelectric power in the future.

History

As far as we can know with any certainty, Iceland was first settled by people of Norse origin coming primarily from the western part of Norway, either directly or through the British Isles. Old Icelandic sources such as the *Book of Settlement* and the *Book of Icelanders* mention that a few Irish hermits (called *papar*) lived in Iceland at the arrival of the Norse settlers, but no conclusive archaeological evidence has confirmed these legends.

According to written sources, the Norse settlement of Iceland started around the year 870—with the year 874 accepted as the traditional date of the arrival of the first permanent settlers. The settlement of Iceland must be seen as an integral part of general Viking expansion to the west, stretching as far as to Greenland and briefly reaching the coast of North America. The leading settlers were for the most part Norwegian chieftains, the early Icelandic sources maintain, escaping the tyranny of the first king of unified Norway. Although this may have motivated some of the Icelandic settlers, population pressure and search for new economic opportunities are more plausible causes for the exodus to Iceland.

The settlers brought with them the economic and social customs of their country of origin, and it was also to Norway that Icelanders looked for a model for their legal system. Thus, around the year 930, Icelanders established a general assembly called Alþingi for the whole country, using Norwegian customs as the basis for their law codes and legal procedures. At Alþingi, which convened for two weeks every summer at a place called Þingvellir in southwestern Iceland, laws were amended and courts were held, making it the most important institution of the Icelandic legal and political system for centuries.

With the establishment of Alþingi, Icelanders developed both a legislative and a judiciary system. They did not, however, create any centralized mechanism for enforcing the law. The most powerful men in the country were the chieftains (*goðar*), or the group of men who held the 36–39 chieftaincies (*goðorð*) in Iceland. In Alþingi, the chieftains carried out the legislative functions and named people into courts, but they had only limited executive functions.

This absence of a centralized state structure led to a gradual dissolution of the Icelandic political system. In the first centuries of its history, wealth and power was relatively equally distributed in Iceland, but during the last decades of the Commonwealth period (930–1262), a few families seized control over all the chieftaincies. After decades of open warfare, in which the most powerful chieftains competed for hegemony in the country, Icelanders accepted the authority of the Norwegian king in the 1260s, in the hope that he would restore peace. With the so-called Old Covenant, which Icelanders approved in the years 1262–64, Iceland became a tributary province in the Norwegian monarchy.

In spite of the violence, Icelandic cultural creativity reached its pinnacle during the 13th century. It was in this century that most of the family sagas were written, in addition to various other literary and historical works. We can trace the start of this literary production to the conversion to Christianity in Iceland, which happened at the start of the second millennium. The church introduced the technology of reading and writing to the Icelandic population, and although most of the Icelandic literature was secular in character, some of the Icelandic religious houses became centers of learning in late medieval Iceland.

During the 14th and 15th centuries the cultural production that characterized the turbulent 13th century declined. For this reason, historical sources for the last period of the Middle Ages are relatively scarce. We know, however, that this was a difficult time in many respects. Two terrible plague epidemics devastated Iceland in the 15th century, and its ecological system gradually deteriorated under a colder climate and overexploitation of the Icelandic vegetation, leading to depletion of the birch woods and soil erosion. Political development in the late Middle Ages in Iceland followed general trends in the Nordic countries. Thus, when the kingdom of Norway entered a union with Denmark in 1380, Iceland became effectively a part of the Danish monarchy. In the mid-16th century, Icelanders converted to Lutheranism under pressure from the royal government. This enhanced the authority of the Danish king in Iceland, because from now on the church was a state institution, under direct control of the king and his officials. Furthermore, the confiscation of the property of Icelandic monasteries made the king the single largest landowner in the country.

Increasing state integration marked political and social development from the late 16th to the late 18th century. From 1602, the king enforced a strict trade monopoly in Iceland, meaning that only Danish merchants, whom he had granted special trading licenses, had the right to trade in Iceland. This tied Iceland more firmly to the mother country, as Denmark dominated all of its economic and political relations with the external world. In 1662, when Icelanders acknowledged the absolutist rule of the Danish monarch, the country became even more dependent upon the Danish state. From then on, all economic and political initiative in Iceland had to come from Copenhagen.

The introduction of absolutism did not lead to a sudden transformation of the Icelandic political and legal system, but in the long run it caused significant changes in Icelandic administration and in the relations between the center and the periphery. In the last decades of the 17th century, Danish authorities reorganized the Icelandic administrative hierarchy and gave it more permanence. As a result, Alþingi lost the last vestiges of its legislative power, evolving into a mere intermediary court; this led to its replacement in the year 1800 by the more effective and professional High Court in Reykjavík.

The 18th century was one of the most difficult periods in the history of Iceland. At the beginning of the century, between a quarter and one-third of the population died in a smallpox epidemic that struck the country in the years 1707–09; close to the century's end, around a quarter of the Icelandic population died in a famine that followed the tremendous Laki eruption of 1783–84. The late 18th century saw, however, the beginning of new trends in the government of Iceland. Inspired by the spirit of the European Enlightenment, Icelandic intellectuals and crown officials studied the plight of the country, writing exhortations with the aim of guiding the popular classes toward the road of progress. These men did not demand political independence for the Icelandic nation, because to them the Danish king was the most likely source of social and intellectual improvement in the country. In the following century, however, their effort inspired a new group of intellectuals who sought the regeneration of Icelandic society. Thus, romantic nationalism enchanted the generation of Icelandic students that came to Copenhagen in the late 1820s and early 1830s. Just as the Danish state was transformed into a nation-state, the Icelandic nationalists requested what they felt to be the natural rights of the Icelandic nation, that is, some form of sovereignty and independence from Denmark.

From the mid-19th until the early 20th century the call for independence formed a basis for all political activity in Iceland. The first response to these requests was offered in 1843, when the king granted the country a separate parliament, carrying the name of the ancient assembly, Alþingi. In the summer of 1845, the newly elected Alþingi met for the first time in Reykjavík. For the next decades it convened for a few weeks every second year, gathering representatives from all around the country. In the beginning, it had no legislative authority, consulting the king on Icelandic financial and legal matters. Alþingi became, however, a unifying symbol for the growing nationalist sentiment in Iceland and served as a platform for the emerging nationalist movement.

From the mid-19th until the early 20th century, Icelanders inched toward their ultimate goal, full independence from Denmark. During its first phase, the undisputed leader of this struggle was the philologist and archivist Jón Sigurðsson. He emerged as a political figure in the early 1840s, guiding Icelandic nationalism until his death in 1879. In 1874, Iceland received its first constitution, abolishing absolutist rule. The constitution granted Alþingi a limited legislative power and secured fundamental democratic rights. The new constitution did not fulfill all the demands of the nationalists, however, as the minister of Iceland was a member of the Danish cabinet and resided in Copenhagen. The effective government of Iceland remained in the hands of the governor of Iceland who was a royal official, responsible only to the king.

In 1901, after decades of intense political struggle, a liberal government came to power in Copenhagen. The new ruling party was much more flexible in its Icelandic policies than its conservative predecessors had been. Thus, in 1904 home rule was established for Iceland, and the ministry of Iceland was transferred from Copenhagen to Reykjavík. This did not satisfy nationalist aspirations in Iceland, however, because the constitution of Iceland still treated the country as a Danish annex. At the end of World War I, a committee of Icelandic and Danish parliamentary representatives solved this dilemma with a bilateral agreement between the two parliaments. In the fall of 1918, a new Act of Union was passed in the Danish and Icelandic parliaments respectively, and it came formally into effect on December 1 of the same year. The act made Iceland a sovereign state sharing king and foreign service with Denmark.

The 20th century has been a time of total transformation for Icelandic society. During the first decades of the century the Icelandic fishing industry mechanized rapidly, with motor boats and trawlers replacing rowboats and schooners. Increasing economic prosperity, changing demographic patterns, and the end of the nationalist struggle called for new political alliances based on novel social realities. Moreover, Iceland became a truly democratic country in the first decades of the century, when women and workers received full rights as citizens. In the beginnig of the 20th century, Iceland became a modern, capitalist society, confirming the general trends in the development of the western world.

The Second World War had a great impact in Iceland, although the country was not a direct participant in the conflict. As it is placed in the mid-Atlantic, the country became crucial for securing communication between the United States and Europe during the turbulent years of the war. To secure the route to its American allies, the British army occupied Iceland in May 1940, a month after the Germans invaded and captured Denmark. The following year, after the government of Iceland had signed a defense treaty with the United States, the American armed forces took over military installations in Iceland. This freed the numerous British soldiers stationed in Iceland for active combat on the European continent and in North Africa, and it moved Iceland decisively into the American sphere of influence.

On June 17, 1944, the Icelandic republic was formally founded at Þingvellir, the place where the old Alþingi had met annually for almost nine centuries. Now, the country could become a full member of the international community, a fact that was later confirmed with its entrance into international organizations such as the United Nations and NATO. When the cold war parted the world into two hostile camps, Iceland sided firmly with the United States and its western allies. Icelanders have always been hesitant, however, to sacrifice the sovereignty they gained through long nationalist strife. Thus, American military presence in Iceland after 1951 was the most divisive political question in the country for decades. Possible membership in the European Union has also faced strong opposition, although Iceland has participated fully in economic and cultural cooperation with its neighbors through the European Free Trade Association (EFTA) and the European Economic Area (EEA) agreement of 1992.

Today, Iceland has most of the characteristics of a modern western society. It has maintained political stability through a democratic process that enjoys almost universal legitimacy. Rapid economic modernization has also secured its inhabitants high living standards, and a comprehensive and highly developed health system has ensured them longevity and one of the lowest rates of infant mortality in the world. Icelanders face, however, a formidable challenge in maintaining their status. First, the Icelandic economy is fairly fragile, as overexploitation threatens the fish stocks that remain Iceland's principal economic resource. Second, it remains to be seen if a country with less than 300,000 inhabitants will be able to manage its foreign relations in a complex and constantly changing world.

THE DICTIONARY

- A -

ABSOLUTISM. Danish absolutism was formally instituted (1660–61) when king Frederick III compelled the Danish aristocracy to renounce the last vestiges of power they wielded in the selection of new kings. To secure the legitimacy of the new regime in Iceland, the Danish governor summoned the most influential men in the country to endorse the king. At the meeting, held at Kópavogur in late July 1662, the Icelandic representatives accepted the absolutist rule, albeit with certain reservations. This did not cause an immediate shift in the Icelandic administration, but gradually the absolutist monarchy abrogated many of the local privileges that limited royal authority in the country. Thus, in the early 18th century Alþingi (q.v.) became a mere court, losing the last vestiges of its legislative functions, and surrendering their traditional right to nominate the two presidents of the court. Following these changes, the Icelandic administration was reorganized to make it more responsive to the government directives and directly dependent on the crown. As in other regions under the Danish monarchy, the country was made a special administrative district (*amt*), with a governor (*stiftamtmaður*, q.v.) living in Copenhagen and a district governor (*amtmaður*, q.v.) residing at Bessastaðir (q.v.) in Iceland.

During the late 18th century, the absolutist system took on its final form in Iceland. The country was divided into three districts, each with one district governor. Above them in the administrative hierarchy was a governor, serving also as district governor in the south district. From 1770 the governor lived in Iceland, but until then the *stiftamtmaður* post had been little more than a ceremonial office. The absolutist system was in effect in Iceland until the early 1870s, or over two decades beyond its abolition in Denmark proper. The constitution of 1874 granted Alþingi limited legislative power and the right to enact its own budget, thus ending the absolutist

11

regime in Iceland. (*See also* CONSTITUTIONS, 1874 –1918; KÓPAVOGUR'S MEETING, THE; LAWMAN)

ACT OF UNION. A legal act passed by the Danish and Icelandic parliaments in 1918 and accepted in a referendum in Iceland the same year. The Act redefined the relationship between the two countries, granting the Icelandic nation full sovereignty in its internal affairs. Hence, the Icelandic nationalist struggle was practically over.

A joint committee, formed by the Danish and Icelandic legislatures, wrote the Act in the summer of 1918. The final negotiations took only a few weeks to complete, closing a long dispute between the two countries. The constitution of 1874 and home rule (q.v.) in 1904 had gradually given Icelanders more independence in their internal affairs. These conciliatory arrangements did not meet Icelandic demands, however, because the Danish government did not acknowledge Iceland as a sovereign state. The Act of Union fulfilled the Icelandic desire for statehood, as its first article proclaimed Iceland and Denmark to be two free and sovereign states, united only by the same king. The Act stipulated, however, that the Danish government would continue to manage Icelandic foreign affairs and guard the Icelandic fishing limits, at least as long as Icelanders felt that they were incapable of managing these issues themselves.

The Act of Union had a profound impact on Icelandic politics and society. On the one hand, it gave the Icelandic nation almost total control over all three branches of its government. The foundation of the Supreme Court of Iceland (q.v.) in 1920 completed this development. On the other, with the end of the nationalist struggle new issues and ideologies began to divide the nation into political groups. Nationalism remained a strong theme in Icelandic politics, but it was no longer the center of all political debates.

According to its 18th article, both the Danish and the Icelandic parliament had the right to revoke the Act of Union at the end of the year 1943, provided that attempts to renegotiate the Act were unsuccessful. As the German occupation of Denmark in 1940 blocked all communications with Copenhagen, the Act had already become entirely ineffectual early in the war, however. Therefore, the Icelandic parliament decided unilaterally to terminate the union with Denmark in 1944 and to declare Iceland an independent republic. This policy received overwhelming support in a referendum held in 1944, and on June 17 of that year, the Republic of Iceland was founded at Þingvellir (q.v.). (*See also* CONSTITUTIONS, 1874–1918; DENMARK (RELATIONS WITH);

DRAFT, THE; NATIONALISM; REPUBLIC OF ICELAND; WORLD WAR II [EFFECTS ON ICELAND])

AGE OF THE STURLUNGS. The last decades of the Commonwealth period (q.v.), or the time from 1200/20 to 1262, are traditionally named after one of the most prominent families in 13th-century Iceland, the Sturlungs. This was a turbulent period when various chieftains competed for political dominance in the country. Gradually, the old social system broke down as the lack of effective executive power rendered the rule of law almost impossible. In 1262–64, when the feuds had broken the power of the ruling families in Iceland and the general population had had its fill of the political upheaval, Icelanders agreed to enter into a contractual alliance with the Norwegian king. This marked the end of the Commonwealth period (q.v.).

The 13th century was not only a time of bloody feuds but also one of the most productive periods in Icelandic literary history. During the Age of the Sturlungs and the following decades, many of the most original family sagas were composed, along with historical works, like the Sturlunga Saga (q.v.) compilation, which gives detailed accounts of the period. Literary production did not end as abruptly as the political feuds, but by the end of the 13th century it had lost most of its creative edge. (*See also* OLD COVENANT; SAGAS; STURLUSON, SNORRI; ÞÓRÐARSON, STURLA)

AKUREYRI. This town, the largest in Iceland outside the Reykjavík (q.v.) area, is often called the capital of northern Iceland. Because of Akureyri's central location, the royal administration chose it as one of the six certified marketplaces in Iceland in 1787. At that time, Akureyri was only a small hamlet of a few huts and one general store, but from the mid-19th century the town began to grow rapidly. As a result, in 1862 it was the first town in Iceland, after Reykjavík, to receive a town charter, providing it with an elected town council and a special town court. As the town grew in size, more services moved to Akureyri, and it became an administrative and cultural center for the surrounding region.

During the first nine decades of the 20th century, the population of Akureyri grew ten-fold, or from 1,370 inhabitants in 1901 to just under 15,000 in 1994. In this period the town developed a strong industrial base while it continued to serve as a commercial center for the prosperous agricultural regions around it. Moreover, in 1928 the Akureyri high school was granted the right to offer university entrance exams, making the town an educational center for the northern and eastern parts of the country. This role was further enhanced in 1987, with the foundation of the University of Akureyri, a small university college specializing in fields such as marine research, nursing, management, and education.

ALÞINGI. The parliament of Iceland, Alþingi, is a central institution in Icelandic history and public life. It traces its history back to the beginning of the Commonwealth period (q.v.), although the modern, democratically elected Alþingi has little in common with its medieval namesake.

The old Alþingi met for the first time around the year 930 on Þingvellir (q.v., "Parliamentary Plains"), about 40 km (25 miles) northeast of Reykjavík. In the beginning, Alþingi was a public gathering, where people from all over the country met for two weeks during the summer. The center of the assembly was Lögrétta, the Law Council, which was dominated by the 39 chieftains. Lögrétta formulated new laws, but the chieftains nominated people to the high court (*fimmtardómur*) and the four so-called quarter courts (*fjórðungsdómar*) at Alþingi. The law-speaker (q.v.) presided over Alþingi until 1271, when his title was changed to lawman (q.v.).

With the union of Iceland and Norway in 1262–64, Alþingi gradually lost much of its prestige, although it remained a unifying symbol for the Icelandic ruling classes. From now on, it was the royal officials that controlled Alþingi, as the chieftaincies were abolished in the late 13th century. From this period until the late 17th century Alþingi held legislative power in conjunction with the king. The role of this assembly was reduced further still after the introduction of absolutism (q.v.) in 1662. Now, its legislative functions were totally abolished, and it became a mere appellate court. In 1798, Alþingi met for the last time at Þingvellir, after convening there every year for nearly nine centuries. After two sessions in the emerging capital, Reykjavík (q.v.), the old Alþingi was abolished in 1800. A permanent High Court (q.v.), staffed with professional judges, appointed by the king replaced it the same year.

King Christian VIII founded the modern Alþingi in 1843 as a consultative assembly for Icelandic affairs. It had 20 elected representatives, one from each county (q.v.) in Iceland and one from the town of Reykjavík, in addition to six members selected by the king. The parliament was to meet every second year for four weeks in the summer to discuss bills introduced by the government and formulate collective petitions to the king. Resolutions passed in Alþingi had no binding authority, but the government usually took them into consideration when it proposed legislative changes to the king.

The constitution of 1874 granted Alþingi limited legislative power in domestic affairs and control over the Icelandic budget. This meant that no bill could become law in Iceland unless a majority in both houses of parliament approved it, but the king had the right to veto all bills passed in Alþingi—a prerogative he used frequently during the last decades of the 19th century. The constitution of 1874 divided Alþingi into two houses; 12 representatives sat in the upper house (until 1915, the king selected six of them, while the rest were popularly elected), and 24 democratically elected representatives sat in the lower house.

Since 1874, Alþingi has slowly become the most important institution of the Icelandic political system. Its primary functions pertain to legislative authority, which it now shares with the president (q.v.) of the republic. Parliament also has strong influence on the executive branch, because the government is responsible to Alþingi, which must also approve the state budget.

Today, regular sessions of Alþingi begin on October 1st every year and last until the following spring. It is composed of 63 members, and since 1990 it meets in one house. All bills presented to Alþingi are discussed in one of its 12 standing committees, and they require three readings in parliament before they are sent to the president for ratification. Alþingi holds its meetings in the parliamentary building, constructed in Reykjavík's center in the years 1880–81.

In the beginning, one representative was elected for each electoral district to a six-year term (shortened to four years in 1920). As demographic patterns began to change in the 20th century, the electoral system tended to favor the rural areas at the expense of the emerging towns around the coast. After numerous attempts to correct the growing imbalance, the system was totally overhauled in 1959. Since then, the country has been divided into eight constituencies in which representatives are elected from party lists. Following a system of proportional representation, each party receives a number of seats in accordance with its share of the popular vote. Since the 1930s, the Icelandic political structure has been relatively stable, with four major parties receiving the lion's share of the votes in most parliamentary elections. (*See also* CABINET; ELECTIONS; GOÐI; PRIME MINISTER)

ALÞÝÐUBLAÐIÐ. This was the organ of the Social Democratic Party (SDP, q.v.). It was founded in 1919 as a daily newspaper serving the SDP. Its first editor was Ólafur Friðriksson, one of the early leaders of the radical arm of the party. The paper has never had a large circulation, and in recent years it has only survived in a reduced form.

AMTMAÐUR. The office of *amtmaður*, or district governor, was established in Iceland in 1684 as part of the general reorganization of the Icelandic administrative system following the introduction of absolutism (q.v.) in 1662. As the governor (*stiftamtmaður*, q.v.) lived in Copenhagen until 1770, the district governor was *de facto* governor of Iceland. In 1770, the administrative hierarchy was reformed again, as the country was divided into two districts instead of one. At the same time, the governor was required to live in Iceland, where he also served as district governor in the southwest district. From that time, the district governor served as a link between the bailiffs in the counties (q.v.) and the governor, collecting information from the local officials and communicating orders from the governor to the bailiffs. In 1787, the district boundaries were redrawn, and the southwest district was split into two parts—the governor serving as district governor of the south district. In 1873, the south and west districts were reunited under one district governor, while the governor (*landshöfðingi*, q.v.) was relieved from his duties as district governor. This arrangement was in force until the district governors' offices were abolished in 1904.

ANIMAL HUSBANDRY. Animal husbandry was for centuries the foundation of the Icelandic economy. The most important domestic animals were sheep and cattle. The former were raised for their milk, wool, and meat, the latter mostly for their milk. Horses were also vital to the peasant economy, especially for transportation over longer distances. Today, animal husbandry is still the most important element of the rural economy, but changing patterns of consumption and improvements in breeding have forced farmers to set strict quotas on their production. Thus, the number of sheep has gone down drastically in recent years, from almost 900,000 head in 1977 to just below 500,000 in 1994. Because of increasing population and urbanization (q.v.), the market for dairy products grew steadily from the early 20th century until the mid 1980s, but constant overproduction has forced farmers to reduce their output in recent years. (*See also* FARMING)

ARASON, JÓN (1484–1550). The last Catholic bishop in Iceland before the Reformation (q.v.) was born in 1484 to a prosperous farmer in northern Iceland. He was ordained a priest in 1507, and after that he rose quickly through the ranks of the church as well as the royal administration in Iceland. In 1522, he was elected bishop in Hólar (q.v.) diocese, and he also served as a bailiff in two districts in northern Iceland. Jón Arason is best known for his staunch opposition to the Lutheran reformation in Iceland, but a Lutheran bishop governed the diocese of Skálholt (q.v.) in southern Iceland from the early 1540s. From 1548 to 1550, Jón Arason maintained a group of armed supporters, imprisoning the bishop in Skálholt and reestablishing monasteries that the Lutherans had closed down in previous years. This led to a total rift with the Danish king Christian III, who was an ardent supporter of Lutheranism. Jón Arason's struggle ended in 1550 when the king's men in Iceland captured him and had him and two of his illegitimate sons executed in Skálholt on November 7, 1550.

To many nationalists of the 19th and 20th centuries, Jón Arason symbolized the struggle of the Icelandic nation against a growing foreign authority. This is certainly an anachronistic opinion, because nationalism in the modern sense of the word did not exist in the 16th century, but the victory of Lutheranism (q.v.) did enhance royal power in Iceland. (*See also* CATHOLICISM)

ARCHIEVES, NATIONAL. *See* NATIONAL ARCHIVES OF ICELAND.

ARI ÞORGILSSON THE "LEARNED." *See* ÞORGILSSON, ARI.

ÁRMANN Á ALÞINGI. The first example in a string of periodicals published by Icelandic students and intellectuals in Copenhagen during the early 19th century. Baldvin Einarsson (1801–33), a son of a farmer in Skagafjörður County in northern Iceland, founded and edited *Ármann á Alþingi* with the aim of providing his countrymen with practical advice on various social, economic, and political issues. It was constructed around a conversation among four fictional Icelanders, each of whom represented certain character traits that the editors found prevalent in society. The journal mixed Icelandic conservatism with the ideals of the European Enlightenment, emphasizing both the traditional values of the Icelandic peasant economy and the possibility of social progress through education and a rational use of Icelandic resources. *Ármann á Alþingi* had little direct influence on Icelandic political life during its short period of existence, but it served as an encouragement for others to follow its example. The first regular issue of *Ármann á Alþingi* came out in 1829, but the journal ceased publication with the fourth issue (1832), following the tragic death of its founder in Copenhagen in February 1833. (*See also* FJÖLNIR; NÝ FÉLAGSRIT)

ARNAMAGNÆAN INSTITUTE. *See* ÁRNI MAGNÚSSON INSTITUTE.

ARNARSON, INGÓLFUR (ninth and 10th centuries). All the medieval sources on the settlement of Iceland suggest that Ingólfur was the name of the first permanent settler of Norse origins in Iceland— there is not a total accord on the name of his father, but by convention he is called Arnarson. Ingólfur is said to have left Norway for Iceland around the time 870–74, calling his farm Reykjavík (q.v.), or "smoke cove." According to the *Book of Settlements* (q.v.), he chose this site because it was there that the posts of his high-seat drifted on land, but he is supposed to have thrown them overboard when he first caught the sight of the island from his ship. Ingólfur Arnarson's decendants retained a high status in Icelandic society, carrying the title *allsherjargoði,* which gave them a special status in Alþingi (q.v.). (*See also* SETTLEMENT PERIOD)

ÁRNI MAGNÚSSON INSTITUTE. The Árni Magnússon Institute was founded as the Icelandic Manuscript Institute (Handritastofnun Íslands) in 1962, but received its current name in 1972. It is named after the Icelandic scholar Árni Magnússon (q.v.) who collected and brought to Copenhagen many of the most valuable vellum and paper manuscripts in Iceland in the late 17th and early 18th centuries. Since the return of the first manuscripts from Copenhagen in 1971, the Árni Magnússon Institute and the Arnamagnæan Institute in Copenhagen have become the main depositories of these cultural treasures and centers of research in Old Norse philology. The main purposes of the Árni Magnússon Institute are to publish scientific editions of manuscripts and pursue research on medieval and early modern literature, but it is also active in folkloric studies. The Árni Magnússon Institute is affiliated with the University of Iceland (q.v.), and its director holds a professorship in the Department of Icelandic Language and Literature at the University. The Insti-tute has, however, a separate budget and a special steering committee. (*See also* MANUSCRIPTS, RETURN OF)

ÁSGEIRSSON, ÁSGEIR (1894–1972). The second president of the Republic of Iceland. Ásgeir Ásgeirsson was born the son of a merchant in Mýrar County. He graduated from secondary school in Reykjavík in 1912 and studied theology at the University of Iceland from 1912 to 1915 and theology and philosophy at the universities of Copenhagen and Uppsala from 1916 to 1917. He taught at the Teachers College in Reykjavík 1918–27 and served as superintendent for Icelandic schools from 1927 to 1931 and between 1934 and 1938. In 1938 he became director of the Fisheries Bank of Iceland, a position he held until he was elected president of Iceland in 1952.

The political career of Ásgeir Ásgeirsson was both long and colorful. He was first elected to parliament for the Progressive Party (PP, q.v.) in 1923, sitting in Alþingi (q.v.) continuously until 1952. In 1931, the PP appointed him minister of finance, and he served as prime minister from 1932 to 1934. At the end of that term, he left the PP but was reelected to Alþingi in 1934 as an independent candidate; in 1937, he joined the Social Democratic Party (q.v.). When Sveinn Björnsson (q.v.), the first president of Iceland, died in 1952, Ásgeir Ásgeirsson entered the presidential race. There he encountered staunch opposition from the two largest political parties in Iceland, the Independence Party (q.v.) and the PP, both of which endorsed Rev. Bjarni Jónsson, a highly regarded minister in Reykjavík. After a fierce campaign, Ásgeir Ásgeirsson won a narrow victory in a three-way race. Ásgeir Ásgeirsson was reelected president without opposition in 1956, 1960, and 1964 but stepped down at the end of his fourth term in 1968. He was generally highly regarded as president, and the controversies surrounding his first election did not affect the cordial relationship that has always existed between the sitting president and the political parties in Iceland. (*See also* PRESIDENT)

ÁSGRÍMSSON, HALLDÓR (1947–   ) The current chairman of the Progressive Party (PP, q.v.) was born in Vopnafjörður in eastern Iceland on September 8, 1947. He graduated from the Cooperative College of Iceland in 1965 and received a licence as a certified accountant in 1970. Halldór Ásgrímsson studied at the Commercial Universities of Bergen, Norway, and Copenhagen from 1971 to 1973. He was appointed assistant professor at the University of Iceland (q.v.) in 1973, but the following year he was elected to parliament for the PP. Halldór Ásgrímsson has served in various coalition governments from the early 1980s; as minister of fisheries from 1983 to 1991, as minister of justice and ecclesiastical affairs 1988–89, and from 1995 as minister of foreign affairs. He was elected vice-chairman of the PP in 1981, and chairman of the party in 1994.

AUÐUNS, AUÐUR (1911–   ). The first woman in Iceland to gain a prominent position in the political establishment. Auður Auðuns was born in Ísafjörður (q.v.), where her father was a businessman and a politician. She graduated from Menntaskólinn í Reykjavík (q.v.) in 1929, and in 1935 she was the first woman to complete a law exam from the University of Iceland (q.v.). She practiced law in her home town Ísafjörður from 1935 to 1936 and served as legal consultant in Reykjavík for the next years. In 1946 she was elected to the City Council of Reykjavík for the Independence Party (q.v.) and served as council president from 1954 to 1959 and again from 1960 to 1970. From 1959 to 1960 she was the first woman to become mayor of Reykjavík. In 1959, Auður Auðuns was elected to Alþingi (q.v.), where she held a seat for Reykjavík until 1974. In 1970 she was the first woman to be appointed to a cabinet post in Iceland, serving as minister of justice and ecclesiastical affairs for the last year of the Reconstruction Government (q.v.).

- B -

BALDVINSSON, JÓN (1882–1938). President of the Icelandic Federation of Labor (IFL, q.v.) and a leader of the Social Democratic Party (SDP, q.v.). Born on December 20, 1882, to a farmer in Ísafjörður County, Jón Baldvinsson learned the printing trade under the tutelage of the editor, politician, and bailiff Skúli Thoroddsen (q.v.), for whom he worked for eight years. From 1905 until 1918, when he became the director of the People's Bakery (Alþýðubrauðgerðin), he worked as a printer in Reykjavík. In March, 1916, at the time of the formation of the IFL, he was chosen as its secretary, and later in the same year, he ousted Ottó N. Þorláksson, the first president of the IFL, in an election for the presidency of the Federation. He served in this post, which automatically made him chairman of the SDP, until his death in 1938. From 1918 to 1924, Jón Baldvinsson sat in the City Council of Reykjavík for the SDP, and he entered parliament for the first time in 1921, where he held a seat until his death in 1938. In 1930 he became one of the first directors of the state-owned Fisheries Bank of Iceland.

Under the leadership of Jón Baldvinsson, the social democratic movement in Iceland took a very moderate course. He was an adamant opponent of revolutionary communism, which led to dissension in the SDP soon after World War I (q.v.). Eventually the radicals abandoned the party to form the Communist Party of Iceland (q.v.) in 1930. Jón Baldvinsson, and the policies he formulated, had a lasting influence on the SDP, as the party has always been fairly moderate compared to its Scandinavian sister parties, and it has consistently remained close to the center in Icelandic politics.

BANKS. *See* CENTRAL BANKING; FINANCIAL INSTITUTIONS.

BENEDIKTSSON, BJARNI (1908–1970). One of the leading politicians of this century in Iceland. Bjarni Benediktsson was born in Reykjavík on April 30, 1908, to a prominent member of the Icelandic parliament. He studied law in Reykjavík and Berlin (1926–32) and was appointed a professor of Law at the University of Iceland (q.v.) in 1932, while only 24 years old. He resigned his professorship in 1940 to become mayor of Reykjavík—a position he held for seven years. He sat in parliament for the Independence Party (IP, q.v.) from 1942 until his death in 1970. Selected to his first ministerial post in 1947, Bjarni Benediktsson served as minister of foreign affairs and justice to 1949, minister of foreign affairs and education 1949–50, minister of foreign affairs and justice 1950–53, and minister of foreign affairs and education 1953–56. When the IP fell from power in 1956, he became editor of the largest newspaper in Iceland, *Morgunblaðið* (q.v.), but with the formation of the Reconstruction Government (q.v.) in 1959, he resumed his former ministerial post. From 1959 to 1963, Bjarni Benediktsson was minister of justice, ecclesiastical affairs, industry, and health, with the exception of the fall of 1961 when he served as prime minister for three months. When Ólafur Thors (q.v.) retired from politics in 1963, Bjarni Benediktsson replaced him as prime minister. At the time of his death in 1970, he had led the government continuously for almost seven years, which was a record in Iceland.

Bjarni Benediktsson was a forceful leader of the largest political party in Iceland. He served as its deputy chairman for many years and, from 1961, as its chairman. Under his leadership, the IP continued its tradition of almost absolute unity, which helped it to retain its large following in local and parliamentary elections. After World War II (q.v.), Bjarni Benediktsson was instrumental in forming the foreign policy of the young republic, leading the country into NATO (q.v.) and to close cooperation with the United States (q.v.). His economic and social views followed the traditions of the IP, with a strong emphasis on free enterprise economics in theory, but a support of an extensive system of welfare programs in practice.

BENEDIKTSSON, EINAR (1864–1940). The poet and entrepreneur Einar Benediktsson was born at Elliðavatn near Reykjavík on October 31, 1864, to Benedikt Sveinsson (q.v.), a judge and politician. He graduated from secondary school in Reykjavík in 1884 and earned his law degree from the University of Copenhagen eight years later. After assisting his father for a few years, he edited the first daily newspaper in Iceland from 1896 to 1898. He was appointed bailiff in Rangárvellir County in 1904 but retired from this post three years later. For the next years, Einar Benediktsson lived for the most part abroad, in Britain, Denmark, and Germany. He was an untiring advocate of economic modernization in his country, promoting, among other things, fantastical plans for the construction of hydroelectric power plants in Iceland. Einar Benediktsson is, however, best known for his literary achievements, as he was a leading poet in Iceland during his lifetime. At first he was under strong influence from realism, and even from socialism, but later individualism and nationalism (q.v.) became prevalent themes in his poetry. During the last years of his life, Einar Benediktsson was a voluntary recluse on his farm on the coast of southwestern Iceland. In 1934, he was appointed professor-at-large by the University of Iceland, honoring his contribution to Icelandic literature, and at his death in 1940, he was the first person to be buried in the national cemetery at Þingvellir (q.v.).

BESSASTAÐIR. The Icelandic presidential residence, located on Álftanes, a small headland to the south of Reykjavík. Bessastaðir, which was an important manor in former times, is first mentioned in the *Sturlunga Saga* (q.v.), which was written in the 13th century. After the death of its owner Snorri Sturluson (q.v.) in 1241, the king of Norway took possession of Bessastaðir, and for centuries it was the abode of the highest royal officials in Iceland. From 1805 to 1846, the only secondary school in Iceland was located at Bessastaðir, but around the mid-century, when Reykjavík (q.v.) emerged as the center of royal administration in Iceland, Bessastaðir lost all of its official functions. In 1941, when Alþingi (q.v.) elected Sveinn Björnsson Governor of Iceland, the owner of Bessastaðir donated the manor to the state and since 1944 it has been the official residence of the president (q.v.) of the republic. The oldest of the buildings now standing at Bessastaðir were constructed for the Danish governor in Iceland during the 1760s, and are thus among the first stone houses to be built in Iceland. (*See also* MENNTA-SKÓLINN Í REYKJAVÍK; RÍKISSTJÓRI)

BJARNHÉÐINSDÓTTIR, BRÍET (1856–1940). One of the founders and early leaders of the Icelandic women's movement, born on September 27, 1856, to a farmer in Húnavatn County in northern Iceland. As was normal for farmers' children at the time, she did not enjoy any formal schooling beyond a year in a special school for girls. The almost total lack of educational opportunities for women at the time alerted her to the existing gender inequalities in Iceland, against which she fought for the remainder of her life.

In 1885, during a brief stay in Reykjavík, Bríet Bjarnhéðinsdóttir published her first article on these issues, but it was only when she moved permanently to the town in 1887 that she established herself as the leading spokeswoman for equal rights in Iceland. From 1895 to 1919 she published and managed a newspaper in Reykjavík, *Kvennablaðið*, which was almost entirely devoted to women's issues, calling for equality of men and women in education and in the workplace. In 1907, she founded the Icelandic Society for Women's Rights (q.v.), which was affiliated with The International Women's Suffrage Alliance. In 1908, or the year when women received the right to sit in local councils, Bríet Bjarnhéðinsdóttir was one of four women elected to the City Council of Reykjavík on a special women's list. She sat on the council for ten years.

Bríet Bjarnhéðinsdóttir was a vigorous advocate for women's rights at a time when formal equality was the main goal of the women's movement in Iceland. By modern standards, her political views were moderate, but her perseverance and enthusiasm make her an example for today's feminists. (*See also* WOMEN'S ALLIANCE)

BJÖRNSSON, SVEINN (1881–1952). The first president (q.v.) of the Republic of Iceland. He was born in Copenhagen on February 27, 1881, the son of a prominent Icelandic journalist and publisher who later became one of the leading politicians of his country. Sveinn Björnsson graduated from secondary school in Reykjavík in 1900 and received a law degree from the University of Copenhagen in 1907. He practiced law in Reykjavík from 1907 to 1920, when he became the first Icelandic ambassador to Denmark. Sveinn Björnsson returned to Iceland in 1924, but in 1926 he was reappointed to his former post in Copenhagen. He held this office until 1941, but as German forces occupied Denmark in 1940, he was summoned to Iceland to advice the Icelandic government on foreign affairs. The following year, Alþingi (q.v.) elected Sveinn Björnsson governor of Iceland, but this was an interim office created to substitute for the functions of the king during the war. When Iceland became an independent republic in 1944, Alþingi elected him Iceland's first president (q.v.). Sveinn Björnsson was reelected in 1948, but he died in 1952 when his second term was coming to an end. For the most part, Sveinn Björnsson played the same role in Icelandic politics as the Danish king had done before. As governor he raised some controversy, however, when he bypassed Alþingi in the formation of a non-partisan government in 1942. (*See also* REPUBLIC OF ICELAND, FOUNDATION OF; RÍKISSTJÓRI; WORLD WAR II [EFFECTS ON ICELAND])

BLACK DEATH. *See* PLAGUE IN ICELAND.

BÓNDI. It is difficult to translate the Icelandic word *bóndi* (pl. *bændur*) into English, both as the meaning of the word in the Icelandic language has changed through time and as it has very different connotations from similar words in English. In medieval texts, the word *bóndi* could best be translated as yeoman or franklin, that is, a freeholder. Thus, first the term involved some form of landownership, although etymologically it means simply a tiller of the earth. In modern Icelandic, the word *bóndi* has lost all of its former reference to the landowning status and includes all persons that head farming households, as long as they either rent or own a substantial tract of land. In this meaning the word *bóndi* can either be translated as peasant or farmer, depending on the social status of the person in question and on his or her relationship to the market. Until recently, *bændur* formed the dominant class in Iceland, both in numbers and social prestige. In the mid-19th century, censuses classified around 80 percent of Icelandic men in their forties as *bændur,* and they dominated parliamentary elections until the 20th century. In recent years the influence of the farmers' class has been declining, both in economic and political terms, following the thorough industrialization and urbanization (q.v.) of Icelandic society. (*See also* FARMING)

BOOK OF ICELANDERS. The *Book of Icelanders* (*Íslendingabók*) is a chronicle of Icelandic history, recording the story of Icelanders from the Settlement period (q.v.) to the early 12th century. The author was Ari Þorgilsson (q.v.) "the Learned," who is thought to have written the book during the years 1122–33. The *Book of Icelanders* recounts the history of the Icelandic settlement and the formation and structure of its legal system in the early 10th century. The author, who was a Catholic priest, lays a great emphasis on the conversion to Christianity (q.v.) of Iceland and the development of the Roman Catholic church. The book had a great influence on the writing of history in medieval Iceland, both because it established the chronology of the early Icelandic history, and because by using the native language rather than Latin, Ari Þorgilsson set the tone for later authors of learned literature in Iceland. (*See also BOOK OF SETTLEMENTS*; SAGAS)

BOOK OF SETTLEMENTS. The *Book of Settlements* (*Landnámabók*) is a description of the discovery and settlement of Iceland, giving accounts of around 430 settlers and their families. Its origin is unknown, because it is not preserved in its original form. It is clear, however, that the first redaction of the *Book of Settlements* dates back to the early 12th century. Today, it is preserved in five redactions, three from the Middle Ages and two from the 17th century. The internal relationship of these redactions has been disputed among scholars; some have traced two of the oldest redactions to a lost version from the early 13th century, but this theory has been challenged by other specialists. Some scholars have also doubted the historical value of the *Book of Settlements*, interpreting it as an attempt by 12th-century chieftains to legitimize their power, rather than as a truthful rendering of the settlement process. Whatever the origins of the *Book of Settlements* may be, or the intentions of its creators, it is at least a testimony of a remarkable interest in the history of Iceland, and of a desire to preserve it in written form. (*See also BOOK OF ICELANDERS*; SETTLEMENT PERIOD)

BROADCASTING. The Icelandic State Broadcasting Service (ISBS) started radio transmissions in Reykjavík in 1930. The state-owned company, which had a monopoly over all broadcasting in Iceland for decades, operated only this one radio channel until 1966. In that year, it added a television channel to its operations, and soon its emissions were received throughout the country.

The ISBS has played a major role in Icelandic cultural life since its foundation. Through its initiative, the Icelandic National Symphony Orchestra was founded in 1950, and in recent years its preferential status has been legitimized with reference to its production of noncommercial cultural programs.

If we do not count the American broadcasting service at the NATO (q.v.) base in Keflavík (q.v.), the state company had no competition until the 1980s, and therefore it did not need to cater specifically to any particular consumer group. Because of an increasing pressure for light entertainment, however, the company launched a new radio channel in 1983, devoting most of its time to popular music and talk shows. In 1985, Alþingi (q.v.) lifted the state monopoly on broadcasting, causing revolutionary changes in this field. Today, three companies compete in the Icelandic television market, and new technology has allowed viewers to receive transmissions from an increasing number of international TV channels. The radio market has undergone similar changes since the diversification of 1985. Thus, in addition to two major companies (the ISBS and the Icelandic Radio Company, which also runs two television channels), a number of small radio stations are now in operation in Iceland, catering mainly to special audiences.

- C -

CABINET. With the home rule (q.v.) of 1904, the office of the minister of Iceland was moved from Copenhagen to Reykjavík. To begin with, the government of Iceland had only one minister, who was formally a member of the Danish cabinet. In 1913, Alþingi (q.v.) passed a law permitting the formation of a cabinet of three ministers in Iceland, and the first such government was formed in 1917. Up to World War II (q.v.), all cabinets consisted of three ministers, but since 1939 their number has grown to around ten ministers. In the period from 1917 to 1995, Iceland has had 31 cabinets, with the average life of two-and-a-half years each.

As a rule, Icelandic cabinets include ministers from two or more parliamentary parties, and the ministers are usually selected from representatives in Alþingi. The president of the cabinet, or the prime minister (q.v.), receives his mandate from the president of the republic (q.v.), but governments are, in fact, normally formed through negotiations between the leaders of different political parties. The role of the president in the formation of cabinets is, therefore, usually more or less symbolic.

CATHOLICISM. When Icelanders converted to Christianity around the year 1000, the country came under the influence of the Roman Catholic church. For the next 550 years, Catholicism was the dominant faith in the country, until Lutheran Protestantism replaced it around the mid-16th century.

Although Iceland formally became a Christian country almost overnight, Catholic dogma and institutions gained acceptance only gradually in the country. The first diocese in Iceland was established at Skálholt (q.v.) in the south in the latter half of the 11th century and the second at Hólar (q.v.) in the north at the beginning of the 12th. At the end of the 11th century, the church ensured its financial independence as Gissur Ísleifsson, bishop at Skálholt, persuaded the various chieftains in the country to allow the church to collect tithes that were divided between the various Catholic institutions. The first monastery in Iceland was founded at Þing-eyri in the early 12th century, and in the late 12th and the 13th century, a few other monasteries and two convents were established in the country. These institutions became centers of learning in Iceland, and they played a pivotal role in the forming of its medi-eval literary culture.

It is difficult to measure the influence of Catholicism on the daily life of medieval Icelanders. The old beliefs seem to have vanished fairly rapidly, however, and in the 12th century the church had already become a relatively powerful institution in Iceland. The relations between the lay elite and the church were often tense, as the church demanded greater moral and political authority than the chieftains were ready to grant; these debates were settled for the most part in late 13th century by the intervention of the Norwegian king and the archbishop in Niðarós (Trondheim), Norway.

In 1550, with the execution of the last medieval Catholic bishop in Iceland, Catholicism was totally eradicated from the country. It was only in the late 19th century that it reemerged through the missionary work of a few Catholic priests who had the primary task of serving French and Belgian fishermen working the Icelandic waters. Today, only around 1 percent of the Icelandic population professes the Roman Catholic faith, but the Catholic church is, however, very active in Iceland. It has founded three hospitals in Iceland, runs a private elementary school in Reykjavík, and maintains a cathedral in Reykjavík. Moreover, on January 14, 1985, John Paul II declared Þorlákur Þórhallsson, bishop in Skálholt from 1178 to 1193, the guardian saint of the Icelandic nation. (*See also* ARASON, JÓN; CONVERSION TO CHRISTIANITY; LUTHERANISM; REFORMATION, THE)

CENSUSES. The first complete census of the Icelandic population was made in 1703, listing all inhabitants of the country by name, place of residence, age, and status. This is an invaluable source for demographic studies in Iceland, and is, in fact, the oldest census of this type that exists for the total population of a whole country. Two more censuses were taken in the 18th century, one in 1769 and another in 1785. The first census of the 19th century was taken in 1801, but it is only from 1835 that the administration conducted censuses on regular basis in Iceland; first every five years, but from 1860, at the beginning of every decade. This practice continued until 1960, when other statistical information made the censuses unnecessary. The last complete census in Iceland was taken in 1981. (*See also* POPULATION)

CENTRAL BANK OF ICELAND. *See* CENTRAL BANKING.

CENTRAL BANKING. The central banking function in Iceland was first established with the founding of Íslandsbanki, the Bank of Iceland, in 1904, but until then the notes of the Danish National Bank had been legal tender in Iceland (in addition to a very limited note issue of the National Bank of Iceland [NBI, q.v.] since 1886). That Alþingi (q.v.) granted the Bank of Iceland a monopoly on note issuing for 30 years was a remarkable decision, in light of the fact that it was a private bank under foreign ownership, established at the zenith of Icelandic nationalism (q.v.). The overriding concern at that time, however, was to provide the Icelandic economy with a separate money supply and, more importantly, its capital-hungry sectors with greatly increased loan capital. Opposition to the bank mounted during World War I (q.v.), due primarily to its money-printing and relaxed lending policies that contributed significantly to pushing inflation (q.v.) to a level far above that of other European countries. In 1921, Alþingi curtailed the Bank's money-issuing rights, and its notes were to be phased out until its privilege expired in 1933, although it was not effected until 1939. The issue of currency was transferred to the NBI in 1927, which set up a separate department to perform the central banking functions in 1928. In 1957, a special management was set up for the central banking department, and three years later ties with the NBI were fully severed. The Central Bank of Iceland (CBI, Seðlabanki Íslands), founded in 1961 as an independent institution, replaced the old department at the NBI.

In addition to its primary function of issuing bank notes and coins, CBI preserves and monitors the foreign reserves of the nation and determines the exchange value of the *króna*, which is subjected to government approval. By a law of 1992, the bank was authorized to let the exchange rate of the *króna* be determined in a foreign exchange market, paving the way for exchange rate policy independent of direct government control. Thus the CBI acts as the government's bank, but it serves as its financial adviser as well. Moreover, it supervises other banking institutions and is able to influence directly their volume of lending by prescribing reserve requirements.

A three-member Board of Governors, appointed by the minister of commerce, administrates the CBI. The CBI has also a Board of Directors, which is a supervisory and advisory body, consisting of five members elected by Alþingi for four-year terms. G. J. (*See also* CURRENCY; FINANCIAL INSTITUTIONS)

CHIEFTAIN. *See* GOÐI.

CITIZENS' PARTY. Two political organizations in Iceland have carried the name Borgaraflokkur, or the Citizens' Party. The first was a short-lived coalition of political groups to the right, formed before elections to Alþingi (q.v.) in 1923. Its electoral success led to the formation of the Conservative Party (q.v.) in the following year. Albert Guðmundsson (q.v.) founded the second Citizens' Party in

1987 when the leadership of the Independence Party (q.v.) forced him to resign his ministerial post. The Citizens' Party won a remarkble victory in the parliamentary elections of 1987, polling 11 percent of the votes cast. After deciding to participate in a coalition government of parties to the left of center from 1989 to 1991, the party disintegrated, and it ceased to exist in 1991.

COAST GUARD. Iceland has never had any military service, and it was only with the foundation of the Icelandic Coast Guard in the 1920s that Icelanders took responsibility for the defense of their territorial waters. Until then the Danish navy had patrolled the sea around Iceland, but the Act of Union (q.v.) of 1918 stipulated that the Icelandic state could take over this function when it chose to do so, either on its own or in cooperation with the Danish navy. The first step toward this goal was taken in 1920 when one vessel was brought to the Vestmanna Islands (q.v.), at a private initiative, with the purpose of guarding Icelandic fishing limits (q.v.) and to serve as a rescue vessel for the islands' fishing fleet. Five years later, the Icelandic government bought its first gunboat for the same objective, starting operations the following year. The Danish navy continued, however, to play an important role in this respect until the outbreak of the Second World War.

The Icelandic Coast Guard was of crucial importance during the so-called cod wars (q.v.) of the 1950s, 60s, and 70s. During these episodes, its gunboats harassed those who did not respect Icelandic fishing limits, then primarily British trawlers. Today, the Coast Guard continues to police the sea around Iceland, and it also performs important rescue services inside and outside Icelandic territorial waters.

In spite of its important tasks, the fleet of the Coast Guard has always been small. At the height of the last cod war, it operated seven patrol boats, but it is down to three at present. The Coast Guard owns also one aircraft and three helicopters.

COD WARS. The Icelandic fishing banks have attracted European fishermen for centuries, causing serious frictions over fishing rights. In his study of the history of these confrontations, the Icelandic historian Björn Þorsteinsson has counted as many as ten cod wars since the Middle Ages, in all of which British fishermen have played a prominent part. The first five of these disputes took place in the period from the early 15th to the early 16th centuries (1415–1532), as the Danish monarchy sought to establish control over the government and trade in Iceland. For Icelanders, the main objective in this period was to prevent the foreign fishermen from establishing permanent stations in Iceland, because many feared that they would unsettle the native social and economic system.

The modern cod wars have all been fought over the extension and protection of Icelandic fishing limits (q.v.). The primary cause for them all was the fact that new fishing techniques made it increasingly undesirable for Icelanders to allow free access to the fishing grounds around the country. The first of the modern cod wars took place at the end of the 19th century when the British government sent a small squadron to Iceland to investigate alleged encroachment upon the liberties of British trawlers around the Icelandic coast. This episode ended in 1901 when the Danish and British governments signed a treaty granting British trawlers permission to fish anywhere outside three nautical miles from the Icelandic coast.

In the years 1952–75 the Icelandic government extended the fishing limits unilaterally from three to 200 nautical miles in four steps. Various governments contested these extensions, but no nation reacted as forcefully as the British. By sending a fleet to protect their trawlers from the harassment of the Icelandic Coast Guard (q.v.), and by economic pressure, the British government tried to force Icelanders to change their position, failing on all four occasions. The last cod war ended in 1976 with a treaty between Iceland and the United Kingdom (q.v.), where the latter acknowledged the 200-mile fishing limits around Iceland. (*See also* FISHERIES)

COMMONWEALTH PERIOD. The common term for the period in Icelandic history from the foundation of Alþingi (q.v.) in 930 until the passing of the Old Covenant (q.v., 1262–64) is the Commonwealth period, or Þjóðveldisöld in Icelandic. This was culturally a very productive period, but politically a turbulent one. Thus, most of the great works of Icelandic medieval literature were written in this period, from the historical chronicles of the early 12th century to the family sagas (q.v.) and contemporary sagas of the 13th.

A growing struggle between various clans for political hegemony in Iceland marks the history of this period. With the foundation of Alþingi, the country was given a unified law code, but the absence of an executive branch for the whole country fueled open warfare in Iceland, primarily in the 13th century. In the beginning, the population was divided into 36–39 chieftaincies (*goðorð*) of equal status, but later the most powerful magnates appropriated many such chieftaincies and governed large regions by the force of their wealth and power. During the last part of the Commonwealth period, or the Age of the Sturlungs (q.v.), the country plunged into almost total chaos, bringing some of the leading families in Iceland toward extinction. Hence, Icelanders pledged allegiance to the Norwegian king and paid taxes in return for pacification of the country. The Commonwealth period ended when Icelanders accepted a union with Norway in 1262–64. (*See also* GRÁGÁS; JÓNSBÓK; SAGAS; STURLUNGA SAGA)

COMMUNE. The traditional term for a local commune in Iceland is *hreppur.* The origin of communes is unclear, but they seem to have been founded early in the Commonwealth period (q.v.). From the beginning, the main function of the communes was to administrate the poor relief and to organize common tasks of the peasant economy, like driving the sheep from mountain pastures in the fall. Originally, the communes were independent entities, governed by so-called *hreppstjórar* (overseers), elected by the taxpaying peasants from their own ranks. When the monarchy grew stronger after the end of the Middle Ages, the king began to assume more command over the local government. Thus, bailiffs selected the overseers, for the most part, after the end of the Middle Ages. In the early 19th century the overseers became virtually state officials, as their number was reduced from three to five to one or two in each commune; the law stipulated that they should be appointed by the bailiffs and the district governors.

During the last 125 years, the system of local government has gone through radical changes, reflecting the general social and political development of the country. In 1872, a new legislation established democratically elected local councils in the communes, while it separated the administrative functions of the overseer from the government of the commune. This has made the communal government more responsive to the needs of its inhabitants, and now they play important roles in the administration of local issues such as education, leisure activities, communications, power supply, and support for local businesses. Above all, however, the demographic transformation of the last century transformed the communes in Iceland. Thus, the smallest communes of today have less inhabitants than ever before, a number having less than 100 inhabitants, while the population of the most populous commune, Reykjavík (q.v.), is almost double that of the whole country in 1850. For this reason, the state has attempted to reduce the number of communes in Iceland, in order to strengthen their ability to deal with the various administrative tasks of modern society. Although this effort has only been partially successful so far, as the traditional municipal divisions have a strong sentimental value in Iceland, the number of local communes has decreased markedly in recent years. Thus, the total number of municipalities fell from 224 in 1980 to 165 in 1997, and this development will almost certainly continue in the future.

COMMUNICATIONS. The location of the country and the sparseness of the population make transportation of cargo and passengers imperative for Iceland's economy, particularly because the lack of most raw materials and the homogeneity of the economy makes the population totally dependent upon foreign trade. Until the late 19th century, however, the Icelandic transportation network was extremely primitive. Roads were almost nonexistent, making the use of vehicles all but impossible. Since then, the modernization of the economy has called for a total transformation, establishing safe and frequent communications between various parts of the country and with foreign countries. Thus, the first major bridge to be constructed in Iceland was completed in 1891, and Iceland's first steamship company, the Icelandic Steamship Company (q.v.), was founded in 1914.

In the 20th century, general changes in technology have revolutionized the system of communications in Iceland. In this respect, the country has followed a similar track with its neighboring countries. At the present, Iceland is connected with both Europe and America through air and on sea, and satellites link the country directly with all of the world. This dramatic improvement in communications has greatly enhanced economic development in Iceland, as rapid transmission of information and materials has allowed Icelandic producers to take full advantage of international markets for their goods. (*See also* ICELANDAIR)

COMMUNIST PARTY OF ICELAND (CPI). After World War I (q.v.) and the Bolshevik Revolution in Russia in 1917, there was a growing sympathy for revolutionary Marxism among Icelandic social democrats. Under the chairmanship of Jón Baldvinsson (q.v.), the Icelandic Federation of Labor (q.v.) and the Social Democratic Party (SDP, q.v.) took a strong opposition to these ideas. As soon as 1922, the Social Democratic Union in Reykjavík split into two factions, one of which espoused a revolutionary line, while the other remained loyal to the moderate opinions of the SDP. The two factions differed on a number of issues, most of which were typical of the rift between social democratic and communist parties in Europe in the interwar period. Domestic politics also caused dissension in the SDP, for the radical members of the SDP opposed the party's cooperation with the government of the Progressive Party (q.v.) formed in the summer of 1927. In the end, no compromise was possible between the two flanks of the SDP, and in 1930 splinter groups from the SDP and other radicals formed the Communist Party of Iceland (Kommúnistaflokkur Íslands), advocating a Marxist revolution. The party received only limited support in the beginning, or 3 percent of the votes cast in 1931, but its following increased rapidly during the years of the Great Depression (q.v.). Thus, the party received 7.5 percent of the votes in the parliamentary elections of 1933, and 8.5 percent in 1937. In the 1937 elections, the last elections in which the CPI took part under that name, the party had its first three representatives elected to parliament. In 1938, the CPI was dissolved to form a new party with a splinter group from the SDP, called the Socialist Unity Party (q.v.). This was in accordance with the resolutions of the Comintern congress of 1935 that called for a united front against fascism in Iceland. (*See also* OLGEIRSSON, EINAR; VALDI-MARSSON, HÉÐINN)

CONFEDERATION OF ICELANDIC EMPLOYERS (CIE). In 1934, 82 employers founded the CIE in Reykjavík, naming it Vinnu-veitendafélag Íslands, but later it received its current name, Vinnuveitendasamband Íslands. The task of the CIE, which was formed at the time of heightened tensions between employers and workers during the Great Depression (q.v.), was to organize employers in their negotiations with labor unions, to secure tranquility in the work place by preventing strikes, and to promote the general interests of employers in Iceland. At the present, the CIE represents around 3,000 employers in the private sector.

Today, the CIE serves as a negotiating partner in disputes with labor unions representing workers in different economic sectors and from all parts of the country. In this capacity, it has had enormous influence on economic policy in recent years, as the agreements between the Icelandic Federation of Labor (q.v.) and the CIE have often required a substantial commitment from the public authorities. The result has been a marked decrease in levels of inflation (q.v.), which since the early 1990s has led to more stability in the economic sphere than was present in the preceding decade.

CONSERVATIVE PARTY (CP). A group of 20 representatives in Alþingi (q.v.) formed the CP, Íhaldsflokkurinn, on February 24, 1924. A strong belief in free enterprise characterized the party platform, and its objective was both to reduce and to balance the state budget. Less than a month after its foundation, the CP formed a cabinet (q.v.), pursuing its agenda with vigor for the next three years. The government lost its majority in the parliamentary elections of 1927, however, although the CP retained its position as the largest party in the country, receiving 42 percent of the votes cast. But as the electoral system favored the rural constituencies, the Progressive Party (q.v.) won more seats in parliament than the CP. In 1929, the CP coalesced with the small Liberal Party to form the Independence Party (IP, q.v.). Jón Þorláksson (q.v.), who had served as chairman of the CP from its beginning, became the first leader of the IP in 1929.

CONSTITUTION OF THE REPUBLIC OF ICELAND (1944). After the total severance from Denmark, the Republic of Iceland was established on June 17, 1944. As a result, a new constitution had to be passed in order to define the functions and role of the office of president (q.v.). The writers of the constitution opted for a weak presidency, while public authority was vested primarily in government and parliament, to which the executive branch is responsible. Except for the provisions on the presidency, the constitution of 1944 followed closely the example of earlier constitutions, building on traditions set during Danish rule. Since its introduction, Alþingi (q.v.) has made a few minor amendments to the constitution, most of which concern parliamentary elections and the structure of Alþingi. (*See also* ALÞINGI; CONSTITUTIONS, 1874–1918)

CONSTITUTIONS, 1874–1918. Icelanders received their first constitution in 1874, the same year they commemorated the 1,000th anniversary of the settlement of Iceland. This came after a long tug-of-war between the Danish government and the Icelandic representatives in Alþingi (q.v.), the former wanting to tie Iceland more closely to the Danish state, the latter wanting only to retain a union with Denmark through personal ties to the king. The constitution of 1874 awarded Alþingi limited legislative power and full sovereignty over the Icelandic budget. The king, however, had absolute veto on all legislation passed in the parliament—a prerogative he used frequently during the next decades—and total control over the executive branch of government in Iceland. As before, Icelanders did not elect representatives to the Danish legislature, and they had, therefore, no influence on the government of the Danish state. For this reason, the constitution of 1874 did not subject Icelanders to general state taxes.

The constitution of 1874 was accepted with great resentment in Iceland and caused fierce debates in the country, primarily because it confirmed the hated Status Laws (q.v.) set in 1871 and did not provide for any independent executive branch under the control of Alþingi. Two major amendments corrected these shortcomings, however—one in 1902–04 and another in 1918–20. The first of these revisions granted Iceland home rule (q.v.), which came into effect in 1904. The second came as a result of the Act of Union (q.v.) in 1918, which gave Iceland the status of an independent and sovereign state. Another major amendment, enacted in 1915, granted women the right to vote in parliamentary elections.

In spite of its shortcomings, the constitution of 1874 remains the foundation for civil government and social life in Iceland, and most of its provisions are still valid. It was based on a firm belief in the importance of personal liberties, freedom of expression, religious liberty, and democratic representation in parliament. Thus, it endorsed the principles of democracy, building upon the political traditions of Western Europe. (*See also* CONSTITUTION OF THE REPUBLIC OF ICELAND (1944); DENMARK [RELATIONS WITH])

CONSTITUTIVE ASSEMBLY. In 1848, King Frederick VII of Denmark renounced his absolute power in the Danish monarchy and convened a constitutive assembly to write a constitution for the state. The same year, after receiving numerous petitions from Iceland, the king promised Icelanders that the constitution would not come into force in Iceland until they had deliberated on the matter in a constitutive assembly of their own. Elections for the assembly were held in the summer of 1850, but the meeting was held in Reykjavík from July 4 to August 9 of the following year.

The promise of a special constitutive assembly (*þjóðfundur*) kindled high hopes in Iceland, and many expected that the new constitution would grant Iceland virtual autonomy in its domestic affairs. At the assembly, the great majority of the Icelandic representatives, under the leadership of the scholar Jón Sigurðsson (q.v.), adhered firmly to this opinion. According to the royal bill presented to the assembly, however, Iceland was to become an integral part of the new democratic Danish state; Icelanders were to elect representatives to the Danish parliament, and Alþingi (q.v.) was only to have the same authority as other regional councils in the monarchy. As the two sides could find no middle ground, the Danish governor of Iceland dissolved the meeting before the representatives had reached any conclusion.

As the constitutive assembly ended in an impasse, Iceland remained effectively under Danish absolutism (q.v.) until king Christian IX granted the the country a special constitution in 1874. For Icelanders, the assembly was not without significance, however, because it forced them to consider their status in the state. Their conclusion was unequivocal; in the long run, nothing short of full sovereignty would be accepted. This set the tone for Icelandic politics for the next decades, and until the Act of Union (q.v.) of 1918, fervent nationalism (q.v.) dominated Icelandic political discourse. (*See also* CONSTITUTIONS, 1874–1918; HOME RULE; ICELANDIC NATIONALIST MOVEMENT)

CONVERSION TO CHRISTIANITY. Until the late 10th century, Icelanders practiced the old Scandinavian religion, worshipping Norse deities like Óðinn and Þór. During the last two decades of the 10th century, an organized Christianizing effort began in Iceland. This was part of an undertaking, directed from Germany, to convert the Scandinavian countries to the Christian faith. Icelanders had come into earlier contact with Christianity, however, as some of the settlers had been converted before coming to Iceland, but no organized congregation existed in the country before the end of the first millennium.

The early missionaries met with only limited success, although they were able to convert some influential chieftains to their religion. But in the summer of 999 or 1000, two missionaries came to Alþingi (q.v.) with direct orders from Ólafur Tryggvason king of Norway to Christianize the Icelandic population. According to the *Book of Icelanders* (q.v.), this split the men gathered in Alþingi into two religious camps, but after careful considerations the leader of the non-Christian group encouraged those present to accept the Christian faith and to abandon the old religion. This was a pragmatic decision, made to preserve peace in the country, because many feared that a religious split would result in a civil war. Therefore, the new religious settlement took a realistic approach, allowing Icelanders to continue some of their old religious practices in secret. Formally, however, from the time of the conversion, the Christian faith was to be the sole religion recognized in the country. (*See also* CATHOLICISM)

COOPERATIVE MOVEMENT, THE. The Icelandic cooperative movement has its roots in Þingey County in northeastern Iceland, where the first cooperative society was founded in 1882. Following the example of similar farmers' associations that were organized in many regions of Iceland during the 19th century, the first cooperative society was to coordinate the trade of farmers in the district with the purpose of increasing the market value of their products and of lowering the prices of the goods they had to purchase. During the last decades of the 19th century, a number of such societies were founded in Iceland, especially in its northern part. One of the incentives for this development was a growing prosperity brought to this part of the country by an active trade in live sheep that were exported directly to Britain in the late 19th century. In 1902, a precursor of the Federation of Icelandic Cooperative Societies (Samband íslenskra samvinnufélaga), commonly known in Iceland by its acronym SÍS, was founded in Þingey County as three local cooperatives joined their forces. During the next decade, a number of cooperative societies in the northeast entered the Federation, but this was a time of rapid expansion of the cooperative movement in general. Moreover, its influence grew drastically during World War I (q.v.), especially because the foundation of the Progressive Party (q.v.) in 1917 gained it a powerful political ally in parliament.

In 1917, the Federation moved its headquarters from Akureyri to Reykjavík (qq.v.), where in the next few years it built up one of the largest commercial enterprises in Iceland. Thus, the Federation acquired a dominant position in trade with farmers in Iceland, acting both as a wholesale importer for the many cooperative societies around the country and as an exporter of the goods that the farmers produced.

The prosperity of the cooperative movement continued in the years following World War II. Its political connections and the loyalty of its members secured the movement a strong position in a strictly regulated market Thus, the Federation moved into new spheres of operation, such as importing cars and machines and exporting fish, in addition to owning totally or a large number of shares in a bank, the largest insurance company in Iceland, a merchant shipping company, and the largest oil-distribution company in Iceland.

In the late 1980s this economic giant hit hard times. Heavy debts at a time of drastic rise in interest rates caused this crisis; a problem that was heightened by the grave difficulties in farming (q.v.) at the time. For this reason, the Federation was more or less dissolved in 1990, as it split into a number of independent companies. Today, some individual cooperative societies are still strong in their local markets, but the cooperative movement as a whole has totally lost both its political clout and its dominant status in the economy and society.

COUNTY. The traditional administrative and juridical district in Iceland is the *sýsla,* or county. The term itself was first used in *Jónsbók* (q.v.), the code of law enacted in 1281, but it was only at the close of the Middle Ages that the geographical division of the country into counties was finalized. In each county there was a bailiff (*sýslumaður*), who served as district judge, sheriff, and representative of the state in the county. The office of bailiff was, therefore, one of the most important administrative posts in Iceland, because the bailiffs were often the only royal officials in their respective districts.

With growing centralization and urbanization in Iceland, the authority of the bailiffs has changed. It was only in 1992, however, that the legal foundation of the office was reformed with a total separation of the judicial and executive branches in the local districts. Thus, the country is now divided into eight judicial districts, each served by a district court. At the same time, the function of the bailiffs has been restricted to serving the executive branch; they collect taxes and head the district police.

Iceland's division into counties has not changed much since the 16th century, although the subdivision of the larger districts has varied through time. At the present, Iceland is divided into 23 counties, which are administrated by 18 bailiffs. In the 1992 administrative reform, the office of town magistrate (*bæjarfógeti*) was abolished, and they received the same title as the bailiffs (*sýslumaður*), although their district is not called county (*sýsla*). The total number of bailiffs is, therefore, 27.

CURRENCY. The Icelandic monetary unit is *króna* (pl. *krónur*), which is divided into 100 *aurar* (sing. *eyrir*). As Danish currency laws applied to Iceland during the 19th century, the króna replaced the old *rigsbankdal* in 1873, as it did in the Danish state in general. It was related to gold, and the value fixed at 1 króna = 0.4032258 g of fine gold. After the suspension of the gold standard in 1914, the króna followed the fluctuations of the Danish krone until 1920, when it was depreciated in order to correct the effects of high inflation during and after World War I (q.v.). It was not until 1922 that banks officially acknowledged the new rate, and the Icelandic króna could be said to have gained independent status.

Persistent high inflation (q.v.) after 1960 led to a rapid depreciation of the króna. On January 1, 1981, a comprehensive currency reform came into effect, including the multiplication of the value of the króna by one hundred, so that one new króna became the equivalent of 100 old krónur. At the same time a new set of notes and coins replaced the old one. Much lower inflation at the end of the 1980s and in the first half of the 1990s has raised hopes of the currency becoming more stable than it was for most of the postwar period. G. J. (*See also* CENTRAL BANKING)

- D -

DAGBLAÐIÐ VÍSIR (DV). The oldest newspaper in Iceland that is still in publication, founded as *Vísir* in 1910. *Vísir* was for a long time the only afternoon daily in Iceland, but in 1975 a rival afternoon paper, *Dagbladið,* started publication in Reykjavík under the direction of Jónas Kristjánsson, a former editor of *Vísir.* After a few years of fierce competition, the two papers merged under the name *Dagbladið Vísir,* or DV as it is commonly known today. DV has no affiliation with a political party, although *Vísir* was always close to the Independence Party (q.v.) in its opinions. DV currently publishes around 50,000 copies, six days a week.

DAGUR. The only daily newspaper published outside of Reykjavík. *Dagur* was founded in 1918 in Akureyri (q.v.) at the initiative of the politician Jónas Jónsson (q.v.). The paper, which supported the Progressive Party (PP, q.v.), was published twice a month in the beginning but weekly from 1919 to 1985. In 1985, it changed to a daily newspaper, severing its ties with the PP. Like all the smaller newspapers in Iceland, *Dagur* has suffered grave financial difficulties in recent years. Therefore it merged in 1996 it with the other PP newspaper, *Tíminn* (q.v.), and the two newspapers are now published under the name *Dagur-Tíminn.*

DENMARK (RELATIONS WITH). The long Danish rule over Iceland began in 1380 when Norway became a Danish dependency, following a merger of the royal houses of the two countries. From that time until the foundation of the Republic of Iceland (q.v.) in 1944, Iceland was tied to the Danish monarchy.

Because of Iceland's geographic isolation, the union with Denmark had little immediate influence on the Icelandic social and political system. With the Lutheran Reformation (q.v.), which was completed in 1550, the Danish state demonstrated, however, that it could force through a drastic change against the determined opposition of its Icelandic subjects. In the 17th century, the monarchy increased its power in Iceland considerably, first with the introduction of the hated monopoly trade (q.v.) in 1602 and later with the establishment of absolutist rule in 1662. From that time until the granting of the first democratic constitution to Iceland in 1874, the Danish king controlled totally both the administration and the legislative process, although in practice he had to rely on the advice and information of his Icelandic administrators for most of his decisions on Icelandic matters.

From the time of the Constitution of 1874 (q.v.) until the final severance of all ties with Denmark in 1944, various Icelandic institutions gradually took over most of the functions of the Danish king. The constitution gave Alþingi (q.v.) limited legislative power and total control over public finances in Iceland. With home rule (q.v.) in 1904, the executive power in Icelandic domestic affairs was moved from Copenhagen to Iceland, and from 1918 to 1944 the king held only a symbolic authority in these matters.

The Icelandic population seemed generally to be content with the Danish rule for most of the half millennium it lasted. One reason for this was the fact that the king usually demanded little from his Icelandic subjects; royal taxes were light and the Danish king never required Icelanders to serve as soldiers in his army. Moreover, most officials in Iceland, except for the governor, were of Icelandic decent, and for that reason Icelandic was the official language in both church and courts. With the growing nationalist sentiment of the 19th century, the union with Denmark became more onerous in the eyes of the Icelandic population, however, and the Constitutive Assembly (q.v.) of 1851 rejected being included Iceland in a Danish nation-state. After that, the nationalists based their demands on claims of past injustice by the Danish government, and for a period of time there was widespread anti-Danish sentiment in Iceland. The generous terms of Icelandic independence, and sympathy for Icelandic sentiments in Denmark, have almost totally healed all grudges toward the former mother country. Today, Iceland has strong cultural ties with Denmark, and the Danish is still an obligatory subject in Icelandic elementary and secondary schools. (*See also* ACT OF UNION; DRAFT, THE; ICELANDIC NATIONALIST MOVEMENT, THE; NATIONALISM; STATUS LAWS)

DIRECTORATE OF FISHERIES. A government agency created in 1992 to implement laws and regulations regarding fisheries and fish processing in Iceland. The function of the Directorate (Fiskistofa) is to ensure effective administration and organization of fisheries' management (q.v.) and supervision of the fishing industry in Iceland. In this capacity, the Directorate determines the annual fishing quotas for all fishing vessels in Iceland, controls the transfer of such quotas between ships, imposes penalties for illegal catches, collects information on each vessel's landings, publishes and gathers statistics on the fishing industry, and supervises monitoring on board fishing vessels and in the various fishing ports in Iceland. Moreover, the Directorate issues licences for fishing plants and oversees their production. The Directorate plays a pivotal role in the development of the Icelandic fishing industry and, consequently, for the economy in general. (*See also* FISHERIES; FISHERIES MANAGEMENT; MARINE RESEARCH INSTITUTE)

DISTRICT GOVERNOR. *See* AMTMAÐUR.

DRAFT, THE. The politics of the Home Rule period (q.v., 1904–18) were marked by the efforts of the Danish and Icelandic parliaments to reach an agreement on how to restructure the relationship between the two countries. Icelanders had always disputed the Status Laws (q.v.) of 1871, which defined Iceland's position in the Danish monarchy, in part because the Danish parliament had passed the statute without consenting with Alþingi (q.v.). In 1908, a committee of Danish and Icelandic parliamentary representatives wrote a draft for new legislation on the issue, which was to be discussed in the two parliaments. The king dissolved Alþingi in the spring of 1908, because a new parliament was to vote on the bill. The opponents of the "Draft" won a clear victory in heated elections in the fall of 1908, leading to its defeat in parliament the following year.

The debates on the Draft in 1908 set the course for Icelandic politics in the following decade. First, they led to a reorganization of the Icelandic party system, where new alliances were formed on the basis of people's opinion of the Draft. Second, they helped to define the ultimate goal of Icelandic politics; that is, anything short of full sovereignty was deemed to be insufficient. In the end, the Danish parliament accepted this fact, and with the Act of Union (q.v.) in 1918, Icelandic sovereignty was fully recognized. (*See also* DENMARK (RELATIONS WITH); HOME RULE; NATIONALISM)

- E -

EDDIC POETRY. A term used for one of the two main categories of Old Norse poetry (the other is skaldic poetry, q.v.). The two major genres of eddic poetry are mythical poetry, such as *Hávamál* and *Völuspá,* and heroic poetry dealing with Old Germanic legends stemming from the time of struggles between Huns, Goths, and Germanic tribes in the fourth and fifth centuries. The former genre is specifically Nordic, serving as the best source available on Old Norse religious beliefs, while poems of the latter type are related to other Germanic poetry of this kind. The main source for eddic poetry is one Icelandic manuscript, called *Codex Regius,* dating from the late 13th century, but the genesis of its poems is unknown.

EDUCATION. Despite the fact that Iceland has had relatively high rates of literacy (q.v.), at least since the 18th century, its school system is more or less a 20th-century creation. Thus, the first comprehensive legislation to stipulate compulsory schooling in Iceland was passed in 1907, requiring most children of the ages 10–14 to attend school for a minimum of six months a year. This legislation reflected a profound transformation that took place in social and economic life during the late 19th and early 20th centuries, because it was only with the growth of fishing villages and towns around the coast that the foundation of elementary schools was possible.

There is a longer tradition for secondary education in Iceland, as its history can be traced back to the bishops' schools in Skálholt and Hólar (qq.v.), founded in the 11th and 12th centuries respectively. These schools were primarily religious seminaries, or Latin schools, preparing clergymen for offices in the church. At the beginning of the 19th century, the two Latin schools merged, moving permanently to Reykjavík in 1846. With the foundation of a theological college in Reykjavík in 1847, the Latin school in Reykjavík became a regular gymnasium, preparing its students for a university entrance exam. Gradually, increasing demands for professional education transformed the elite character of secondary education in Iceland, and in the 1920s the secondary school in Akureyri (q.v.) received the right to prepare students for university studies. During the latter half of the 20th century the secondary school system has diversified greatly. Today over 20 institutions, spread around the country, have the right to offer university exams, and a great majority of Icelanders now receive some form of secondary education.

The system of vocational and trade schools in Iceland has its origins in the late 19th century. A growing interest in economic improvements led to the foundation of the first special schools for farmers around 1880. In the next few decades a number of vocational schools were founded—the Nautical School in Reykjavík in 1891, Reykjavík Trades' School in 1904, and the Commercial School of Iceland in 1904, to name a few examples. Finally, as part of the school reform legislation of 1907, a teacher training college was founded in Reykjavík in the following year, with the purpose of educating elementary school teachers.

Until the latter half of the 19th century, the University of Copenhagen served as the national university for Iceland. With the foundation of the colleges of theology (1847), medicine

(1876), and law (1908), a large part of university-level professional education moved into the country, however. The foundation of the University of Iceland (q.v.) in 1911 was a further step in that direction, and it has gradually developed into the largest educational institution in Iceland. In recent years, a number of college- or university-level institutions have been founded in Iceland, usually on the basis of existing specialized schools (for example, the Teacher Training College was upgraded to the University College of Education in 1971). Moreover, in 1987, the state established a small university in Akureyri (q.v.) in its effort to decentralize university education in Iceland.

Today, it is compulsory for all Icelandic children to attend school from the ages of six to 16. The state runs nearly all the Icelandic educational system; all public elementary schools are free of charge and secondary schools, universities, and colleges charge only minimum fees for tuition. (*See also* LITERACY; MENNTASKÓLINN Í REYKJAVÍK)

EIRÍKSSON, JÓN (1728–1787). One of the most influential Icelanders of the 18th century was born to a farmer in Skaftafell County on August 31, 1728. In 1743, he enrolled in the Latin school at Skál-holt (q.v.), where a Danish Lutheran minister, Ludvig Harboe, took him under his wing. Harboe was stationed in Iceland at the time on a special mission from the Danish church authorities, surveying Icelandic religious life and the moral conduct and education of the inhabitants. When Harboe was appointed bishop of Trondheim in Norway, Jón Eiríksson went with him, never to return to Iceland. He finished secondary school in Norway, and in 1748 he enrolled in the University of Copenhagen. Soon he abandoned his plans of becoming a theologian, studying philology and philosophy, and later law, at the university. A year after earning his law degree in 1758, he accepted a teaching position in law at Sorø Academy in Denmark—a post he held until 1771. Upon leaving his teaching position, Jón Eiríksson moved to Copenhagen to work in the newly established Norwegian section of the Ministry of Finance (Finanskollegiet, later Rentekammeret). For the remainder of his life, he held high posts in the royal ministries in Copenhagen.

Throughout much of his career, Jón Eiríksson was a key figure in the administration of Icelandic affairs in the capital, supporting actively the efforts of men like Skúli Magnússon (q.v.), who sought to diversify the economy. In addition to his career as a royal official, he held various other appointments; he served as an assessor in the Danish Supreme Court from 1779 and head librarian of the Royal Library from 1781. In the end, a heavy workload and personal disappointments caused the deterioration of his mental health, leading to his suicide in 1787.

Jón Eiríksson gained respect for his remarkable energy and intelligence, on the basis of which he reached high rank in the administrative hierarchy. He remained an Icelandic patriot throughout his life, writing extensively on economic and cultural affairs. Thus, although Jón Eiríksson remained a loyal servant of the king to the end of his life, the nationalist intellectuals of the 19th and 20th centuries revered him greatly for his contributions to Icelandic social and economic development. (*See also* INN-RÉTTINGARNAR)

EIRÍKSSON, LEIFUR (10th and 11th centuries). This adventurer was born around the year 970 on a farm in western Iceland. The son of Eiríkur Þorvaldsson, the founder of the Norse settlement in Greenland (q.v.), Leifur Eiríksson moved with his father to the new colony in 986. Around the year 1000, when he was on his way from Norway to Greenland, Leifur Eiríksson is said to have drifted from his course and to have hit an unknown land to the west of Greenland—that is, the mainland of North America. One part of this "new world" he named Vinland (q.v.), meaning either "Vine Land" or "Meadow Land." According to legend, Leifur Eiríksson spent one winter in Vinland, returning to Greenland in the following spring and bringing back a load of timber. On his way to Greenland, he is said to have rescued people from a shipwreck, a deed that earned him the nickname *heppni* (Lucky). Leifur Eiríksson is supposed to have died around the year 1020.

ELDJÁRN, KRISTJÁN (1916–1982). The third president of the Icelandic republic was born in Eyjafjörður County in northern Iceland on December 6, 1916. Kristján Eldjárn entered secondary school in Akureyri (q.v.) in 1931, and graduated five years later. After studying archaeology at the University of Copenhagen, he returned to Iceland in 1939 at the outbreak of World War II. Kristján Eldjárn completed a master's degree in Icelandic studies at the University of Iceland in 1944, and in 1957, he defended a doctoral dissertation at the University of Iceland.

In 1945, Kristján Eldjárn became an assistant at the Icelandic National Museum. Two years later, he was appointed director of the Museum. In that capacity he served as the leading authority on all archaeological research in Iceland for over two decades. Kristján Eldjárn held this position until he entered the presidential race of 1968.

The elections of 1968 marked a watershed in Icelandic presidential politics. Kristján Eldjárn had never taken an active part in party politics, but he defeated Gunnar Thoroddsen (q.v.), an accomplished politician with strong ties to the old establishment. His convincing victory—receiving almost two-thirds of the votes cast—demonstrated the voters' preference for a nonpartisan pres-ident. Kristján Eldjárn challenged the idea that presidents should be elderly statesmen, and the same holds true of his successor, Vigdís Finnbogadóttir (q.v.). Kristján Eldjárn ran unopposed in 1972 and 1976, but retired at the end of his third term.

Kristján Eldjárn was a popular president and his only controversial decision came late in his last term: in 1990 he handed his former opponent, Gunnar Thoroddsen, the mandate to form a government. This decision was in clear opposition to the will of the majority of Gunnar Thoroddsen's Independence Party (q.v.). After Kristján Eldjárn retired, the University of Iceland awarded him an honorary professorship, but his death in 1982 prevented him from pursuing a further academic career. (*See also* PRESIDENT OF THE REPUBLIC)

ELECTIONS. With the foundation of modern Alþingi (q.v.) in 1843–45 democratic elections were introduced into Icelandic society. Since then, the democratic process and popular representation have become the dominant forms of political legitimation in Iceland, as the national parliament, local councils, and the president of the republic are all selected through popular vote. Election turnout is usually very high (commonly between 85 and 90 percent), although no one is required by law to cast his or her ballot.

In the first Icelandic parliamentary elections, held in 1844, the franchise was limited to male property holders over 25 years of age, but in 1857 it was expanded to include almost all farmers and some cottars in coastal towns. Women received the right to vote in a few successive steps in the period 1882–1920, and economic restrictions on the franchise were gradually lifted during the first decades of the 20th century, final vestiges of which were abolished in 1934. Hence, the franchise was extended to nearly the entire adult population. In 1934, the voting age in parliamentary elections was moved down from 25 to 21 years of age, and in 1967 to the age of 20. Today, all Icelandic citizens who have reached the age of 18 on the day of elections, and do not have a criminal record, are eligible to vote.

Until the end of the 19th century, parliamentary elections in Iceland were organized on a strictly personal basis. The first formal political parties emerged around the turn of the century, focusing first and foremost on the struggle for independence. During World War I (q.v.) and the Great Depression (q.v.) the party system went through a radical transformation, with the foundation of parties based on social interest and political ideologies. Since then, the party system has been relatively stable, normally with four major parties competing for the popular votes both in parliamentary and local elections and fairly strong loyalty to their respective parties among the voters. In recent years, this stability seems to have eroded, however. First, the introduction of a system of proportional representation in 1959 gave small groups the opportunity to have representatives elected to parliament. Second, the demographic and social changes since World War II (q.v.) have transformed the socio-economic structure of the population. Third, the end of the cold war has rendered many of the dividing lines in Icelandic politics obsolete. This trend can be seen in the success of the Women's Alliance (q.v.) in recent elections, as its feminist agenda has allowed the party to draw support from former voters of all the established political parties. (*See also* CABINET)

EMIGRATION. From the end of the Settlement period (q.v.) until the mid-19th century, Iceland's geographic location rendered migration to and from the country rather difficult. However, massive emigration from Europe to America in the late 19th century tempted many Icelanders to seek their fortunes abroad. Thus, in the late 1850s and early 1860s a small group of people, who had converted to the Mormon faith, immigrated to Utah, and another group went to Brazil in the 1860s. It was only after 1870, however, that emigration began for real. This was a time of improved technology in communications, and the efforts of encouraging agents provided people with the opportunity and incentive to emigrate to North America. Emigration reached its peak in the late-1880s, with around 2,000 persons—or almost 3 percent of the Icelandic population—emigrating in 1887. The last wave of emigrants left the country around the turn of the century, but emigration practically ended at the beginning of the First World War. Over 14,000 persons are known to have immigrated to America in the period 1870–1914, which is a considerable number for a country that had a population of only 78,000 in 1900.

The causes of Icelandic emigration to America were similar to those in other European countries; that is, a combination of factors pulling people to the new world and pushing them from their old countries. The rapidly expanding economies of the United States and Canada offered opportunities that did not exist in Iceland, especially during the economic difficulties of the late

19th century. Also growing overpopulation in the Icelandic countryside made it difficult for people to find employment in farming (q.v.), forcing them either to emigrate or to move to the fishing villages around the coast. Furthermore, climatic condi-tions were very unfavorable during the last decades of the 19th century, making it very difficult for farmers to make ends meet. Strong economic growth during the early 20th century, fuelled primarily by a rapid mechanization of the fisheries (q.v.), removed most of the economic reasons for emigration, and slowly the flow to America abated.

Emigration took place in a period of intense nationalist struggle. Hence, there was a great interest among the emigrants to retain their national identity in the new country, despite the fact that economic hardship forced many of them to leave their homeland. For this reason, they established an Icelandic "colony" on the western shores of Lake Winnipeg in Manitoba, Canada. A large group of Icelandic immigrants moved to this area, which was often called New Iceland, and their influence is still prominent in Winnipeg and the surrounding areas. Other centers of Icelandic settlement were North Dakota and Minnesota in the United States.

EMPLOYMENT. During most of the 20th century, the Icelandic labor market has performed remarkably well in terms of rates of employment. Participation rates have been high and unemploy-ment modest to nonexistent in most years. Full employment has been a major macroeconomic objective for a long time, albeit often at the expense of low inflation (q.v.). Earlier employment statistics are imperfect, but estimates indicate that even during the Great Depression (q.v.) the unemployment rate did not exceed 4 percent in the most populous area in the southwest. Moreover, apart from the recession in 1967–70 the rate was below 1 percent from the postwar period up to the late 1980s. Substantial seasonal fluctuations have, however, always set their mark on the labor market, although decreased importance of farming and fisheries (qq.v.) has reduced these effects in recent years. This has caused significant seasonal unemployment, to which workers adjusted with a high degree of regional mobility, most clearly observed in the migration to rural areas in the summer and to urban areas in the winter. The recession that started in 1988, caused by the deterioration in external conditions of the economy as well as poor fish stocks and stagnation in the energy-intensive industries (q.v.), produced an unprecedented rise in the rate of unemployment, up to 4–5 percent in 1993. Although the rates are still considerably lower than those in other European countries, Icelanders have found it difficult to cope with the presence of chronic unemployment in their country. G. J. (*See also* LABOR MARKET)

ENLIGHTENMENT, THE. The Enlightenment had a strong and lasting influence on Icelandic intellectual and social life, as it did in most of Europe. This was never an organized movement in Iceland, but rather a sentiment, or an intellectual outlook. It was influenced by Danish and German thought and dominated Icelandic intellectual life from the mid- and late 18th to the early 19th centuries. The central idea of the Icelandic Enlightenment, and perhaps its only coherent theme, was the belief in progress through human effort. This was an elitist ideal, as the educated few were to introduce and direct progress for the benefit of the masses, but it was also democratic in the sense that social advancement and education was not to be limited to the social elite.

The Enlightenment in Iceland had no definite beginning, but in the works of Eggert Ólafsson (1726–68, q.v.), a naturalist and poet, we can trace all of its basic characteristics. From 1752 to 1757, he and Bjarni Pálsson, the future surgeon general of Iceland, traveled around the country in order to study its nature and economy. His experiences later led him to write scientific treatises on nature and exhortations to the Icelandic peasants, enticing them to break out of their state of lethargy. In the late 18th century it became fashionable for educated officials to write essays on economic issues and to make agricultural experiments, all in the interest of a more rational organization of Icelandic farming (q.v.). These men, most important of whom was the first chief justice of the Icelandic High Court, Magnús Stephensen (qq.v.), were all loyal subjects of the Danish king, and many of them saw the Danish government as the most likely agent to lead Iceland out of its alleged misery. In the first half of the 19th century the Icelandic Enlightenment came to an end, although it has set its mark on Icelandic history ever since. New political currents redefined public debates in Iceland, in part because of the radical changes that were taking place on the political front in Copenhagen. With the advent of nationalism, the poor state of the Icelandic econ-omy was no longer blamed on the intellectual deterioration of the Icelandic peasant class but rather on Danish oppression and the government's ignorance of Icelandic affairs on the one hand, and lack of national sovereignty on the other. In spite of the new emphasis, the early nationalist leaders, like Jón Sigurðsson (q.v.) and the publishers of the journal *Fjölnir* (q.v.), saw them-selves as heirs of the enlightened men of the 18th century. Thus, there was no clear break in Icelandic intellectual history at the end of the Enlightenment, because the issues of economic and cultural progress became an integral part of 19th-century nationalistic discourse, just as they had been in the preceding century. (*See also* NATIONALISM; ROYAL COMMISSIONS OF 1770 AND 1785)

EUROPEAN ECONOMIC AREA (EEA). On May 2, 1992, representatives of the 12 member-nations of the EU (q.v.) and those of EFTA (q.v.) signed an agreement to form a common economic area, called the European Economic Area (EEA). It was to take effect in 1993, but its rejection in a Swiss referendum meant that some of the terms in the agreement had to be renegotiated. After a protracted debate in the Icelandic parliament and protests from the opposition parties, which claimed that the agreement would cause a significant loss of national sovereignty, Alþingi (q.v.) approved the accord in January 1993, making it the last of the signatories' parliaments to vote on the issue. The EEA was a major leap toward integration of the Icelandic economy into the wider European economic system. Icelanders gained virtually complete access to the EU market for their goods, services, capital, and labor, on condition that they make certain financial contributions to EU funds and accept most existing and future EU directives and regulations in the Single-Market Program. This will require legal harmonization in major areas of the economy, a process that is already under way. Of great importance to the Icelandic economy will be a drastic reduction of EU tariffs on marine products, especially filleted fish, but the country is also expected to benefit from the removal of technical barriers, cheaper imports, and the deregulation of the financial market. In addition to its economic links, the EEA agreement has solidified Iceland's contacts with the EU in the field of research and education. Thus, Iceland has acquired full access to educational and research programs such as LEONARDO, SOCRATES, and the Fourth Framework Agreement, which have facilitated scientific cooperation and academic exchange in Europe in recent years. G. J.

EUROPEAN FREE TRADE ASSOCIATION (EFTA). The entry of Iceland into EFTA on March 1, 1970, marked a turning point in its international economic relations. Membership brought the highly protected economy closer to the European market, and duties on most industrial goods were immediately reduced by 30 percent and on raw materials and machinery by 50 percent. By 1981, all tariffs on imports from EFTA countries were virtually abolished, and Iceland obtained duty-free access to the EFTA countries for all products covered by the EFTA convention. These fundamental changes in trade policy have had great impact on the industrial sector during the last twenty years.

The future role of EFTA is somewhat in doubt, however, since four of its largest members opted to leave the Association in order to join the EU (q.v.) in 1994. The signing of the European Economic Area (q.v.) agreement with the EU in 1992 has also changed EFTA's mission, as it has subjected the EFTA countries to many of the EU's regulations and institution. G. J. (*See also* EUROPEAN UNION (EU),(RELATIONS WITH); EUROPEAN ECONOMIC AREA; INDUSTRY)

EUROPEAN UNION (EU), (RELATIONS WITH). Iceland's participation in international economic organizations was one of the most contentious political issues of the 1960s. Membership in the EEC, the precursor to the EU, was high on the agenda in the early years of the decade, but after a protracted debate Iceland applied for membership in EFTA (q.v.) instead. In 1972, Iceland negotiated a free trade agreement with the EEC, taking effect on April 1, 1973, with the same general provisions as EEC's agreements with other EFTA countries. Because of disputes over Iceland's extension of fishing limits (q.v.), however, the EEC suspended tariff reductions for certain fish products until a satisfactory solution was established in 1976. Economic relations with the EU have become ever more important to the Icelandic economy as around 60 to 70 percent of Icelandic exports have been sold on that market in recent years. The expansion of the EU after the ratification of the Maastricht treaty and the formation of the European Economic Area (EEA, q.v.) have again raised the question of joining the EU, but Iceland, in contrast to the other non-EU signatories to the EEA, has not indicated any desire to join the Union. The main reason given for this position is that the EU Common Fisheries Policy is incompatible with Icelandic national interests, but fear for loosing a part of Icelandic national sovereignty also plays a significant part in popular resentment toward EU membership. G. J.

- F -

FARMERS' ASSOCIATIONS. The first farmers' association in Iceland was formed in 1837, for the most part by government officials. With growing interest in progress in farming (q.v.), a number of regional farmers' associations was established in the 19th century to organize improvements in farming techniques and develop education in the field. In 1899, a federation of these farmers' associations was founded, called Búnaðarfélag Íslands. The Federation grew quickly in stature, playing a vital role in the modernization of Icelandic farming in the 20th century. In 1945, a special farmers' union was established (Stéttarsamband bænda), which was to look after the economic interests of the farmers. As the market for agricultural products has been highly regulated, the Farmers' Union has played an important part in forming public policy toward farming and setting market prices. The two associations were closely linked from the beginning, and they merged into one association (Bændasamtök Íslands) in 1995.

FARMING. In general, Iceland is not particularly well-suited for farming. The country's climate makes growing grain almost impossible, and fragile vegetation and long winters limit the development of animal husbandry (q.v.). In spite of these natural restrictions, however, farming was for most of Iceland's history the most important sector of the economy

Various historical sources and archaeological evidence confirm that grain—barley in particular—was cultivated in Iceland during the first centuries of its history, at least in areas most suitable for agriculture. During the late Middle Ages, deteriorating climatic conditions and declining prices on world markets undermined grain production, and it disappeared entirely in the 16th century. Since then, Icelandic farming has been based almost completely on animal husbandry, with sheep, cattle, and horses the most important domestic animals. In large parts of the country, fishing also served as an invaluable source of income for farming households, as farmers and their servants often spent the slack seasons in fishing stations by the coast.

In the late 19th century, over 90 percent of the working population was employed in farming. The natural habitat set its mark on the peasant economy, as farms were usually very small and skirted the inhabitable part of the country. At that time, Icelandic farming organization and techniques had changed little in centuries. With rapid urbanization (q.v.), which started in the latter half of the last century, a domestic market for farming goods came into being, at the same time as a transformation of the labor market (q.v.) reduced the number of farm servants. This has transformed farming production in the last century; mechanization and technological progress have eliminated the farmers' need for hired hands, and farmers are increasingly at the mercy of the urban market.

The social and economic modernization of the 20th century has affected Icelandic farming in all of its aspects. Today, little more than 5 percent of the active population is employed in farming, down from around 33 percent in 1940. In the same period, dairy production has more than doubled, and production of meat has increased over 50 percent. This development was the result of a period of great expansion in Icelandic farming that lasted from the mid-20th century to the late 1970s. This was a time of generous state support of farmers, which was used for enlarging meadows and the purchase of modern farm equipment. In the long run, increased output has created problems for farmers, as it led to chronic over production of milk and mutton, traditionally their most important products. For this reason, farmers have had to reduce their production in recent years, especially because the state has scaled down the cumbersome system of farm subsidies set up during the Great Depression (q.v.). Unfortunately, state-sponsored programs created to diversify farming production have been largely unsuccessful, while high production cost has thwarted most attempts to export farming goods. These economic difficulties, along with the declining political clout of the farming classes, make the future of Icelandic farming rather uncertain at the moment. (*See also* FARMERS' ASSOCIATIONS; LABOR BONDAGE; REGIONAL POLICY)

FEDERATION OF ICELANDIC COOPERATIVES. *See* COOPERATIVE MOVEMENT.

FILM INDUSTRY. In spite of its strong literary tradition, and although films have been popular in Iceland since the early 20th century, the history of the Icelandic cinematographic industry is relatively short. The main reasons for its late development are the small size of the domestic market and a lack of financial resources, which have given imported films a strong advantage over the Icelandic production. There exist, however, a few early films based on Icelandic literary works, beginning with Victor Sjöström's epic film *Mountain-Eyvind and His Wife* (released in 1918), but they were for the most part foreign productions. In the 1950s and 60s, pioneers in Icelandic filmmaking attempted to establish a domestic film industry, either through production of low budget films or in cooperation with Scandinavian partners. Although this period produced some notable motion pictures, such as *Salka Valka* (1954) and *The Girl Gógó* (1962), it failed to pave the way for independent filmmaking.

The year 1979 was a turning point for Icelandic cinema. First, in that year the government laid the foundation for domestic film production through the creation of the Icelandic Film Fund. Second, at the same time, a new generation of cinematographers returned to Iceland after completing their studies abroad. Thus, close to 30 feature-length motion pictures were released in the 1980s, an astonishing number compared to earlier periods.

At first, explosion in filmmaking was sustained by remarkable successes in the domestic market. Early in the decade, it was not uncommon for a film to attract an audience of more than 60,000, or around a quarter of the total population. In recent years, this initial enthusiasm has subsided, making it impossible for producers to rely solely on the domestic market. The critical success of films such as Friðrik Þór Friðriksson's *Children of Nature* (1991) has opened foreign funds to Icelandic directors. This fact, in addition to the foundation of the Nordic Film and Television Fund and increased access to European cultural funds, has made the producers of Icelandic films less dependent upon the domestic market than before, although, as the cost of film production rises, the life of the Icelandic motion picture industry still remains precarious at best.

FINANCIAL INSTITUTIONS. At the present, the Icelandic financial system is comprised of a complex of banking institutions—including a Central Bank, three commercial banks, and 33 savings banks—a postal bank service, dozens of public investment credit funds and state lending funds, an insurance system including private insurance companies, and pension funds, as well as a comprehensive system of social insurance. The banking system developed late in Iceland—the first savings banks were established around 1870 and the first commercial bank opened in 1886—but it entered a phase of rapid expansion at the turn of this century.

Extensive government involvement has characterized the banking system from early on, not only through heavy regulation but also through direct ownership of most of the major banks and investment credit funds. For this reason, the state has exerted considerable influence on credit allocation. The investment funds are of particular interest in this context for their scope and importance, commanding a quarter of the total outstanding credit. A further characteristic of the financial system is that until recently organized markets for money, bonds, and foreign exchange have been virtually nonexistent. Private companies and public bodies obtained outside funds primarily through borrowing from financial institutions, giving the latter an important role in the economic development of Iceland. Since the mid-1980s, the system has undergone an extensive process of liberalization; the commercial banks are now free to decide their own interest rates, while the Central Bank's control over money supply has been extended. External capital controls are slowly being dismantled, and a new private bank, Íslandsbanki (The Bank of Iceland) started operation after a merger of four banks. It is currently the second largest bank in Iceland. Innovative financial services have mushroomed in recent years. The most notable of these are the rapidly expanding equity markets, leasing companies, and mutual funds. Furthermore, The Icelandic Stock Exchange has been operating under the auspices of the Central Bank since 1986, providing a marketplace for debt securities, primarily government and housing bonds, and to a much lesser extent, equities. Lastly, an interbank market in foreign exchange began operation in 1993. G. J. (*See also* CENTRAL BANKING; CURRENCY; NATIONAL BANK OF ICELAND)

FINNBOGADÓTTIR, VIGDÍS (1930–). Fourth president (q.v.) of the Republic of Iceland. Born in Reykjavík on April 15, 1930, Vigdís Finnbogadóttir graduated from Menntaskólinn í Reykjavík (q.v.) in 1949. She studied French literature and drama at the University of Grenoble, the Sorbonne in Paris, and the University of Copenhagen 1949–53 and 1957–58, completing a degree in English and French from the University of Iceland (q.v.) in 1968. From 1962 to 1972, she taught at two secondary schools in Reykjavík, and she was appointed director of the Reykjavík Theater Company in 1972. In 1980 she was elected president of Iceland in a close four-way race. She ran unopposed in 1984 and 1992 and won a landslide victory in 1988, receiving over 90 percent of the votes cast. Vigdís Finnbogadóttir retired from her post as president at the end of her fourth term in 1996.

The election of Vigdís Finnbogadóttir to the highest office of the Icelandic Republic was a significant victory for advocates of equal status for men and women. She proved to be not only a popular president, but also a highly respected stateswoman both at home and abroad. During Vigdís Finnbogadóttir's tenure as president, the office has become more visible than before, as she has travelled extensively to promote the interests of the Icelandic nation and to introduce its culture abroad. She followed closely the footsteps of her predecessor, Kristján Eldjárn (q.v.). In the same way, she was involved in cultural life rather than politics before becoming president, a fact that set a clear mark on her style and emphasis as president.

FISHERIES. While fishing and fish processing have never employed a major part of the Icelandic working population—now accounting for 12 percent of the labor force—fish products constitute around three-quarters of merchandise exports. Thus, the fishing sector is of fundamental importance for the economy and, during this century, it has instigated the modernization of Icelandic society. The strength of the fisheries is based on the fact that the continental shelf surrounding the island is one of the most productive fishing grounds in the world, with cod, haddock, saithe, herring, redfish, and capelin the most important commercial species. Due to various environmental factors, there has always been a large annual fluctuation in the sizes of these species, especially herring, which has effected not only the fisheries and their organization, but the economy in general.

The main fishing grounds are in the southwest coastal waters where demersal species concentrate to spawn in late winter and early spring before moving eastwards and along the west coast to the sea to the north of Iceland. Until the late 19th century, fishing was primarily organized as a subsidiary occupation of the rural population. Most fishermen were recruited from the rural male population, who migrated toward the coastal regions during the main fishing season in late winter—which happened to be the slack season in farming (q.v.). Only a minority of households had fishing as its main source of income, and primarily fishing farmers and crofters in coastal areas near the main fishing grounds. As early as the 15th century, Alþingi (q.v.) introduced legal restrictions— such as labor bondage (q.v.) and a demand for minimum property for those who wanted to establish a household outside the rural areas—that hampered the development of independent fisheries in Iceland. The authorities enforced these restrictions in one form or another until the first years of the 20th century. Furthermore, the rhythm of the fisheries varied by seasons, because of the migration of cod around the coast. This made it extremely difficult for people to have fisheries as their primary means of living throughout the year. The level of technology contributed to this situation; fishing techniques remained primitive for centuries, and fishing was carried out on small rowboats with crews of two to six men using handlines. As the boats had to return to harbor every night, fishing was confined to coastal areas that the fishermen could reach in one day. The biggest boats were twelve-oar boats; hardly any decked vessels existed until the late 19th century. The principal fish products were dried fish (stockfish) and liver oil, which as a result of higher prices and expanding markets at home and abroad replaced cloth (*vaðmál*) as the main export staple by the middle of the 14th century. Exports of salt cod started in the 1760s, with the opening of the Spanish market, and had become the dominant export article by the 1830s.

In the second half of the 19th century the fishing sector improved substantially. The major contributing factors were better market opportunities abroad, increased accumulation of capital, improved fishing techniques, and changes in the institutional framework of the economy. The number of decked vessels increased rapidly toward the end of the century, bait became more available with the introduction of freezing techniques, and harbors and other facilities were greatly improved. At the beginning of the 20th century, mechanization of the fishing fleet revolutionized the fisheries. Motorboats and trawlers replaced decked vessels and rowboats during the first quarter of the century, changing fishing into an all-year activity and multiplying fish catches. Transformation of fishing gear also contributed to this development, with trawls on trawlers and bigger boats and the so-called purse-seine in herring fishing. Fish processing changed more slowly, however, and salt fish dominated the fish exports until the Great Depression (q.v.) and the collapse of the markets in Spain and Italy in the late 1930s. A desperate search for new marketable products led to a greater emphasis on herring fishing, but of more lasting importance was the rapid shift to the production of frozen fish for the American market. Now, the principal export commodities are frozen fillets (37 percent of all fish exports in 1991), salt fish and herring (20 percent), iced demersal species (14 percent), and shrimp (8 percent). A great increase in the resource base with the extension of the fishing limits (q.v.) and an enormous technological advance in both fishing and fish processing has characterized the postwar period. In 1995, the fishing fleet consisted of over 800 vessels standing at a total of 123,000 gross registered metric tons, including well over 100 powerful trawlers with advanced fishing gear. The most important changes in fish processing in recent years are the increase in freezing and processing of fish at sea and containerized shipping of fresh fish to European markets. G. J. (*See also* COD WARS; FISHERIES MANAGEMENT)

FISHERIES MANAGEMENT. Signs of overfishing in Icelandic waters, due partly to almost open admission to the fishing grounds, were a matter of great concern in the immediate postwar period. In 1948, the passing in Alþingi (q.v.) of the so-called Scientific Conservation of the Fisheries of the Continental Shelf Act provided a legal framework for fisheries management. This pioneering Act gave the government authority to implement measures to prevent depletion of fish stocks. In the following decades, the most important measures regarding the preservation and management of fish stocks centered around extension of fishing limits (q.v.). The extension to 200 miles in 1976 brought commercial fishing around the country under Icelandic jurisdiction and, hence, laid the responsibility for conservation solely in the hands of the Icelandic government. With the closing of Icelandic waters to other nations, it has been the rapidly expanding Icelandic fishing fleet, especially after 1970, that has posed the greatest threat to the fish stocks around the Icelandic coast. During the early 1980s, a sharp decline in cod stock led to adoption of transferable quotas for individual vessels, based on annual catches between 1981 and 1983. The aim was to limit the total catch, encourage more efficient fishing operations through transfers of fishing rights between vessels, and invite ship owners to take older vessels out of registration. Since the system's introduction, the authorities have extended and reformed it in various ways. Under its present form, the Ministry of Fisheries allocates every vessel percentage "quota share" in the total allowed catch of all regulated species, which now includes all the main commercial species. In deciding the allowed catch, which covers each fishing year (September 1 to August 31), the Ministry follows the recommendations of the Marine Research Institute (q.v.). This system has halted the expansion of the fishing fleet, leading to a steady decline in the number of fishing vessels. G. J. (*See also* COD WARS; DIRECTORATE OF FISHERIES; FISHERIES)

FISHING LIMITS. As fishing has been the major economic activity in Iceland for the last century, regulation of fishing limits has been a great concern in recent years. In 1901, a treaty between the Danish government, which was in charge of Icelandic foreign affairs at the time, and the United Kingdom (q.v.) set the limits for the territorial waters around Iceland at three nautical miles. This was a clear retreat from earlier regulations, because until then relatively wide but ill-defined fishing limits had helped to protect the fishing grounds. Thus, the 1901 treaty opened the fjords and bays to European trawlers, while they had earlier been closed to foreign fishermen. This change came at a critical juncture, because new technology in fishing made it increasingly imperative for Iceland to protect its fishing grounds. As British trawlers swarmed Icelandic waters, they hampered small Icelandic boats and threatened the breeding grounds of some of the most valuable species around the country. After World War II (q.v.), the Icelandic government subsidized a large-scale modernization of its fishing fleet at the same time as foreign trawlers returned to Icelandic fishing grounds following a respite imposed by the war. This situation required new regulations on fishing in order to prevent an inevitable depletion of fish stocks. The prevailing idea in Europe at the time was to prevent individual states from setting unilateral rules restricting fishing outside of three-mile territorial waters. Rather, the theory was that regional organizations should determine such conservationist measures, allotting quotas to interested nations. The Icelandic government rejected these ideas and opted for expansion of its fishing limits. Following the example of some Latin American nations, Alþingi (q.v.) and the sitting government set the course toward control over the entire continental area around the country. From 1952 to 1975, the government used The Scientific Conservation of the Fisheries of the Continental Shelf Act, issued on April 5, 1948, to extend the fishing limits to 200 nautical miles. This happened in four successive steps: from three to four nautical miles in 1952, to 12 miles in 1958, to 50 miles in 1972, and to 200 miles in 1975. All these actions caused confrontations—so-called cod wars (q.v.)—between Iceland and other interested nations, especially Great Britain.

The objectives of the policy were two-fold. First, fish is clearly a limited resource that is sensitive to overfishing. Thus, a stringent policy of preservation, based on scientific research, has to be employed in order to prevent depletion of fish stocks. The expansion of the fishing limits has allowed Icelandic research institutions to formulate and enforce such policies in Icelandic waters. Second, the expansion has given Icelandic fishermen monopoly over the rich Icelandic fishing grounds. This has gradually increased their share of the catch in Icelandic waters, from around 50 percent in the 1950s to over 90 percent in the 1980s. (*See also* COAST GUARD; FISHERIES; FISHERIES MANAGEMENT)

FJÖLNIR. A periodical that became a leading organ for Icelandic nationalism in its formative stage. The first volume of the journal was issued in Copenhagen in 1835, promising to contribute to the awakening of the nation from its alleged slumber. The editors were four young Icelandic intellectuals, all students at, or recent graduates of, the University of Copenhagen. At the time of its publication, *Fjölnir* was controversial. Its aggressive style evoked strong reactions among some Icelanders, while many simply ignored the journal. *Fjölnir* had, however, a lasting influence on the Icelandic nationalist movement (q.v.), and it is generally regarded to have played a major part in the development of nationalist sentiment. Thus, although many contemporaries found the journal both eccentric and uncompromising in its views on aesthetics and orthography, its emphasis on language and literature was important in projecting these issues into the core of Icelandic national identity. The last issue of *Fjölnir* was published in 1847, but by that time all of the original editors had left the editorial group. (*See also ÁRMANN Á ALÞINGI; NÝ FÉLAGSRIT*)

- G -

GAMLI SÁTTMÁLI. *See* OLD COVENANT.

GEYSIR. A spring of gushing hot water in Árnes County, in southern Iceland, which has given its name to this natural phenomenon in many languages (the word is, for example, "geyser" both in English and French). The name comes originally from the noun *gos* or the verb *gjósa*, both of which can be translated as "gush" in English.

Geysir is a one m-deep (three ft.) bowl, its surface 20 m (65 ft.) in diameter. From this bowl, a pipe, one m in diameter, descends 23 m (75 ft.) below the surface. It was probably formed by an earthquake in the late 13th century. For centuries, it gushed water as high as 70–80 m (225–260 ft.) in the air, but in the last decades these spouts have become both infrequent and less impressive than before. The spring remains, however, one of the most renowned tourist attractions in Iceland.

GÍSLADÓTTIR, INGIBJÖRG SÓLRÚN (1954–). The most notable young politician in Icelandic leftist politics was born in Reykjavík on December 31, 1954. After completing secondary school in 1974, Ingibjörg Sólrún Gísladóttir studied history and literature at the Universities of Iceland (q.v.) and Copenhagen. In 1982, she was elected to the City Council of Reykjavík for the new Women's Ticket, where she served until 1988. Ingibjörg Sólrún Gísladóttir entered national politics in 1991 when she was elected to parliament from the Women's Alliance (q.v.). In Alþingi (q.v.) she gained respect for her independent views and her strong performance in political debates. In the local elections of 1994, she became the unifying symbol of the parties to the left of the Independence Party (IP, q.v.) in Reykjavík, leading them to victory in elections for the City Council for only the second time in its history. After the elections, Ingibjörg Sólrún Gísladóttir became mayor of Reykjavík, the second woman in the history of the city to carry that title. With this victory, she has set a strong mark on

Icelandic politics; not only was she instrumental in uniting the parties on the left, which have long professed their desire to build a united front without much success, but her popularity was also the main reason for their victory in the traditional stronghold of the IP.

GOÐI. The most powerful men in Iceland during the Commonwealth period (q.v.) were the chieftains (sing. *goði,* pl. *goðar*), or the group of men who held the so-called chieftaincies (*goðorð*). Originally, around the year 930, these chieftaincies were 36 in number, but in 965 three were added to make 39 in all. Etymologically, the word *goði* is derived from *goð,* or god, which has led many to believe that they had served some religious function before the introduction of Christianity in Iceland. In fact, we know little about pre-Christian religious practices in Iceland, because few reliable sources about them exist. Thus this role of the chieftains is debated. The *goðar* were, however, certainly the most prominent leaders of the old Icelandic society. In Alþingi (q.v.), they carried out the legislative functions and named people into courts, while each spring they directed local assemblies in their districts.

To begin with, all *goðar* had equal status, and each free man had the right and duty to follow a *goði* of his choice. Originally the chieftaincy was not a geographic unit, but a contractual relationship between patrons and clients. During the 12th and 13th centuries, as certain individuals and families became dominant in Iceland, the chieftaincies became more or less fixed, and a few families collected all the *goði* titles in their hands. After 1220, this led to open warfare between the most powerful chieftains in Iceland, as they scrambled for hegemony in the country. In the end, this caused political and social chaos, which ended only when the country became a part of the Norwegian monarchy in 1262–64. A little later, shortly after Icelanders accepted a new legal code in 1271–73, the *goðorð* were abolished. After that, Iceland was gradually divided into geographically defined counties (q.v.), called *sýsla,* which were administrated by royal officials, bailiffs (*sýslumenn*). (*See also* AGE OF THE STURLUNGS)

GOÐORÐ. *See* GOÐI.

GOVERNMENT OF THE LABORING CLASSES. "Stjórn hinna vinnandi stétta," or the Government of the Laboring Classes, was a coalition government of the Progressive Party (PP, q.v.) and the Social Democratic Party (SDP, q.v.). It was formed in late July, 1934, under the leadership of Hermann Jónasson (q.v.) from the PP. This was the first government in which the SDP took part, but the party had supported the minority government of the PP from 1927 to 1931. The main objective of the government was to reduce the unemployment rate, which had remained very high for some years because of the Great Depression (q.v.). The coalition parties also instituted a wide range of changes with social legislation. The parliament passed legislation to regulate the market for meat and dairy products in 1934, founded the State Social Security Institute in 1936, and recognized the negotiation rights of labor unions in 1938.

Although the two parties mostly represented the two largest classes of working people in Iceland, that is, workers in towns and small farmers in the countryside, their programs differed on many issues. Thus, the SDP advocated nationalization of many key industries, especially in the fishing sector, while the PP wanted to strengthen the cooperative movement (q.v.) rather than increase the role of the state in economic life. During the last year of the government, the two parties were increasingly at odds over these issues, and in spite of a secure parliamentary majority, it resigned in March 1938.

GOVERNOR. See HIRÐSTJÓRI; LANDSHÖFÐINGI; RÍKISSTJÓRI; STIFTAMTMAÐUR.

GOVERNOR'S PERIOD. The period from 1873 to 1904 is commonly known as the Governor's period (Landshöfðingjatímabilið). It takes its name from the title of the governor's office, *landshöfð-ingi* (q.v.), which was introduced in 1873 and abolished with home rule (q.v.) in 1904. The governor took a very prominent place in Icelandic political debates at the end of the 19th century, because he had a very strong position in the government of the country. The person ultimately responsible for the administration of Iceland was, however, the minister of Icelandic affairs in Copenhagen—a post always held by the Danish minister of justice.

What characterized this period in Icelandic history is, first, a growing economic diversification, which appeared particularly in increasing emphasis on the fisheries (q.v.). As a result, there was a steady population growth in the small fishing villages around the coast, and Reykjavík (q.v.) became the first real town in the country in this period. The main reasons for this change were population pressure in the countryside, the difficult climatic conditions for farming (q.v.), and technological advancement in the fishing industry. Second, a strong nationalist sentiment set its mark on political life during the Governor's period. There was deep discontent in Iceland, especially concerning the status of the country in the monarchy, where a clear majority of politically active persons in Iceland demanded more independence from Denmark. During the 1880s and early 1890s, members of parliament spent a great deal of energy in a fairly futile struggle for a new constitution, and Alþingi (q.v.) attempted unsuccessfully to persuade the conservative government in Copenhagen to transfer more of executive authority over Icelandic affairs to Reykjavík. As the period came to a close, parliament became more conciliatory in its opinions toward the Danish government, because no radical changes in the status of Iceland seemed possible. The fall of the conservative Danish government in 1901 changed this situation completely. With more liberal politicians in power in Copenhagen, the Danish government accepted home rule for Iceland in 1904, and the governor's office was abolished. (*See also* CONSTITUTIONS, 1874–1918; STATUS LAWS; STIFTAMTMAÐUR)

GRÁGÁS. The laws of the Icelandic Commonwealth (q.v.), preserved in two manuscripts dated from around the mid-13th century, are commonly named *Grágás,* meaning "gray goose." This name is a fairly late creation, from the 16th century, and its origins are unclear. The two existing *Grágás* manuscripts, called *Codex Regius* and *Staðarhólsbók,* are not identical in content, but together they provide a clear picture of a legal tradition in Iceland that started with the decision in Alþingi (q.v.) in 1117 to write down the Icelandic laws. Thus, the *Grágás* law codes are more literary in style than similar codes in Scandinavia, and the extreme details on various issues indicate that revisions and elaborations had taken place from the time when the laws existed only in oral form. The *Grágás* laws are based, however, on Scandinavian legal traditions, where the intention is to cover all possible scenarios rather than to construct general rules that apply to various situations. In 1271–73, after Iceland entered into union with Norway, a law book called *Járnsíða* superseded *Grágás,* but it was written at the behest of King Magnús Hákonarson of Norway. One decade later, *Jónsbók* (q.v.) replaced *Járnsíða,* and it was to serve as the basis for the Icelandic legal system for centuries. (*See also* COMMONWEALTH PERIOD)

GREAT DEPRESSION, THE. The first effects of the Wall Street Stock Crisis of 1929 and the ensuing crisis in international exchange hit Iceland in 1930. After that, Icelanders endured an economic slump for almost a decade. The main causes for the depression were a steep fall in export prices for Icelandic goods (between 40 and 50 percent between 1929–33) on the one hand, and various restrictions on the flow of merchandise to and from the international markets on the other. The outbreak of the Spanish Civil War in 1936 prolonged the Great Depression in Iceland, because the war closed down the most lucrative market for Icelandic goods (35 percent of Icelandic exports—mostly salt cod—went to Spain in 1926–30, compared with 2.6 percent in 1936–40). The chronic problem of unemployment ended only with World War II (q.v.), when British and American forces stationed in Iceland provided abundant employment to Icelandic workers.

The Great Depression affected Icelandic society in various ways. High unemployment led to increasing political polarization in the country, with a growing radicalization of the labor movement and rising popularity of the Communist Party and the Socialist Unity Party in elections (qq.v.). The Depression had a lasting influence on the structure of the economy, because the changes in international trade forced the country to seek new opportunities in the world markets. Moreover, in these years the state dramatically increased its participation in the economy, both by direct ownership of various businesses and through its money and tariff policies. In these fields, Icelanders felt the effects of the Great Depression long after the economic difficulties had ended. (*See also* GOVERNMENT OF THE LABORING CLASSES; GÚTTÓSLAGURINN; TRADE, FOREIGN)

GREENLAND (NORSE SETTLEMENT IN). In the late 10th century, as Iceland was becoming more fully settled, Norsemen expanded their settlements further to the west, exploring the island of Greenland. According to Icelandic sagas, the first Norse settler on the island was Eiríkur Þorvaldsson, who fled Iceland in 985 or 986 after having been sentenced for killing a man. He gave the name Greenland to his new home, allegedly to attract prospective settlers. The Norse settlers inhabited two regions in Greenland, calling them the Western and Eastern Settlements respectively, although both of them were on the southwestern coast of the island. During the first centuries of their existence, the Norse settlements in Greenland seem to have prospered; this is indicated by the ruins of a cathedral and other buildings in their center at Garðar. During the 14th and 15th centuries, contacts with Greenlanders became more sporadic and, for some reason, the Norse settlements on Greenland disappeared entirely sometime between the early 15th and late 16th centuries. (*See also* EIRÍKSSON, LEIFUR; VINLAND)

GRÍMSSON, ÓLAFUR RAGNAR (1943–   ). Politician and a former professor at the University of Iceland (q.v.). Born on May 14, 1943, in Ísafjörður in northwest Iceland, Ólafur R. Grímsson graduated from Menntaskólinn í Reykjavík (q.v.) in 1962. He completed a B.A. degree in economics and political science from the University of Manchester in 1965 and a Ph.D. in political science from the same university in 1970. In 1970, he was appointed assistant professor in political science at the University of Iceland and full professor three years later. In 1978, Ólafur R. Grímsson was elected to parliament for the People's Alliance (PA, q.v.) for the first time, but failed to win reelection for his third term in 1983. Although he did not sit in Alþingi (q.v.) at the time, he became chairman of Parliamentarians for Global Action, an international organization of parliamentary representatives in 1984. From 1988 to 1991 he served as minister of finance, reentering Alþingi in 1991.

Ólafur R. Grímsson's political career has been both colorful and controversial. He sat on the steering committee of the Progressive Party (PP, q.v.) from 1971 to 1973, but left the PP in 1974 with a group of activists from its left wing, joining the Union of Liberals and Leftists (ULL, q.v.). He served as chairman of the steering committee of ULL 1974–75, before he changed parties once again and joined the PA. His rise in the PA was rapid; he was elected to parliament for the party in 1978, became chairman of its parliamentary group in 1980–83, chairman of its steering committee 1983–87, and finally party chairman from 1987 to 1995. During his tenure as chairman of the PA, Ólafur R. Grímsson attempted to change the emphasis of the party. This was, in part, the result of the changing scene in international politics at the conclusion of the cold war, but it was also a response to new currents in the socialist movement in Iceland. Some of the new policies, such as the more positive view on Icelandic membership in NATO (q.v.), were very controversial in the party, dividing it into rival flanks.

GRÖNDAL, BENEDIKT (1924–   ). This former politician and prime minister was born in Ísafjörður County on July 7, 1924. Benedikt Gröndal completed his secondary education in Reykjavík in 1943 and enrolled in Harvard University the same year. After receiving a B.A. degree in history from Harvard in 1946, Benedikt Gröndal studied for one year at Oxford University. After completing his studies, he returned to Iceland to work for the Social Democratic newspaper *Alþýðublaðið* (q.v.), first as a journalist but later as editor-in-chief. In 1956, he was elected to parliament for the Social

Democratic Party (SDP, q.v.) for the first time, retaining his seat until he retired from politics in 1982. In 1974, he was elected chairman of the SDP but was ousted from this post in 1980 by Kjartan Jóhannsson (q.v.). Benedikt Gröndal served as minister of foreign affairs from 1978 to 1980, and as prime minister for a few months in 1979–80. When retiring from politics, Benedikt Gröndal was appointed ambassador, serving in different countries from 1982 to 1991.

GUÐMUNDSSON, ALBERT (1923–1994). A former professional soccer player and politician, born in Reykjavík on October 5, 1923. Albert Guðmundsson graduated from the Cooperative College in Reykjavík in 1944 and from Skerry's College in Glasgow, Scotland, in 1946. From 1947 to 1956, he played professional soccer with various teams in Britain, France, and Italy. In 1965, after retiring from sports, Albert Guðmundsson started a successful wholesale firm in Reykjavík. His active involvement in politics began in 1970, when he was elected to Reykjavík's city council for the Independence Party (IP, q.v.). Four years later he entered Alþingi (q.v.) as a representative for the IP, serving as minister of finance 1983–85 and minister of industries 1985–87. In 1987, the leadership of the IP forced him to resign his ministerial post because of accusations of tax evasion. As a response, he quit the party to form his own political organization, the Citizens' Party (q.v.). The new party won a resounding victory in the 1987 election, taking 11 percent of the votes cast and sending seven representatives to Alþingi. In 1989, Albert Guðmundsson was appointed ambassador to France, a post he held until just before his death in 1994.

The political strength of Albert Guðmundsson lay in his ability to communicate with the "common man," and his populist policies earned him respect and trust among leading members of the labor movement. Thus, while he never gained full acceptance from the elite of the IP, Albert Guðmundsson remained popular among its general voters.

GUÐMUNDSSON, VALTÝR (1860–1928). This scholar and politician was born in Húnavatn County on March 11, 1860. After graduating from secondary school in Reykjavík in 1883, Valtýr Guðmundsson began his studies of Old Norse at the University of Copenhagen. He completed a master's degree from this university in 1887 and defended his doctoral thesis in 1889. From 1890, he taught Icelandic history and literature at the University of Copenhagen, becoming a full professor in Icelandic Language and Literature in 1920.

In Iceland, Valtýr Guðmundsson is not primarily remembered for his distinguished academic career, but for his political activities. He was elected to Alþingi (q.v.) for the first time in 1894. The following year, he caused a sensation when he suggested a novel solution to the constitutional crisis. He encouraged the parliament to adopt a pragmatic approach in the nationalist struggle, demanding only what the Danish conservative government would possibly accept. In his view, material progress was more important than political independence, for the time being at least. In the next few years, Valtýr Guðmundsson was able to gain majority support in Alþingi for his conciliatory approach. Unfortunately for him, however, the same year as his proposition finally passed through Alþingi (1901), a new government came to power in Copenhagen and accepted home rule (q.v.) for Iceland. This was more than Valtýr Guðmundsson had demanded, and the king selected his nemesis, Hannes Hafstein (q.v.), to head the first home rule government. Although Valtýr Guðmundsson sat in parliament almost continuously until 1913, he did not have much influence on Icelandic politics for the remainder of his life. (*See also* CONSTITUTIONS, 1874–1918; GOVERNOR'S PERIOD; STATUS LAWS)

GUNNARSSON, TRYGGVI (1835–1917). One of the most influential Icelanders of his time, both as a pioneer in commerce and as the director of the National Bank of Iceland (NBI, q.v.). Tryggvi Gunnarsson was born in Þingey County in northern Iceland on October 18, 1835. As a young man, he learned carpentry from his uncle, and he practiced this trade for a number of years. In 1859, Tryggvi Gunnarsson married and started farming in his county of birth. At this time, most Icelandic trade was in the hands of Danish merchants, many of whom were extremely unpopular in Iceland. For this reason, at the end of the 1860s a number of farmers in northern Iceland formed an association in the region, with the purpose of taking trade into their own hands. Tryggvi Gunnarsson was one of the leaders of this group, and from 1873 he served as director of the trading company, which was called Gránufélagið (the Grána Company). In the next few years, Tryggvi Gunnarsson rose to prominence in Iceland, both as the manager of an expanding enterprise and as a member of Alþingi (q.v.). In parliament, he was a close ally of Jón Sigurðsson (q.v.), the leader of Icelandic nationalism. Tryggvi Gunnarsson's nationalist fervor cooled down considerably, however, in his later years. After 1880, the prosperity of the farmers' trading company declined rapidly, both because of the general economic depression in the country and declining support among farmers with a growing competition from the cooperative movement (q.v.). Tryggvi Gunnarsson left the directorship in 1893 to become manager of the NBI. He held this position until 1909 when his political rivals ousted him from the post.

Tryggvi Gunnarsson was very influential in Icelandic society during the last decades of the 19th century. As director of the Grána Company, he introduced new trading practices in his district, and as the manager of NBI, his lending policies helped promote the growth of the fishing industry. His projects as a building contractor, managing the building of the parliamentary house in Reykjavík and the construction of the first major bridge in Iceland (Ölfusá Bridge), have also secured his place in Icelandic history.

GÚTTÓSLAGURINN. This violent scuffle in Reykjavík (q.v.) between the police and a group of workers and radicals is one of the best-known incidents of the Great Depression (q.v.). The riots began in early November 1932, when leftists and laborers demonstrated against a planned reduction of salaries for workers employed in a program of relief works. The labor unions resisted this reduction, both because the relief works were a major source of revenue for the unemployed in Reykjavík, and because they feared that the proposed decrease in wages would affect the level of salaries for the working class in general. On the afternoon of November 9, police and demonstrators clashed inside and outside the meeting hall of Reykjavík's city council, and in the end between 20 and 30 persons were injured. The riots ended when the city council and the government yielded to the workers' demands.

GYLFASON, VILMUNDUR (1948–1983). One of the most controversial politicians in Iceland in recent years. He was born on August 7, 1948, in Reykjavík to one of the leaders of the Social Democratic Party (SDP, q.v.). Vilmundur Gylfason graduated from Menntaskólinn í Reykjavík (q.v.) in 1968, completed a B.A. degree in history at the University of Manchester in 1971, and a M.A. degree at the University of Exeter in 1973. From 1973 until his death, Vilmundur Gylfason taught in Menntaskólinn í Reykjavík. In 1978 he was elected to Alþingi (q.v.) for the SDP, and his vigorous campaign helped the party in winning its largest electoral victory in its history. He served as minister of justice, ecclesiastical affairs, and education from 1979 to 1980. During these years Vilmundur Gylfason advocated radical changes for the political and administrative systems, calling for direct elections of political leaders in order to reduce the power of both parliament and the political parties. These ideas met with limited support among professional politicians, even in his own party. For that reason he left the SPD in 1982 to form a new political organization in the following year, the Social Democratic Alliance (SDA, q.v.), which he led in the 1983 parliamentary elections. In spite of hasty preparations, the new party gained four representatives in these elections, but after Vilmundur Gylfason's early death in the spring of 1983, the SDA quickly disintegrated.

Vilmundur Gylfason fought for a total transformation of the Icelandic political system, which he saw as stagnated and outdated. But his popularity was based more on his campaign style and personal charisma than on the ideas he propounded. His energetic performance in the media, both in television and in print helped him to captivate and excite people in a way that no Icelandic politician has done for a long time.

- H -

HAFSTEIN, HANNES (1861–1922). The first minister of the Home Rule period (q.v.) was born in Eyjafjörður County in the north to the district governor of the North and East District of Iceland. He graduated from secondary school in Reykjavík in 1880 and completed a law degree from the University of Copenhagen in 1886. After practicing law and working as secretary for the governor in Reykjavík, he assumed the position of bailiff in Ísafjörður County in 1895. He sat in parliament for this county in 1901 but was elected as representative for Eyjafjörður County in 1903. Hannes Hafstein became a leader of the Home Rule Party (HRP, q.v.), which was formed as a loose federation of representatives in parliament shortly before 1900. When the Danish government awarded the country home rule (q.v.) in 1904, Hannes Hafstein, as the leader of the majority party in Alþingi, was appointed minister of Iceland. He resigned from this post in 1909, after the HRP had lost its majority in parliamentary elections the year before. As he stepped down, Hannes Hafstein was appointed director of the Bank of Iceland (Íslandsbanki), where he served until he resumed the ministerial post in 1912. In 1914, he was forced to resign again when the parliamentary group that stood behind him dissolved. He resumed the directorship of the Bank of Iceland, but deteriorating health forced him to retire from public life in 1917.

Hannes Hafstein caught attention for his poetry and energetic performance as a public official, and he rose rapidly to the highest post in Icelandic politics. As a minister, he emphasized issues of social and economic progress, but he was ousted when the advocates of fervent nationalism (q.v.) swept the parliamentary elections of 1908. It was only with the Act of Union (q.v.) that the electorate was ready to turn away from the politics of nationalism, but then Hannes Hafstein had left the political scene. (*See also* DRAFT THE; GUÐMUNDSSON, VALTÝR)

HAFSTEIN, JÓHANN (1915–1980). This politician was born in Akureyri (q.v.) on September 19, 1915, to the bailiff of Eyjafjörður County. After graduating from the secondary school in Akureyri in 1934, Jóhann Hafstein studied law at the University of Iceland (q.v.), completing a law degree in 1937. For a few years, he worked for the Independence Party (IP, q.v.), first as its emissary and from 1942 to 1952 as its managing director. Elected to Alþingi (q.v.) for the IP in 1946, he served as one of its representatives for Reykjavík for over three decades. He was a member of Reykjavík's city council from 1946 to 1958 and from 1952 to 1963, the director of the Fisheries Bank of Iceland. Jóhann Hafstein held his first ministerial post for a brief period in 1961, but from 1963 to 1970 he served as minister of justice for the IP in the Reconstruction Government (q.v.). At the death of Bjarni Benediktsson (q.v.) in 1970, Jóhann Hafstein succeeded him as chairman of the IP and prime minister, but his cabinet had to resign after defeat in the parliamentary elections of 1971. Two years later Jóhann Hafstein lost his office as party chairman of the IP to Geir Hallgrímsson (q.v.), and his political career was effectively over.

HALLGRÍMSSON, GEIR (1925–1990). Former mayor of Reykjavík, prime minister, and director of the Central Bank of Iceland. Geir Hallgrímsson was born in Reykjavík on December 16, 1925. After completing a law degree from the University of Iceland (q.v.) in 1948, he studied for a year at Harvard Law School. In 1948–59, Geir Hallgrímsson practiced law in Reykjavík. He was appointed mayor of Reykjavík for the Independence Party (IP, q.v.) in 1959, a position he held until 1972. Elected to parliament for the IP in 1970, he became its chairman in 1973. In 1974, he formed a coalition government with the participation of the IP and the Progressive Party (PP, q.v.), serving as prime minister for four years. The government lost its majority in the elections of 1978, but from 1983 to 1986 Geir Hallgrímsson served as minister of foreign affairs in a new coalition government with the PP. He stepped down as chairman of the IP in 1983 when challenged by Þorsteinn Pálsson (q.v.) and withdrew from politics three years later. During his last years, he served as director of the Central

Bank of Iceland. A cautious politician, Geir Hallgrímsson was highly respected as mayor of Reykjavík, but he lacked the necessary charisma or force to lead effectively the largest party in Iceland.

HALLGRÍMSSON, JÓNAS (1807–1845). This naturalist and poet was born in Eyjafjörður County on November 16, 1807, to a country pastor. After finishing a university entrance exam at Bessastaðir (q.v.) in 1829, Jónas Hallgrímsson worked as a clerk for the royal treasurer for Iceland in Reykjavík. Three years later, in the fall of 1832, he enrolled in the University of Copenhagen with the intention of studying law. Before completing his law degree, Jónas Hallgrímsson changed to the study of natural history, at the same time as he became involved in Icelandic student politics in Copenhagen. In 1834–35, he was one of the founders of *Fjölnir* (q.v.), a periodical devoted to aesthetics in literature and to the development of Icelandic culture and society in general. From 1837 to 1842 he travelled extensively in Iceland, studying its nature and economy. He dedicated his last years to the publication of the results of his research but had completed none of this material at the time of his early death in 1845.

Jónas Hallgrímsson is known today as one of Iceland's greatest poets. His love for Icelandic nature and history are recurrent themes in his poetry, and he expressed sentiments that were of great importance to the Icelandic nationalist movement (q.v.).

HANNIBALSSON, JÓN BALDVIN (1939–   ). One of the most prominent politicians in Iceland of the 1980s and 1990s. Born in Ísafjörður on February 21, 1939, to Hannibal Valdimarsson (q.v.), a schoolmaster and labor leader in this fishing town in northwest Iceland, Jón Baldvin Hannibalsson completed a secondary school exam in 1958. In 1963, he received an M.A. degree in economics from the University of Edinburgh and became an elementary school teacher in Reykjavík the following year. From 1970 to 1979 he was a principal of the secondary school in Ísafjörður, where he became active in local politics, serving on the town council for the Social Democratic Party (SDP, q.v.). In 1979, he became editor of *Alþýðublaðið* (q.v.), the organ of the SDP. He entered parliament in 1982 and was elected chairman of the SDP in 1984, ousting Kjartan Jóhannsson (q.v.). After a short stint as minister of finance in 1987–88 in a government headed by Þorsteinn Pálsson (q.v.) of the Independence Party (q.v.), he became minister of foreign affairs in 1988, a position he retained from 1991 to 1995 in the first government of Davíð Oddsson (q.v.). As minister of foreign affairs, Jón B. Hannibalsson was a passionate advocate of close cooperation with the EU (q.v.), and he was one of the main instigators of the negotiations that led to the European Economic Area (q.v.) agreement between the EU and EFTA (q.v.).

Jón Baldvin Hannibalsson has been a controversial politician, even inside his own party. Under his leadership, the SDP has continued its centrist course, and the party has severed most of its ties with the labor movement. During the early 1990s there was a growing friction between him and the left wing of the SDP. This friction ended when his most vocal opponents, led by the party's vice-chairwoman, Jóhanna Sigurðardóttir (q.v.), resigned from the SDP in 1994, forming Þjóðvaki (q.v., National Awakening) in January of the following year.

HEIMASTJÓRNARTÍMINN. *See* HOME RULE PERIOD.

HEKLA. This mountain, which is perhaps the best-known volcano in Iceland, is located in Rangárvellir County in southern Iceland. Hekla rises just under 1,500 m (4,900 ft.) above sea level and has been built up through repeated eruptions on a 40 km-long (25 mi.) fissure—the mountain itself is about 10 km (6 mi.) long. Hekla is a relatively young mountain, at least in geological terms, but it has been very active throughout its short history. The first known eruption took place around 6,600 years ago, and at least sixteen eruptions have been recorded since the settlement of Iceland.

In the Middle Ages, people sometimes considered Hekla to be the entrance to Hell, a fable that was underlined by the havoc it wreaked upon neighboring regions and sometimes upon large parts of the country. In 1104, scientists believe that a huge eruption in Hekla destroyed the whole community of Þjórsárdalur to the west of the volcano, and in 1300, 1693, and 1766, pumice and poisonous ashes from the volcano caused widespread devastation. The last major eruption of Hekla took place in 1947–48. The eruptions of 1971, 1980–81, and 1991 were all relatively insignificant.

HERMANNSSON, HALLDÓR (1878–1958). Former curator of the Fiske Icelandic Collection and professor at Cornell University. Halldór Hermannsson was born on January 6, 1878, to the bailiff of Rangárvellir County. After graduating from secondary school in Reykjavík in 1898, he entered the University of Copenhagen to study law. During the summer of 1899, Halldór Hermannsson met Daniel Willard Fiske, formerly the head librarian of Cornell University and traveled with him to Florence to assist with his collection of Icelandic books. In 1905, the year after Fiske's death,

Halldór Hermannsson became the first curator of the Fiske Icelandic Collection at Cornell, which Fiske had established by donating his books and a part of his legacy. Along with his position as a curator, Halldór Hermannsson taught Old Norse and modern Icelandic at Cornell University and, in 1924, the university promoted him to a full professorship in Scandinavian languages. Under his direction, the Fiske Icelandic Collection flourished, and it is now one of the largest collections of Icelandic books outside Iceland. He founded and edited the series *Islandica,* where he published a number of studies on various aspects of Icelandic history and culture. Halldór Hermannsson retired from his position at the Fiske Collection in 1948 and died in Ithaca, New York, ten years later.

HERMANNSSON, STEINGRÍMUR (1928–   ). Iceland's most influential politician of the 1980s was born in Reykjavík on June 22, 1928. Steingrímur Hermannsson, who is the son of Hermann Jónasson (q.v.), the leader of the Progressive Party (PP, q.v.) for almost three decades, was introduced to politics at an early age. He began his career, however, as an engineer, receiving a B.S. degree in electrical engineering from Illinois Institute of Technology in 1951, and an M.S. degree from California Institute of Technology in Pasadena one year later. After serving as an engineer in Iceland and the United States, he was appointed director of the Icelandic Research Council in 1957. Steingrímur Hermannsson was first elected to parliament for the PP in 1971, becoming secretary of the party in the same year and its chairman in 1979. He served as minister in a number of cabinets from the late 1970s and through the 1980s; first as minister of justice, ecclesiastical affairs, and agriculture (1978–79), later as minister of fisheries and communications (1980–83), prime minister (1983–87 and 1988–91), and minister of foreign affairs (1987–88). When appointed director of the Central Bank of Iceland (q.v.) in 1994, he retired from politics, giving up both his seat in parliament and the leadership of the PP.

In politics, the 1980s were, in many respects, the decade of the PP, and Steingrímur Hermannsson's popularity contributed greatly to the strong position of the party. He served as prime minister for most of the decade, sometimes forming coalition governments with the parties on the left and sometimes with the Independence Party (q.v.) on the right. This is a testimony to his ability to negotiate between different political opinions. Moreover, in opinion polls people repeatedly voted him the most popular politician in Iceland, in part because of his skill in conveying an image of flexibility and resolution that appealed to voters.

HIÐ ÍSLENSKA BÓKMENNTAFÉLAG. *See* ICELANDIC LITER-ARY SOCIETY.

HIGH COURT. Established on July 11, 1800, after the suppression of Alþingi (q.v.), the Icelandic High Court (Landsyfirréttur) met for the first time in August 1801. The High Court was the highest court in Iceland, but its rulings could be appealed to the Supreme Court in Copenhagen. Three justices served in the High Court, one of whom was chief justice, and it met in Reykjavík. The High Court met for the last time in December 1919, and it was replaced by the Supreme Court (q.v.) of Iceland in the following year.

HIRÐSTJÓRI. The highest royal office in Iceland was named *hirðstjóri* from 1270 until the mid-16th century, when the title changed to *höfuðsmaður.* The literal meaning of the term *hirðstjóri* is courtier, or a man of the court, and at first the function of the office was to lead the king's men in Iceland. In the beginning, the number of *hirðstjóri* fluctuated, and they were, as a rule, Icelandic by birth. From the 14th century until the office was abolished in 1683, many foreigners served as *hirðstjóri* or *höfuðsmaður,* using Bessastaðir (q.v.) as their official residence. From that time on, the function of the office was more clearly defined than before, making it the pinnacle of the administrative system in Iceland.

HÖFUÐSMAÐUR. *See* HIRÐSTJÓRI.

HÓLAR. A farm in Skagafjörður County in northwestern Iceland. It became the second episcopal seat in Iceland in 1106, serving as the residence for the bishop for northern Iceland until 1798. In 1801, Danish church authorities formally abolished the Hólar diocese and put the whole country under one bishop placed in Reykjavík. For seven centuries, Hólar was a center of religious and cultural life in its district. For most of this period the bishop ran a Latin school for boys and young men at Hólar. Jón Arason (q.v.), the last Catholic bishop at Hólar, founded the first printing press in Iceland there around the year 1530.

At the beginning of the 19th century, Hólar lost its former prestige and became a regular church farm. In the early 1880s, Skagafjörður County bought Hólar in order to turn the farm into an agricultural college. Similar to Skálholt (q.v.), the other former episcopal seat in Iceland, the Lutheran church has striven in recent years to restore some of the old standing of Hólar; thus, its 18th-century church has recently been renovated and is now the residence of one of Iceland's two suffragan bishops. (*See also* CATHOLICISM; LUTHERANISM)

HOME RULE. With the Constitution of 1874, Alþingi (q.v.) acquired limited legislative power and full control over public expenditure in Iceland, although the executive power remained totally in the hands of the Danish government and officials appointed by the king. Moreover, the minister of Icelandic affairs sat in the Danish cabinet and, as it turned out, this ministry remained the responsibility of the Danish minister of justice. Icelanders were very dissatisfied with this arrangement, both because they felt that a Danish minister was unable to comprehend Icelandic needs and aspirations, and because they preferred to have a minister that was responsible to their own parliament, Alþingi.

From 1881 to 1903, the revision of the constitution remained the central issue of political debates in Iceland. The conservative government in Denmark rejected all demands for constitutional revision, but when the government fell in 1901, the doors opened for reorganization of the Icelandic executive branch. In 1903, the king ratified a new constitution, granting Iceland home rule. The following year, the king appointed Hannes Hafstein (q.v.) the first Icelandic minister. Formally he was a member of the Danish government, but as he resided in Reykjavík his participation in cabinet meetings remained sporadic. Moreover, he was responsible to Alþingi but not to the Danish parliament, meaning that he did not resign when the cabinet lost its majority in the Danish parliament. However, when Hannes Hafstein proved to have lost his majority in Alþingi in 1909, he had to resign. This confirmed that the home rule government adhered to the principles of representative government. Although home rule made the government more responsive to the desires of Icelanders, it did not satisfy their demands for independence. The constitution did not revoke the Status Laws (q.v.) of 1871, and it required the Icelandic minister to present all bills passed in Alþingi to the Danish cabinet. For this reason, the Home Rule period (q.v.) was a time of intense nationalist mobilization in Iceland, reaching its peak with the debates about the "Draft" (q.v.) in 1908. With the Act of Union (q.v.) of 1918, Iceland became a sovereign state in union with Denmark, and the Home Rule period (q.v.) came to an end. (*See also* CONSTITUTIONS, 1874–1918; GUÐMUNDSSON, VALTÝR; HOME RULE PARTY)

HOME RULE PARTY (HRP). A party uniting the opponents of Valtýr Guðmundsson (q.v.) at the end of the 19th century. One of the main tenets of the HRP was a demand for home rule (q.v.) in Iceland, and with the transfer of government from Copenhagen to Reykjavík in 1904, Hannes Hafstein (q.v.), the leader of HRP, became the first minister to reside in Iceland. The HRP lost its majority in Alþingi (q.v.) in 1908, and Hannes Hafstein resigned the following year. Like all the political parties of its time, the HRP was more a loose federation than an organized political party. From 1912 the HRP was very unstable, because some of its leading members left the party to form new political groups. During World War I (q.v.), the political system in Iceland was reorganized along class lines, and the Act of Union (q.v.) in 1918 rendered the pre-war parties obsolete. The HRP participated in parliamentary elections for the last time in 1919, but its former leaders were instrumental in the formation of the Conservative Party (q.v.) in 1924. (*See also* DRAFT, THE; HOME RULE PERIOD)

HOME RULE PERIOD. The period from 1904 to 1918 is called the Home Rule period (Heimastjórnartíminn). It opened on February 1, 1904, when the Ministry of Icelandic Affairs moved to Reykjavík from Copenhagen, and it ended on December 1, 1918, when Iceland became a sovereign state. Strong economic growth, fueled by a rapid mechanization of the fisheries (q.v.), characterized the Home Rule period. This period was a time of fervent nationalism (q.v.), reaching its high point in 1908. In that year, the voters turned down an offer for a new constitution (the so-called "Draft", q.v.), because it did not declare Iceland a sovereign state. Finally, with the Act of Union (q.v.) of 1918 the Danish government gave in to Icelandic demands, accepting Icelandic sovereignty. (*See also* HOME RULE; HOME RULE PARTY; STATUS LAWS)

HREPPUR. *See* COMMUNE.

- I -

ICELANDAIR. Icelandair (Flugleiðir), the largest airline in Iceland, was formed in 1973 with the merger of Flugfélag Íslands and Loftleiðir (Icelandair and Icelandic Airlines). Prior to the merger, the two airlines had waged a controlled but emotionally charged competition. Icelandair, the older of the two companies (established in 1937), specialized in domestic flights, in addition to serving the routes to Scandinavia and the British Isles. Icelandic Airlines were better known internationally, however, primarily for their inexpensive transatlantic flights, connecting Iceland with both the United States and the European continent. In the long run, the small Icelandic market could not sustain two airlines, and the two competitors merged, uniting the domestic and international routes. In spite of the merger, Icelandair has often faced great economic difficulties. Its survival is crucial for the Icelandic economy, however, and a thorough overhaul of its fleet and a major reduction of its operating costs in the late 1980s and early 1990s have made it financially profitable again. Icelandair seems, therefore, to be able to continue providing Iceland with the necessary links to the surrounding world.

ICELANDIC FEDERATION OF LABOR (IFL). Representatives from various unions of unskilled laborers, fishermen, and artisans formed this general organization of Icelandic labor, Alþýðusamband Íslands, on March 12, 1916. The aims of the federation were to guard the interests of its members in negotiations with employers and to serve as a political party, advocating social democratic ideals in Iceland.

In the beginning, no clear distinction was made between the IFL and the Social Democratic Party (SDP, q.v.)—thus the president of the IFL served also as chairman of the SDP. Since the links between the two organizations were severed in 1940–42, the IFL has not been aligned with any political party but focuses on economic and social issues of its working class members. The IFL plays a major role in negotiating salaries between workers and employers, and it administrates various services for its members. Today, the IFL has over 66,000 members in 238 separate unions, making it the largest association in Iceland. The current president of the IFL is Grétar Þorsteinsson. (*See also* CONFEDERATION OF ICELANDIC EMPLOYERS; LABOR MARKET; LABOR MOVEMENT)

ICELANDIC HISTORICAL ASSOCIATION (IHA). Sögufélag, or the IHA, was founded in 1902, for the purpose of publishing Icelandic historical sources. True to its original goal, the IHA has published the acts of the old Alþingi (q.v.), the rulings of the High Court (q.v.), and the documents of the Royal Commission of 1770 (q.v.). In recent years, the IHA has also published a number of historical monographs and collections of essays. Through the years, three journals have been issued under the auspices of the IHA, *Blanda* (1918–53), *Saga* (1950–   ), and *Ný saga* (1987–   ).

ICELANDIC LANGUAGE. Icelandic is one of the Nordic languages, which together form a defined subgroup of the Germanic languages. It originates in a "parent language," usually called Proto-Nordic, which was spoken in an area covering the area from central Scandinavia and Denmark to the river Ejder in modern Schleswig, Germany. On the basis of historical evidence, it seems probable that Old Icelandic, or Old Norse as it is commonly named, is primarily derived from West Norwegian dialects. A few loanwords of Celtic origin came into the language early on, and a number of words, mostly from Latin and Greek, were adopted after the conversion to Christianity (q.v.) after the year 1000.

Because of the isolation of the country, the Icelandic language changed only gradually through the centuries. From the 14th century it began, therefore, to become distinguishable from Norwegian, mostly because the latter changed at a much more rapid pace than Icelandic. The grammatical structure and syntax of modern Icelandic is very similar to the language of the Saga Age, and the basic vocabulary is remarkably well preserved. A modern Icelander can, for example, read the medieval sagas (q.v.) with relative ease.

During the struggle for independence, linguistic conservatism became a matter of great pride for Icelandic nationalists. To them, this proved that modern Icelandic culture was truer to its origins than the cultures of the other Nordic countries and, consequently, that Icelanders had preserved the parent form of all the Scandinavian languages. For this reason, there was a great effort in the 19th and the early 20th centuries to "purify" the language, or to eliminate as many traces of Danish influence as possible. This effort has been fairly successful, as Icelandic is still more resistant to foreign loanwords than most European languages. The outcome of this policy of language purification is not certain, however, as it has proven to be increasingly difficult to isolate the language from the world dominance of the English language. (*See also* ICELANDIC LITERARY SOCIETY; NATIONALISM)

ICELANDIC LITERARY SOCIETY (ILS). At the initiative of the Danish philologist Rasmus Christian Rask (q.v.), Hið íslenska bókmenntafélag, or the Icelandic Literary Society, was founded in Copenhagen in 1816. The society originally had one section in Copenhagen and another in Iceland, reflecting the importance of the Danish capital for Icelandic cultural life at the time. The goal of the society was to contribute to the protection and development of the Icelandic language (q.v.) and culture through the publication of educating and enlightening literature; thus it combined influences from the Enlightenment of the 18th century and the emerging romanticism of the 19th. The incentive for this enterprise was

Rask's fear for the future of the Icelandic language, but during a visit to Iceland in 1813, he predicted that it would perish in the next one hundred years.

Since its foundation, publication has been the center of ILS's activities. In 1817, in its second year, the Literary Society launched a journal called *Íslenzk sagnablöð*, but a decade later the journal *Skírnir* replaced it. This journal has been published continuously ever since. During its long history, the ILS has also published a great variety of books on subjects such as Icelandic literature, history, economy, law, and popular science, emphasizing instruction aimed at the general public. In the beginning, the center of this activity was in Copenhagen, but after the death of Jón Sigurðsson (q.v.), who was the president of ILS's Copenhagen section from 1851 to 1879, a campaign started for its transfer to Reykjavík. It was only in 1911, however, that the two sections merged in Reykjavík.

At the present, the ILS is not as dominant in its field as it was during the last century, but it is still one of the most active publishers of scholarly literature and books of educational value for the general public in Iceland.

ICELANDIC NATIONALIST MOVEMENT. Icelandic nationalism (q.v.) did not engender an organized political movement until the last decades of Danish rule in Iceland, but from the late 1830s and the early 1840s it became a dominant theme in Icelandic politics. The original demands of Icelandic nationalism were formulated by students and intellectuals in Copenhagen, soon under the leadership of the philologist and archivist Jón Sigurðsson (q.v.). From 1845, he emerged as the most forceful spokesman of Icelandic nationalism in Alþingi (q.v.), and he set the tone for the Constituent Assembly (q.v.) held in Reykjavík in 1851. At this meeting, Icelanders rejected all participation in Danish nation-state, calling for home rule and legislative power to be bestowed upon the Icelandic parliament, Alþingi.

During the 1860s, nationalist policies had clear popular support in parliamentary elections, and Jón Sigurðsson remained the unquestioned leader of the nationalist movement. In 1871–74, the Danish government handed Alþingi limited legislative power in Icelandic internal affairs, although the king retained full prerogative to veto all bills passed in Alþingi. This did not satisfy the nationalists, and their fight for sovereignty continued. Efforts to amend the constitution of 1874 dominated parliamentary politics during the last two decades of the 19th century, ending with the establishment of home rule (q.v.) in 1904. The nationalist struggle reached its pinnacle in 1908, however, when the so-called "Draft" (q.v.) for a new constitution was rejected in parliamentary elections on the grounds that it did not acknowledge Icelandic national rights. After the passing of the Act of Union (q.v.) in 1918, nationalism became less prevalent in Icelandic politics, as the Act fulfilled most nationalist demands, but the foundation of the Republic of Iceland (q.v.) in 1944 has to be seen as a logical conclusion of the nationalist struggle.

The nationalist movement was never organized in a unified association in Iceland, but nationalist sentiments remained the defining factors in Icelandic politics from the mid-19th century to the end of World War I (q.v.). It is not surprising, therefore, that nationalism remains an important theme in Icelandic politics to this day, as the early nationalist leaders, Jón Sigurðsson in particular, have gained near saintly status in Icelandic history.

ICELANDIC REVOLUTION, THE. On June 25, 1809, a British soap merchant by the name of Samuel Phelps arrested Count Trampe, the Danish governor in Reykjavík (q.v.), and deposed him from his post. The reason for Phelps's action was Trampe's unwillingness to grant him permission to trade in Iceland, a measure that threatened the merchant's commercial venture in the country. Phelps's "revolution" took a drastic turn, however, when Jörgen Jörgensen (q.v.), a Danish interpreter in his service, assumed the role of Governor of Iceland. In two proclamations, issued on June 26, 1809, the new ruler of Iceland proposed revolutionary changes in the administration. The country was declared free and independent under British protection. Jörgensen's intention was to establish a legislative assembly in the spirit of the old Alþingi (q.v.), with democratically elected representatives from the various districts in Iceland. To secure his popularity, the new governor lowered all taxes in Iceland, while he promised to introduce stiff price controls on grain. Jörgensen reiterated these proclamations on July 11 of the same year, when he promised to convoke a constituent assembly of elected representatives on July 1 of the following year. At the same time, he declared himself "protector," or virtual absolute ruler, of the island for the next year.

The revolutionary government met little resistance in Iceland. Jörgensen promised to retain all royal officials of Icelandic descent, provided that they sent him a declaration of allegiance. As the Danish government had no defensive forces in the country, and communications with Copenhagen were sporadic at the time because of the Napoleonic Wars, many officials saw no point in resisting the usurper. His rule lasted only nine weeks, however, as a British naval captain patrolling Icelandic waters brought it to an end in late August 1809. In the captain's opinion, Phelps and his company had transgressed British laws, because he did not consider Iceland an enemy of Britain. On August 22, 1809, Danish rule was reestablished in Iceland, and shortly thereafter the "revolutionaries" were brought back to Britain.

The Revolution did not have much influence on the course of Icelandic history, although the summer of 1809 is certainly among its most memorable periods. Jörgensen completely failed to incite Icelanders, and his revolutionary rhetoric horrified men like Sir Joseph Banks, the British naturalist and explorer, who had long attempted to persuade the British government to annex Iceland. Thus, when the former authorities were back in control, Iceland returned quietly to the Danish sphere of influence, although the British government continued to control Icelandic trade throughout the Napoleonic Wars. (*See also* UNITED KINGDOM [RELATIONS WITH])

ICELANDIC SOCIETY FOR WOMEN'S RIGHTS (ISWR). The ISWR (Kvenréttindafélag Íslands) was founded in 1907, in Reykjavík, at the incentive of Bríet Bjarnhéðinsdóttir (q.v.), the early champion of women's rights in Iceland. In the beginning, the main purpose of the ISWR, which was affiliated with the International Alliance of Women, was to fight for the en-franchisement of women. The ISWR achieved an astounding vic-tory in 1908 when four women were elected to Reykjavík's city council from an all-female list, as the previous year's charter for the city of Reykjavík had just given women the right to vote in local elections. For the next few years, Alþingi (q.v.) removed many of the legal barriers denying women full citizenship. In 1911, it granted women equality with men in education and full access to offices in the civil service, and in 1915–20 they received equal suffrage in parliamentary elections. The ISWR was active in promoting all of these issues.

Until 1926, the ISWR took a prominent position in politics, offering special tickets in many local and parliamentary elections. But as the modern Icelandic party system took form, political allegiances began to split the ISWR. For this reason, the Society changed its policy and became a nonpartisan organization, uniting women from all political parties. Since then, the ISWR has remained a strong advocate of women's rights in the workplace and the public arena, in addition to supporting various charitable organizations working for women. (*See also* ELECTIONS; WOMEN'S ALLIANCE)

ICELANDIC STEAMSHIP COMPANY (ISC). The first Icelandic shipping company, Eimskipafélag Íslands, or the Icelandic Steamship Company, was founded in January 1914. The ISC, which was the first major public shareholding company in Iceland, was created through a well-organized campaign instigated by a group of entrepreneurs in Reykjavík. Their goal was to free transportation to and from Iceland on sea from a virtual Danish monopoly. The effort was very successful, as the number of founding shareholders was over 13,000, or around 13 percent of the Icelandic population at the time. In 1915, the ISC started scheduled sailing between Iceland and Europe on two new vessels, and it has remained Iceland's largest transportation company ever since. From its founding, the ISC had very strong nationalistic overtones. For the inhabitants of an isolated island, control over communications with the neighboring countries played a central role for the national identity; at the same time, the ISC's success boosted Icelandic confidence at an important juncture in the struggle for independence.

INDEPENDENCE PARTY (IP). Two different political organizations have carried the name Sjálfstæðisflokkur, or Independence Party, in the 20th century. The former was established as an electoral alliance before the parliamentary elections of 1908, and it became a formal political party in February, 1909. Although the party existed for the next 17 years, it was always marked by deep divisions. In 1915, the party split into two groups; one (called the IP *þversum*) advocated an intransigent position in the struggle for Icelandic sovereignty, while the other (the IP *langsum*) was more pragmatic in its approach to these questions.

In 1923–24, a group of representatives, both from the former Home Rule Party (q.v.) and the IP's parliamentary group, united in the formation of new parties to the right of the political spectrum, leading to the establishment of the Conservative Party (CP, q.v.) in 1924. Thus, the old IP was dissolved in 1926, when one of its two remaining representatives in Alþingi (q.v.) joined the Progressive Party (PP, q.v.), and the other founded the Liberal Party.

The second party to bear the name IP has been the largest political party in Iceland since its foundation in 1929. It was formed on May 25 of that year through a merger of the CP and the small Liberal Party. This happened as a response to the growing strength of parties at the center and the left of the political spectrum, that is the PP and the Social Democratic Party (SDP, q.v.). The new party inherited its name from the defunct IP, but it had little more than that in common with its old namesake.

Since its foundation, the IP has incorporated diverse ideological tenets. In their original declaration, its founders aimed at full separation from Denmark and professed a strong belief in social progress, and they thought that individual liberty was the best strategy to attain both goals. The party has always emphasized its support of free enterprise policies in the economic sphere, and it prefers private initiative to state enterprise in most areas of social life. In practice, the party has always been flexible on these issues. Because of its size, it spans a wide political field, both in ideological and social terms. Thus, the IP draws support from the far-right and the moderate center, from towns as well as from the countryside, and even if it is often seen as pro-business, it has a strong representation in the leadership of the labor movement. Although the IP originally advocated strong nationalist views, no political party has been as resolute in its support of the American military presence in Keflavík (q.v.).

In its first parliamentary elections (1931) the IP captured nearly 44 percent of the popular vote. For the next four decades its support was fairly stable, usually ranging from 37 to 42 percent. Strong popular support has made the party a major force in Icelandic politics, both on a national level and in local councils.

The 1980s were a difficult period for the IP. Due to a struggle over its leadership, the support of the party dwindled, and it seemed to be heading toward a permanent split. In 1980, Gunnar Thoroddsen (q.v.), one of its longtime leaders and its deputy-chairman at the time, broke from the IP to head a coalition government of the PP, the People's Alliance (PA, q.v.), and three IP representatives in parliament. In the 1987 elections, Albert Guðmundsson (q.v.), another leading member of the party, left the IP to form his own party, the Citizens' Party (q.v.). As a result, the support of the party fell to an all-time low in the polls. It received only 27 percent of the votes cast in the 1987 parliamentary elections. The party came to the 1991 elections reunited, however, under the leadership of Davíð Oddsson (q.v.), the mayor of Reykjavík, receiving just under 40 percent of the popular vote that year. The party formed a coalition government with the SDP in 1991, following the pattern of the Reconstruction Government (q.v.) of 1959–71. It lost some ground in the 1995 parliamentary elections, but its government retained a slim majority all the same. In order to strengthen its parliamentary majority, the leadership of the IP chose to change partners, forming a new coalition government with the PP under the premiership of Davíð Oddsson.

INDUSTRIALIZATION. Using higher rates of growth and structural changes in the economy as the two main, albeit narrow, criteria in defining industrialization, its initial phase in Iceland can be dated to the turn of the 20th century. Unfortunately, national income data is nonexistent prior to 1901 and is unreliable before 1945. The historical evidence indicates, however, that the economy entered a period of accelerated growth around 1890, based on increased exports of fish products and, to a lesser extent, of agricultural products. Export earnings showed an increase of 35 percent in the 1890s compared with the previous decade and the available national income data that indicate an annual growth rate of 3.9 percent in the period 1901–14, which is well above the European average. Important contributory factors to this growth were expanding overseas markets for fish products and steadily improving terms of trade from 1894 onwards. The growth of the fisheries (q.v.) and higher returns attracted both domestic and foreign capital and paved the way for the use of modern technology, first decked vessels and later motorboats and trawlers.

The move from the primary into the secondary economic sector, an important criterion of industrialization, was fairly slow during the early phases of the economic transformation of Iceland. The catalyst for growth was, and still is, fishing and fish processing rather than manufacturing industry, making industrialization a somewhat ambiguous label for economic change in Iceland. The share of farming (q.v.) in employment dropped continuously from the late 19th century, or from 80 percent in 1870 to 32 percent in 1940, while the rates for the fisheries, including fish processing, rose from 13 to 18 percent and for industry from 3 to 12 percent in the same period. The proportion of the national income derived from farming declined from 45 percent in 1901 to 18 percent in 1940, the respective figures for the fisheries being 30 and 27 percent. The industrial process reversed the traditional roles of the two main sectors within the overall economic structure. The fisheries ceased to be primarily parttime employment of the rural population and became the main livelihood for a growing section of the urban labor force, which normally supplemented its earnings with casual farm work and construction work during slack seasons in the fisheries.

Industrialization, defined rather narrowly above, was only part of a more general and lengthy process, transforming Iceland into a modern capitalist society. Essential to this process were factors like new sources of energy (imported coal and oil and hydroelectric power), the development of a transportation system, the liberalization of foreign trade, the emergence of modern financial institutions, the creation of a free labor market, the shift toward freehold farming, and other changes in the institutional framework of the economy. G. J. (*See also* INDUSTRIES, ENERGY-IN-TENSIVE; INDUSTRY)

INDUSTRIES, ENERGY-INTENSIVE. Interest in exploiting the enormous energy of Icelandic rivers and geothermal areas on a grand scale first arose around the year 1900, but it was not until after World War II (q.v.) that the first large energy-intensive factory was built in Iceland. Financed mainly through Marshall Aid (q.v.), the fertilizer plant (later the state fertilizer plant) at Gufunes, in the vicinity of Reykjavík, started operation in 1954. It used approximately 140–150 GWh a year, supplied by the Írafoss power plant on the river Sog, built in conjunction with the project.

Industrial policy in the 1960s concentrated on developing the energy-intensive sector. A diatomite plant at Mývatn, opened in 1968, represented the first large-scale application of geothermal energy for industrial purposes in Iceland. An aluminum factory near the town of Hafnarfjörður started operation in 1969, supplied with hydroelectric power from the newly established, publicly owned Landsvirkjun, or the National Power Company of Iceland (q.v.). The production capacity of the plant has increased from 60,000 to almost 100,000 tons of aluminum per year, requiring up to 1,500 GWh, and the company has decided to enlarge the factory even further in the next few years. A ferrosilicon plant situated in Hvalfjörður, to the north of Reykjavík, was commissioned in 1979, with a capacity of 58,000 tons, using 500–600 GWh p.a. These three factories are all at least partly foreign-owned.

A desire to diversify the Icelandic economy and to harness the vast but unused resources of hydroelectric and geothermal energy has motivated the promotion of energy-intensive industry. Today, this sector uses over 50 percent of all electricity consumed in Iceland. Its products account for 15–20 percent of all exports, but its contribution to the national income is much lower than these figures imply, because most of the raw materials used in the energy-intensive industries are imported, and the processes are capital-intensive rather than labor-intensive. For this reason, the sector's share of the labor force is only around 1 percent. These industries have, however, reduced the dependence on fish exports and have had a stabilizing effect on economic growth and foreign currency earnings. The operating returns of the industries concerned have, on the other hand, varied greatly, and the question of foreign investment in Icelandic industries has often been an issue of great political controversy, although it has

abated somewhat in recent years. G. J. (*See also* INDUSTRIALI-
ZATION; INDUSTRY)

INDUSTRY. The small resource base and limited specialization in the
work force offered few opportunities for the development of
manufacturing industries in Iceland during most of its history. In
general, each household processed the materials produced on the
farm, such as wool, hides, milk, meat, and fish, thus fulfilling the
needs of the household for clothes and food. Some of the household production was exported, notably socks, mittens, and other
knitted fabrics, salted mutton, and dried and salt fish. With urbanization and growing division of labor during the second half of the
19th century, specialized artisans—carpenters, blacksmiths, stone
masons, saddle makers, bakers, shoemakers—took over many of
these functions. The advent of steam and electrical power after
the turn of the 20th century gave rise to more diversified, modern
industries, such as textile factories, creameries and dairies, and
herring and fish factories. Moreover, light industry producing
goods for the domestic market expanded rapidly under the comprehensive protection policy of the so-called "Government of the
Laboring Classes" (q.v.) of 1934–38.

During the 1970s, industry entered a new phase in Iceland.
This happened with the emergence of energy-intensive industries
(q.v.) and the reduction of various restrictions on foreign trade and
currency transactions, leading to an intensified competition with
imported industrial goods. This trend became more evident when
Iceland entered the European Free Trade Association (EFTA, q.v.)
in 1970, but tariffs on the production of other EFTA coun-tries were
to be removed gradually over a decade. The duty-free access of
Icelandic industrial products to markets in the EFTA countries has
encouraged export industries, which were feeble before 1970. The
last two decades have been a trial period. National income derived
from industry (12–13 percent) and the share of industrial goods in
total exports (about 20 percent) has, on the whole, stagnated while
industrial employment has, in relative terms, shrunk considerably
with the consequent rise in productivity. Industries producing
goods for the domestic market have not fared well in competition,
in particular the manufacture of textiles, clothing, and furniture.
The main reasons for this are reduced protection against foreign
imports and the high exchange rate of the Icelandic currency.
Manufacturing and export of woolen goods used to be a significant
element in the Icelandic economy, but it has been hard hit in recent
years. In contrast, other export industries, such as industries related
to the fisheries (notably the production of fishing gear and fish

processing equipment) and the energy-intensive industry, have progressed considerably in recent years. G. J. (*See also* INDUS-TRIALIZATION)

INFLATION. Iceland suffered higher rates of inflation than most European countries during the postwar period. Already in the 1950s, the annual rate was more than double that of the other European OECD countries (9 percent versus 4 percent), and the disparity continued to grow in the following decades, culminating in an 84 percent rise in consumer prices in 1983. In the following year, however, the inflation rate fell below 30 percent. The persistent high inflation after World War II (q.v.) reflects the dependence of the economy on foreign trade and the heavy weight of fish products in total exports. Large fluctuations in fish catches and export prices have often generated swings in national income on a much larger scale than in other European countries. During periods of rising export values, salaries in the fishing industry tend to rise rapidly, a trend that was later transmitted into higher wage claims in other economic sectors. The subsequent price/wage-spiral, eventually led to a decline in profitability in the export industries, to which the government responded by devaluing the currency. Generally, economic policy was geared toward adjusting the economy to inflation by limiting its most harmful effects, rather than to fighting inflation. This was clearly demonstrated in the relaxed fiscal and monetary policies of the 1970s and 1980s and the general indexing of wages, loans, and deposits to inflation.

This economic cycle dominated the development of prices until the late 1980s when inflation dropped sharply, or from 25 percent in 1988 to 1.5 percent in 1994. This drastic change is a combined result of the recession that plagued Iceland in the years 1988-96, wage agreements between the Icelandic Federation of Labor and the Confederation of Icelandic Employers (qq.v.), and a shift in government policy orientation. In recent years the state has placed more emphasis on low inflation than high employment, using tight monetary and fiscal policy to fight the pressure of inflation. G. J.

INGÓLFUR ARNARSON. *See* ARNARSON, INGÓLFUR.

INNRÉTTINGAR. An industrial project contrived by a number of influential Icelanders in 1751 at the suggestion of Skúli Magnússon (q.v.), the royal treasurer of Iceland. The original purpose was to reorganize the Icelandic economy and improve the lot of the nation. The Danish government contributed substantial sums of money to the project, which started operating small textile workshops in Reykjavík in the early 1750s, thus laying the foundation for the development of the future capital of Iceland. In the beginning, the company experimented with processing and exporting sulfur and with improving fishing techniques, but from early on it emphasized the production of woolen cloth. For various reasons, the company was never profitable, and most of its ventures were only shortlived. In 1764, a Danish merchant company took over the textile workshops in Reykjavík, and in 1774 they became a royal property. The workshops were sold in 1787 and finally closed down in 1802–03; this can be viewed as the end of the Innréttingar project. Seen purely as an economic investment, the Innréttingar was a clear disaster, but it must also be viewed as symbolic of new economic thinking in Iceland and Copenhagen, the belief in economic and social progress through the efforts of the state. Furthermore, it served the purpose of channeling new methods to textile production, and perhaps also the processing of salt cod, to Iceland. (*See also* EIRÍKSSON, JÓN; ENLIGHTENMENT; MONOPOLY TRADE)

ÍSAFJÖRÐUR. The largest town in northwestern Iceland traces its beginning to the late 16th century, when it became a station for foreign merchants. During the period of monopoly trade (q.v.), it became the most important commercial center in the Western Fjords. After the mid-19th century, the town began to grow, and from the late 19th century to the beginning of the 20th, it was the second largest town in Iceland. In this period of expansion, fishing on decked vessels became the foundation of the town's economy. The town benefited from its proximity to some of Iceland's richest fishing grounds.

The population of Ísafjörður increased steadily from the late 19th century to the beginning of World War II (q.v.), rising from 350 inhabitants in 1850 to just under 3,300 in 1940. Since then, the population has remained more or less stationary. Fishing remains the mainstay of Ísafjörður's economy, but with improved communications the rugged nature of this part of Iceland is also becoming a major tourist attraction.

- J -

JENSEN, THOR (1863–1947). This entrepreneur and shipowner was born in Denmark on December 3, 1863, to a Danish carpenter. He moved to Iceland in 1878, to work as an assistant to a merchant in the northwest part of the country. From 1886 to 1901 he ran general stores, first in the towns of Borgarnes and Akranes in western Iceland and later in the town of Hafnarfjörður to the south of Reykjavík (q.v.). In 1901, Thor Jensen moved to Reykjavík, and soon he became one of the most enterprising shipowners in the capital. He was one of the founders of the trawler company Alliance in 1905 and served as its director until 1910. In 1912, he founded the trawler company Kveldúlfur, which later became one of the largest firms in Iceland. In spite of his role in what can be called the Icelandic industrial revolution, Thor Jensen always had a strong interest in farming. Thus, late in life, he retired from his trawler company to run a large farm outside of Reykjavík, specializing in milk production for the growing town. This venture was not well received by his competitors, and in 1934 small farmers used their political clout to pass legislation that rendered capitalist development in agriculture more or less impossible. Thor Jensen was one of few Danes who became fully integrated into Icelandic society; he married an Icelander and their son, Ólafur Thors (q.v.), was one of the leading Icelandic politicians of the 20th century.

JÓHANNESSON, ÓLAFUR (1913–1984). The politician and legal scholar Ólafur Jóhannesson was born in Skagafjörður County in northern Iceland to a peasant family. In 1935, after graduating from secondary school in Akureyri, he enrolled in the University of Iceland (q.v.), completing a law degree in 1939. From 1939 to 1947, Ólafur Jóhannesson practiced law in Reykjavík and worked for SÍS, the Federation of the Icelandic Cooperative Societies. In 1947 he was appointed professor of law at the University of Iceland (q.v.), where he taught until he became prime minister in 1971. He wrote extensively on legal issues during his university years, establishing himself as a leading authority on Icelandic constitutional law.

Ólafur Jóhannesson became a professional politician fairly late in life. In 1959, he was elected to Alþingi (q.v.) for the Progressive Party (PP, q.v.), where he served until his death in 1984. He was elected deputy-chairman of the party in 1960 and its chairman in 1968. After the fall of the Reconstruction Government (q.v.) in the 1971 parliamentary elections, he, as the leader of the largest opposition party, was appointed to form a new coalition government. For the next twelve years he held ministerial posts continuously, except for a brief period from late 1979 to early 1980. He served as prime minister from 1971 to 1974 and again in 1978–79, as minister of justice, ecclesiastic affairs, and commerce from 1974 to 1978, and as minister of foreign affairs 1980–83. Ólafur Jóhannesson was a memorable and sometimes controversial politician, and under his leadership the PP was able to regain its status as a major force in Icelandic politics. This is a remarkable feat, because the population of the countryside, where the party has had its traditional base of support, has shrunk steadily since World War II (q.v.). (*See also* LEFT-WING GOVERNMENT)

JÓHANNSSON, KJARTAN (1939–   ). Former minister of fisheries and trade and the present director of EFTA (q.v.). Born in Reykjavík on December 19, 1939, Kjartan Jóhannsson studied civil engineering at the Royal Technical University in Stockholm, completing his degree in 1963. In 1965, he received an M.S. degree in microeconomics from Illinois Institute of Technology in Chicago and a Ph.D. degree from the same institution in 1969. He was appointed associate professor at the University of Iceland (q.v.) in 1974. The same year he was elected both deputy-chairman of the Social Democratic Party (SDP, q.v.) and a member of the town council of his home town, Hafnarfjörður. Kjartan Jóhannsson was elected to Alþingi (q.v.) in 1978 and served as minister of fisheries from 1978 to 1980 and minister of trade from 1979 to 1980. He was elected chairman of the SDP in 1980, but Jón Baldvin Hannibalsson (q.v.) defeated him in his bid for reelection in 1984. In 1989, Kjartan Jóhannsson left domestic politics to become the Icelandic ambassador to EFTA, and in 1993 he was appointed director of the organization.

JÓNASSON, HERMANN (1896–1976). One of the leading figures in Icelandic politics from the early 1930s to the late 1950s. Hermann Jónasson was born on December 25, 1896, to a farmer in Skagafjörður County in northwestern Iceland. After completing a law degree at the University of Iceland (q.v.) in 1924, he worked as a deputy in the office of the district judge for Reykjavík (*bæjarfógeti*), and in 1928, following a reorganization of the judiciary administration in the capital, he was appointed chief of Reykjavík's police. Hermann Jónasson was elected to parliament for the first time in 1934 for the Progressive Party (PP, q.v.), defeating the former chairman of the party, Tryggvi Þórhallsson. The same year, Hermann Jónasson became prime minister in the so-called Government of the Laboring Classes (q.v.), which was a coalition government of the PP and the Social Democratic Party (SDP, q.v.). For more than two decades, he remained one of the most prominent politicians in Iceland. He served as prime minister in two governments from 1934 to 1942, and again from 1956 to 1958, and as minister of agriculture from 1950 to 1953. Although he was *de facto* leader of the PP from 1934 to the early 1960s, he was only elected its chairman in 1944; he held that position until 1962. Hermann Jónasson retired from politics in 1967.

JÓNSBÓK. A written law code, called "Jón's Book" after the law-speaker (q.v.) Jón Einarsson, one of its authors. The code was first accepted in Alþingi (q.v.) in 1281, superseding the existing law book, called *Járnsíða.* After certain amendments and revisions had been made to the original version of *Jónsbók,* at the request of Icelanders, it took its final form in the early 14th century. In this form, it remained valid for around 400 years, until absolutism (q.v.) was introduced in Iceland. Some of its clauses, especially those dealing with farming (q.v.) and land use, are still in force today. The strength of *Jónsbók* lies in the fact that it was able to adapt general revisions of Norwegian laws written in the 1270s to Icelandic conditions. Moreover, *Jónsbók's* durability must be seen as a testimony to the relative stagnation and conservatism of Icelandic society in the past.

   Jónsbók is not preserved in an original redaction, but the code exists in numerous medieval and later manuscripts. It was one of the first secular books to be printed in Iceland (1578), which is a clear indication of its popularity, and it remained one of the most widely read books in Iceland for centuries. (*See also* GRÁGÁS)

JÓNSSON, ARNGRÍMUR (1568–1648). A Lutheran minister and scholar. He was born to a prosperous farmer in Húnavatn County, northern Iceland, in 1568. When he was eight years old, Arngrímur Jónsson moved to Hólar (q.v.), to study under the influential bishop, his relative, Guðbrandur Þorláksson (q.v.). After graduating from the diocese school at Hólar in 1585, he continued his studies in Copenhagen. In the summer of 1589, he returned to Iceland and became headmaster of the Hólar school. He held this position for a few years, but from around 1598 until his death in 1648 he served as a rural pastor in northern Iceland. Arngrímur Jónsson was one of the most learned men in Iceland during his lifetime. His first work was a short essay in Latin on the nature and history of Iceland (1593), written to correct erroneous information in contemporary foreign literature. In 1609, he published a book on Icelandic history in Latin, called *Chrymogæa,* introducing the country and its medieval historical literature to European scholars. Arngrímur Jónsson formed good contacts with

Danish colleagues of his time, writing in the spirit of European humanism.

JÓNSSON, JÓNAS (1885–1968). One of the most influential politicians in Iceland in the interwar period. He was born to a poor peasant family at Hrifla in Þingey County, in northeast Iceland (therefore he is commonly known as "Jónas from Hrifla"). Jónas Jónsson's poverty prevented him from entering secondary school in Reykjavík, as was required for all who aspired to a career in the government bureaucracy. In 1906, he received a grant from Alþingi (q.v.) to study abroad, and he spent the next three years in Denmark, Germany, and England. In this period he attended a Danish folk high school, a teacher college in Copenhagen, and Ruskin College in Oxford.

Upon returning to Iceland, Jónas Jónsson received a teaching position in the new Teacher Training College in Reykjavík, a position he held for nine years (1909–18). During this period he wrote a survey of Icelandic history, which was used as a textbook in all elementary schools in Iceland for decades and formed the historical perspective of generations of Icelanders. In 1918, he became the first headmaster of the Cooperative College in Reykjavík, a position he held until his retirement in 1955.

Jónas Jónsson entered politics at a time when the modern party system in Iceland was emerging. As the nationalist struggle was approaching its end, economic and social interests, rather than the relationship with Denmark, became the focus of political debate in the country. Jónas Jónsson viewed it as his mission to further these issues and therefore became one of the founders of the Icelandic Federation of Labor (q.v.) in 1916, which was to be both a political organization for workers and a trade union. In the years 1916–19 he was also the driving force behind the formation of the Progressive Party (PP, q.v.), which under his influence became the political arm of the cooperative movement (q.v.), although no formal ties existed between the party and the Federation of Icelandic Cooperatives.

Jónas Jónsson's political career was long and colorful. He sat in parliament from 1922 to 1949, served as chairman of the PP in the period 1934–44 and as minister of justice, education, and ecclesiastical affairs from 1927 to 1932. Jónas Jónsson proved to be a vigorous and shrewd organizer, propagandist, and ideologue for the PP, and he used his power effectively, especially during his stint as minister. He was an extremely prolific essayist, writing on various issues in journals and newspapers (in *Tíminn*, q.v. in particular). Moreover, he maintained close personal contacts with people in all parts of the country and used this network to gather information and disseminate his ideas. Because of his fierce and often ruthless oratory, he was a controversial figure, hated by his opponents but revered by his admirers. The pinnacle of Jónas Jónsson's political career came in the late 1920s and early 30s, but after that he became more and more isolated in his party, and his influence waned. Although his authority did not last for long, few—if any—20th-century politicians have had such a long-lasting influence on the course of Icelandic history.

JÖRGENSEN, JÖRGEN (1780–1841). A Danish adventurer, known for his leading role in the so-called Icelandic "Revolution" (q.v.). Born in Copenhagen in 1780, the son of a prominent watchmaker to the Danish court, Jörgensen was apprenticed to an English collier at the age of 14, serving on British ships for over a decade. During this time, he partook in expeditions to far-off places, including South Africa and Australia. After returning to Denmark in 1806, Jörgensen became a commander on a Danish privateer, but was taken captive by a British man-of-war in early spring of 1808. As the young commander had friends in high places in London, his captivity was fairly relaxed. Later that year, Jörgensen became acquainted with an English soap merchant, Samuel Phelps, who was in desperate need of fats for his soap boiling manufacture. Jörgensen brought to his attention Iceland, which was more or less isolated at the time because of the Napoleonic Wars and produced tallow in considerable quantities. Phelps sent two trading expeditions to Iceland in 1809, with Jörgensen serving as an interpreter.

The second expedition arrived in Iceland in late June, but upon its arrival the Danish governor of Iceland, Count F. C. Trampe, banned all commerce between his subjects and the English merchants. As this was both in direct violation of Trampe's agreement with a British officer earlier the same month, and threatened his mission, Phelps saw no other alternative but to arrest and depose the governor on June 25. Subsequently, Jörgensen took over the governor's office, and thus began one of the most bizarre episodes in Icelandic history. The new governor, or "Protector" as he called himself, promised revolutionary changes in the administration of Icelandic affairs, cutting all ties with Denmark, and threatened to depose all officials who refused to obey his orders. This government was only short-lived, however, as a British naval officer declared Jörgensen's actions illegal on August 22, 1809. Jörgensen was brought back to England and charged with violation of his parole, as he was still formally a prisoner of war at the time of his journey to Iceland. Jörgensen, who never returned to Iceland, died in 1841 in Hobart, on the island of Tasmania.

JÓSEFSSON, LÚÐVÍK A. (1914–1994). For many years, one of the most influential leftist politicians in Iceland. Lúðvík Jósefsson was born on June 16, 1914, into a fisherman's family in Neskaupsstaður, Suður-Múli County, a fishing town on the east coast of Iceland. He completed a high school exam in Akureyri (q.v.) in 1933 and taught at the elementary school in his hometown from 1934 to 1943. From 1944 to 1952, he worked for fishing companies in Neskaupsstaður, serving as director of the Community Fishing Company 1948–52.

For over half a century, Neskaupsstaður has been known as a staunch socialist stronghold, and Lúðvík Jósefsson was instrumental in founding that legacy. He was elected to the town council for the newly formed Socialist Unity Party (SUP, q.v.) in 1938 and to parliament for the same party in 1942. He sat in the town council of Neskaupsstaður for the SUP and the People's Alliance (PA, q.v.) until 1970 and in Alþingi (q.v.) until 1979. He served as president of the PA from 1977 to 1980 and as the leader of its parliamentary group from 1961 to 1971, and again 1975–79. The fisheries (q.v.) were always his main area of interest, and he served as minister of fisheries and commerce in the first two so-called Left-Wing Governments (q.v.), or from 1956 to 1958 and from 1971 to 1974. In this capacity, he was a leading advocate of the extension of the fishing limits (q.v.), first from four to 12 nautical miles, and later from 12 to 50 miles. After his retirement from active politics, Lúðvík Jósefsson served as a member of the Board of Directors of the National Bank of Iceland (q.v.) for a number of years.

- K -

KEFLAVÍK. A small fishing port on the southwest coast of Iceland. Keflavík was an important station for seasonal fishermen in the past, based on its proximity to important spawning grounds for cod. During World War II (q.v.), Keflavík assumed a new role, as a barren heath in its outskirts became the site for an airport that became a major link in transporting goods between the United States and Europe. At the end of the war, the United States government asked for a long-term lease of the airport, but this received no support in Iceland at the time. The reason for this rejection was the nationalistic euphoria in the country following the foundation of the republic in 1944 and the sentiment that the presence of a foreign military was not wanted in peacetime. In 1946 the Icelandic parliament ratified a treaty with the government of the United States in which the latter promised to withdraw the American forces from Iceland and to hand the control of Keflavík Airport over to the Icelandic government. At the same time, a civilian company was entrusted with the operation of the airport, at the behest of the United States Department of Defense, and the American military was given free access to its utilities in order to facilitate communications between the United States and its forces in Germany. Three years later, as Iceland became a founding member of NATO (q.v.), the Icelandic government reiterated its firm intention of not allowing a foreign army to be stationed in Iceland in times of peace. In 1951, as the cold war escalated with the emerging crisis of the Korean War, the Icelandic government struck a defense agreement with its American counterpart. Since then, the United States has stationed up to 5,000 men in Keflavík.

Today, Keflavík is best known for its airport, which is used by the military and the majority of international flights. Although the fisheries are still important for the town, the various services required by the airport and the military base have become the foundation of the town's economy. This is clearly reflected in the rapid growth of the town and its surrounding communities, as their combined population has increased from around 3,500 to 15,500 since the end of World War II.

KJARVAL, JÓHANNES SVEINSSON (1885–1972). A pioneer in Icelandic painting and the most popular painter in 20th-century Iceland. Jóhannes Kjarval was born on October 15, 1885, into a poor peasant family in southeast Iceland. He came to Reykjavík in 1901, attending high school for a time and taking private lessons in drawing. In 1908, he opened his first exhibition in Reykjavík, and three years later he set out on a journey to Europe to study art. Kjarval spent most of the following decade abroad, first in London, then primarily in Copenhagen. In 1914, he enrolled in the Royal Academy of Art in Copenhagen, where he studied until 1918. Four years later, he moved back to Iceland, where he gradually rose to prominence among native artists. By the mid-1930s, he was generally considered the national painter of Iceland, a position he acquired primarily for his interpretation of Icelandic nature and landscapes. For this reason, the city of

Reykjavík opened an art museum in 1972 carrying Kjarval's name and celebrating his art.

KÓPAVOGUR'S MEETING, THE. A meeting held at Kópavogur, to the south of Reykjavík, on July 28, 1662. It was held at the request of Henrik Bjelke, the governor of Iceland (*höfuðsmaður*), who summoned all royal officials in Iceland, the two Icelandic bishops, many ministers of the church, and representatives of the farming elite to pay homage to King Frederick III of Denmark and accept his absolutist rule on behalf of his Icelandic subjects. At the Kópavogur's meeting, the 109 Icelanders present signed a declaration repealing many of the privileges that had been guaranteed in the Old Covenant (q.v.) of 1262–64 between Icelanders and Norwegian King Hákon Hákonarson. From now on, the king had *de jure* all legislative and executive authority in Iceland, and Alþingi (q.v.) became a mere court. During the nationalist struggle of the early 20th century, historians maintained that the Icelandic leaders were forced to sign the document at Kópavogur, but there is little direct evidence to prove that assertion. (*See also* ABSOLUTISM; STIFTAMTMAÐUR)

KRÓNA. *See* CURRENCY.

- L -

LABOR BONDAGE. The labor market in preindustrial Iceland was strictly regulated by law and custom. For centuries, legal restrictions (*vistarband*) were in force to control the number of crofters (*þurrabúðarmenn*), lodgers (*húsmenn*), and casual laborers (*lausamenn*). These restrictions were set to prevent a drain of the labor supply from farming to fisheries (qq.v.) and to battle pauperism by keeping down the number of crofters. Moreover, the social regulations expressed a general belief in the merit of farm service for young people in Iceland, and they were defended as a necessary bulwark against anarchy and social dissolution.

The legal codes of the Commonwealth period (q.v.) obliged dependent persons to have a fixed home on the basis of annual contracts with farmers. Initially, the law did not require people to work for the master of the house, but with time this obligation evolved into labor service. Exempted were crofters and casual laborers, the latter on the condition that they possessed a certain minimum amount of property. Píningsdómur, a decree passed in Alþingi (q.v.) in 1490, obliged crofters to keep livestock and have access to a plot of land. The decree also contains an important clause, prohibiting foreign merchants from maintaining stations in Iceland over the winter, reflecting the fear of foreign competition in the labor market. In 1783, a royal decree severely tightened labor bondage, banning altogether the class of casual laborers and allowing only lodgers and crofters to take on casual work. Casual laborers regained legal status in 1863, but only on the condition that they pay a considerable fee to the authorities for the permission. At the same time, restrictions on lodgers and crofters were relaxed to a certain degree. The growth of the nonagrarian sector and increased competition for labor after the mid-19th century upset traditional work patterns and pushed up wages in Iceland. Mounting opposition to labor bondage, increasing awareness among farmers of the economic disadvantages of such restrictions on personal liberty, and difficulties in enforcing the law at a time of growing population pressure and economic crisis in the rural areas, led to its virtual abolition in 1894, followed by the ending of most legal restrictions on crofters and lodgers in 1907. G. J. (*See also* LABOR MARKET)

LABOR MARKET. One of the most striking characteristics of the Icelandic labor market is its small size, as there were only around 40,000 people economically active in 1910 and just under 150,000 in 1990. The country has, however, experienced structural changes in employment similar to those in neighboring countries in this century. Agriculture's share in the labor force dropped from 50 percent to 5 percent between 1910 and 1990, while manufacturing's (fish processing not included) share rose from just under 5 percent to 13 percent, commerce's from 3 percent to 15 percent, and public services' from 2 percent to 18 percent. The fisheries and fish processing have experienced a slight drop in this period, or 17 percent in 1910 to 13 percent in 1990. Self-employed persons and small employers have always been numerous in Iceland; nearly 60 percent of Icelandic employers today have less than four employees.

Traditionally, a high rate of labor force participation has characterized the Icelandic labor market. With the unemployment rate rarely rising above 4 percent in the period since the Second World War, the participation rate has been one of the highest in the OECD countries, while the average workweek has been one of the longest in the Western world. The rapid entry of women into the labor market has pushed the participation rate upward in recent decades, and now they constitute 47 percent of the total labor force. Thus, the participation rate for women went up from about 33 percent to 77 percent between 1960 and 1992. The participation rates for both the young and the elderly are also very high, in part because a social security pension is not collectable until the age of 67, and most private pension payments begin at the age of 70.

Iceland, along with the other Nordic countries, is among the most highly unionized in the world. Yet, this has not caused wage inflexibility; wages in Iceland seem, indeed, to be very sensitive to conditions in the labor market. The flexibility of the labor market is also demonstrated in fairly smooth geographical and occupational adjustment to employment situations—the latter feature undoubtedly related to the high level of education. G. J. (*See also* EMPLOYMENT; ICELANDIC FEDERATION OF LABOR; LABOR BONDAGE; LABOR MOVEMENT)

LABOR MOVEMENT. The first labor unions emerged during the last decade of the 19th century. Fishermen were the first to organize themselves from 1894 onwards in the so-called Bárufélög, which were modeled on the temperance movement. The flurry of trade union activity around and after the turn of the century, including the foundation of Dagsbrún, the biggest union of unskilled laborers in Iceland, in 1906, culminated in the establishment of the Icelandic Federation of Labor (IFL), (q.v.) in 1916. By 1940, approximately 70 to 80 percent of the working population belonged to unions, largely as a consequence of the strong position the unions achieved in the early 1930s. During these years, Alþingi (q.v.) passed laws securing union members a priority to work and prohibiting employers from paying wages below those negotiated by the unions. The same trend has continued since World War II (q.v.), and in 1994 more than 100,000 people, or three-quarters of all employed persons in Iceland, were members of labor unions. The largest labor organization is the IFL, with 66,000 members, covering most blue collar workers employed in the private sector. The second largest is the Federation of State and Municipal Employees, with 17,000 members.

In its early days the labor movement concentrated its campaign on better pay, improved conditions, and recognition of individual unions as legitimate bargaining partners. The latter demand was not fully achieved until the 1930s. Increased political mobilization among the laboring classes was also a part of its goals, but the Social Democratic Party (SDP, q.v.) was formed as the political wing of the IFL in 1916. In the early 1940s, the labor movement severed its ties with the SDP, when radical socialists on the left and conservatives on the right demanded equal status in the IFL.

Militancy has not been widespread in the labor movement, at least not since World War II, but strikes have been frequent, particularly during the inflationary years of the 1960s and 70s. A tit for tat relationship developed between the movement and the government; the former using strikes to maintain or raise living standards, the latter in turn resorting to devaluation of the currency (q.v.) to reduce the real purchasing power of wages. In recent years, labor negotiations between the IFL and the Confederation of Icelandic Employers (q.v.) have broken this stalemate, and the former has accepted a limited rise in wages in return for both low levels of inflation, and relative stability in the exchange rates of the Icelandic currency. G. J. (*See also* GOVERNMENT OF THE LABORING CLASSES; LABOR MARKET)

LAKI ERUPTION. On June 8, 1783, an enormous volcanic eruption began in Lakagígar, a row of craters located on a fissure to the southwest of the Vatnajökull (q.v.) glacier. In the summer of 1783, lava flooded to the south from the craters, covering large tracts of farmland in nearby Skaftafell County. Even worse, wind spread ashes and poisonous gases from the eruption site over much of northern Iceland, killing livestock and driving people from their homes. The eruption itself ended in February 1784, but its effects crippled the Icelandic economy for over a year afterwards. The period from 1783 to 1785, called Móðuharðindi, or Famine of the Mist—receiving its name from the haze created during the eruption—was one of the most trying periods in Icelandic history. As cattle and sheep perished, either from consuming volcanic ashes or from lack of forage in the winter, people suffered from serious food shortages during the years 1784 and 1785. In these two years, thousands of Icelanders died from hunger and disease, leading to a serious population decline in Iceland—from around 49,000 inhabitants in 1783 to just under 39,000 in 1786. Thus, in 1786 the population of Iceland reached the lowest point recorded in its demographic history, and for this reason some contemporary commentators raised serious doubts about the viability of Icelandic society in the future. (*See also* POPULATION)

LANDFÓGETI. The Danish king established the office of Royal Treasurer of Iceland, or *landfógeti,* in 1683 as a part of the reorganization of the administrative system in Iceland following the introduction of absolutism (q.v.). The *landfógeti* was the chief financial administrator in Iceland, collecting taxes and rents of royal property. He was often entrusted with other duties, such as policing the region around Reykjavík. In 1806 the office of *landfógeti* and *bæjarfógeti* (bailiff) in Reykjavík were formally united, but in 1874 these offices were separated again. The office of *landfógeti* was abolished in 1904 when Iceland obtained home rule (q.v.). (*See also* MAGNÚSSON, SKÚLI)

LANDSHÖFÐINGI. In 1872, a royal decree changed the name of the office of governor in Iceland from *stiftamtmaður* (q.v.) to *landshöfðingi.* This was a part of a general reform of the Icelandic administrative system, following the passing of the Status Laws (q.v.) in 1871. Three men held this important office from 1873 until it was abolished in 1904: Hilmar Finsen (1873–83), Bergur Thorberg (1883–86), and Magnús Stephensen (q.v., 1886–1904). The last two were Icelanders by birth.

The *landshöfðingi* was the pinnacle of the Danish administrative hierarchy in Iceland and served directly under the minister of Icelandic affairs in Copenhagen—a post that was always held by the Danish minister of justice. His role was to execute the government policy in Iceland, advise the government on Icelandic affairs, and serve as a link between the officials beneath him in Iceland and the ministeries in Copenhagen. The *landshöfðingi* represented the king in Alþingi (q.v.) but could not be dismissed by parliament. Thus, he was a central figure in Icelandic political and social life; therefore the period from 1873 to 1904 is generally named after the office, or landshöfðingjatímabilið (the Governor's period, q.v.).

LANDSHÖFÐINGJATÍMABILIÐ. *See* GOVERNOR'S PERIOD.

LAWMAN. An office (*lögmaður*) established in 1271, shortly after Iceland entered into a union with Norway. The lawman presided over Alþingi (q.v.), and its proceedings were illegal without his presence. The lawmen also served as presidents of the courts in Alþingi, selected jurors, and directed the different functions of the assembly. There was initially only one lawman in Iceland, but from 1277 until Alþingi was abolished in 1800, they were two at a time, one for the northwestern part of the country, another for the southeastern part.

From the beginning, it was unclear who should choose the lawmen. Formally, this was the prerogative of the king, or his representatives in Iceland, but until the late 17th century Alþingi had, as a rule, a decisive influence on the nomination of a new lawman. Alþingi insisted that the lawmen should be Icelandic by birth, and usually they were. With the introduction of absolutism (q.v.), the Danish king began to nominate the lawmen without consulting

Alþingi, and he continued to do so until the office was abolished at the end of the 18th century. (*See also* LAW-SPEAKER)

LAW-SPEAKER. The president of Alþingi (q.v.) during the Commonwealth period (q.v.) was called *lögsögumaður,* or law-speaker. Originally, he received this title because he had to memorize the law codes and to recite one-third of them at the meetings of Alþingi each summer. This function changed when the law codes were written down in the early 12th century, but the law-speaker continued to direct the meetings of Alþingi, convene juries, and preside over Lögrétta, the central institution of Alþingi. In 1271, the office of law-speaker was abolished with the introduction of Járnsíða, a new law code of Norwegian origin. (*See also* LAW-MAN)

LAXNESS, HALLDÓR (1902–   ). The master of Icelandic contemporary literature was born Halldór Guðjónsson on April 23, 1902. He grew up on a farm named Laxness in Mosfellsdalur, a farming district to the north of Reykjavík. He published his first novel in 1919, at only seventeen years of age. In the 1920s and 30s, he established himself as the leading author of prose literature in Iceland, although he was a controversial figure in society. His radical views in politics and his unconventional orthography made him unpopular in conservative circles. When awarded the Nobel Prize for literature in 1955, he received international recognition, and since then he has been generally regarded as the greatest author in 20th-century Iceland.

The reason for Halldór Laxness's success has been his unique ability to combine Icelandic literary traditions with cosmopolitan influences. He has travelled widely throughout his long career, establishing contacts and friendship with colleagues in other countries. In the early 1920s he converted to Catholicism, but later he renounced religion and became deeply inspired by socialism. His novels are all firmly rooted in Icelandic experience, and his religious or political opinions have never dominated his writings.

LEFT-WING GOVERNMENT. A term used for coalition governments that united political parties to the left of the Independence Party (IP, q.v.) from the 1950s to the 1970s. The first government to be called this was a cabinet (q.v.) headed by Hermann Jónasson (q.v.) in 1956–58; the second was the first cabinet of Ólafur Jóhannesson (q.v.), succeeding the Reconstruction Government (q.v.) in 1971 and resigning in 1974; and the third was the second cabinet of Ólafur Jóhannesson in 1978–79. The Progressive Party (PP, q.v.) and the People's Alliance (PA, q.v.) participated in all three Left-Wing Governments, the Social Democratic Party (q.v.) in the first and third, and the Union of Liberals and Leftists (q.v.) in the second.

The three Left-Wing Governments do not have much in common, beyond the fact that they were headed by the PP and that they all included ministers from the PA. There is, however, a clear continuity between the first two. Both advocated strong government involvement in the economy, especially by supporting actively the modernization of the fishing fleet and encouraging economic development outside the Reykjavík area. These two governments were also instrumental in the extension of Icelandic fishing limits (q.v.), the first extending the territorial waters to 12 miles and the second to 50 miles. Both declared that their intention was to close down the NATO base in Keflavík (q.v.), although neither was able to keep that promise. A common characteristic of all three Left-Wing Governments was also their instability, because none of them survived for a full four-year term. With the end of the cold war, and the decline of the left-right dichotomy in Icelandic politics, the term Left-Wing Government seems to be outdated and will hardly be revived in the near future.

The Left-Wing Governments hoped to formulate an alternative to the free market policies of the IP. The fact is, however, that the parties on the left did not agree on the content of such a program, and their ambitious plans had the tendency to fuel an escalating inflation (q.v.). (*See also* REGIONAL POLICY)

LEIFUR EIRÍKSSON. *See* EIRÍKSSON, LEIFUR.

LIBRARY, NATIONAL. *See* NATIONAL AND UNIVERSITY LIBRARY OF ICELAND.

LITERACY. Little is known about literacy rates in Iceland before the 18th century, but it is often maintained that the strong literary traditions of late medieval Iceland reflect a widespread ability to read among the general public. Recent studies have demonstrated, however, that the majority of the adult population in Iceland was illiterate at the beginning of the 18th century—women and servants in particular. This situation began to change in the late 17th and the early 18th centuries, when lay and religious authorities, under influence from Pietism (q.v.), began a concerted effort to ensure that everyone would learn to read. The campaign was remarkably successful, given the fact that Iceland had no elementary school system at the time, and literacy had become more or less common in Iceland by the end of the 18th century. Since then, literacy rates in Iceland have been among the highest in the world. (*See also* EDUCATION; LITERATURE)

LITERATURE. Icelandic literature traces its beginning to the early 12th century when Icelandic laws were written down for the first time. Ari Þorgilsson's (q.v.) *Book of Icelanders* (q.v.) is also from this period, but it was written sometime between 1122 and 1133. Icelandic medieval literature reached its peak in the 13th century, however, as during that turbulent century some of the finest literary works of medieval Europe were written here. That was, for example, when most of the family sagas (q.v.) were composed, and Snorri Sturluson (q.v.) wrote the bulk of his works in the 1220s and 30s. In the late medieval period, Icelandic literary tradition changed as the writing of family sagas and historical chronicles came to an end. This did not mean an end to literature in Iceland, however, as most of the extant mythical heroic sagas (*fornaldarsögur*) stem from the 14th and 15th centuries. Moreover, a new form of poetry, called *rímur,* developed in the late medieval period. Influenced by eddic and skaldic poetry (qq.v.) in style and often using the mythical heroic legends and romances as a subject, the *rímur* remained the most popular literary genre in Iceland until the 19th century.

The Reformation (q.v.) had a lasting influence on Icelandic literature. The publication of the Bible in Icelandic (1584) was, for example, crucial in securing the status of Icelandic as a church language, and much of the poetry of the 16th and 17th centuries was religious in character. Moreover, the most influential work of prose in the vernacular of the early modern period was a book of sermons written by Bishop Jón Vídalín (q.v.) and published in 1718–20.

Although printing was introduced relatively early in Iceland (around 1530), it was used mostly by the church until the late 18th century. However, in the last decades of the 18th century, there was a great expansion in the publication of secular works in the Icelandic language. To begin with, they were primarily treatises on practical issues, introducing new methods in farming (q.v.) and exhorting Icelanders to improve their material conditions, but with the romantic nationalism of the 19th century, Icelandic literature was rejuvenated. In the early 19th century, poets like Bjarni Thorarensen and Jónas Hallgrímsson (q.v.) introduced a new voice in Icelandic poetry, and Jón Thoroddsen's (q.v.) *Piltur og stúlka*

(*A Boy and a Girl*), published in 1850, is often regarded as the first modern Icelandic novel.

20th-century Icelandic literature is remarkably strong and varied, considering that Icelandic is spoken by less than 300,000 people. The most notable Icelandic literary figure of this century is, without doubt, Halldór Laxness (q.v.) who received the Nobel Prize for literature in 1955. Moreover, five Icelandic authors have received the Nordic Literary Prize in the last two decades. (*See also* LITERACY; NJÁLS SAGA; STURLUNGA SAGA)

LIVING STANDARDS. In terms of national income, Icelanders have fared well during the postwar period, with gross domestic products (GDP) per capita among the highest in the world in recent decades ($22,900 in 1990). The average annual increase has been 2.6 percent from the end of World War II (q.v.) up until the late 1980s, when the economy entered a recession. Improved living standards can be attributed to a combination of factors, such as more extensive use of the fishing grounds, exploitation of hydroelectric and geothermal energy, high level of investment, adoption of high technology, and a well-educated labor force. Other indicators of living standards, such as average life expectancy, infant mortality, and the number of cars, telephones, and doctors, put Iceland in a very favorable light.

Postwar growth has, however, been uneven, and the great variability of output, unparalleled in the OECD countries, in combination with the consequent fluctuation in real wages, has taught Icelanders not to take their everyday economic situation for granted. In addition to the uncertainty attached to the level of prosperity, it must be noted that the high GDP per capita has been achieved because of the hard work of the population, which has higher participation rates and a longer working day than most European nations. In 1994 the average working week for persons working fulltime was 53.2 hours for men and 43.8 for women. Furthermore, the welfare state (q.v.) has not reached the same levels in Iceland as it has in the other Nordic countries. G. J.

LUTHERANISM. With the Reformation (q.v.), which was completed with the execution of the last medieval Catholic bishop in Iceland, Jón Arason (q.v.), the Evangelical Lutheran Church was established as the only authorized church in Iceland. As in the other Nordic countries, the Lutheran church was under direct control of the state, and the Danish king served as its supreme head. Thus, Lutheran bishops in Iceland were royal officials, although they received most of their revenues from church lands until the late 18th and early 19th centuries.

In the beginning, the Reformation did not transform the structure of church administration in Iceland, except for the suppression of religious houses and the severance of all ties with Rome. The two dioceses, Skálholt and Hólar (qq.v.), were preserved until the end of the 18th century, when they merged, and the bishop's seat moved to Reykjavík. In the long run, however, the Reformation strengthened royal authority in Iceland, both because of the king's position as the head of the church and because the confiscation of the property of the religious houses in Iceland made the king one of the largest landowners in Iceland.

In 1874, the first Icelandic constitution introduced religious freedom, but Lutheranism continues to be the dominant religion in the country. Today, around 95 percent of the population are, at least formally, members of the Lutheran church. Moreover, although the constitution guarantees religious liberty, the fact that the Lutheran church is a state institution gives it a considerable advantage over other religious denominations—the state pays, for example, the salaries of church employees, and the Lutheran bishop plays a strong symbolic role in many public ceremonies, serving as the spiritual head of the Republic of Iceland. (*See also* CATHOLICISM)

- M -

MAGNÚSSON, ÁRNI (1663—1730). Professor, archivist, and collector of manuscripts. Born on November 13, 1663, Árni Magnússon was fostered first by his maternal grandfather and later by his uncle, both of whom were ministers in Dalir County in western Iceland. He studied at the Latin school in Skálholt (q.v.) from 1680 to 1683, and in the fall of 1683 he enrolled in the University of Copenhagen. He studied theology in Copenhagen until the year 1685, in addition to working as an assistant to the renowned Danish Royal Antiquarian Thomas Bartholin. After 1694, Árni Magnússon spent over two years in Germany, and upon returning to Copenhagen in 1697, he was nominated secretary for the royal archives. He was appointed professor at the University of Copenhagen in 1701 but was sent as a royal emissary to Iceland the following year. From 1702 to 1712, Árni Magnússon and Vice-Lawman Páll Vídalín traveled around the country, collecting information on its economic conditions, legal practices, and trade. Under their direction, the first census (q.v.) in Iceland was taken in

1703, listing all inhabitants by name, place of residence, age, and status. In this period, they also completed a description of every farm in Iceland. Árni Magnússon was appointed librarian at the University Library in Copenhagen in 1721, effectively serving as its director. Upon his death in 1730, he bequeathed his manuscript collection to the University of Copenhagen, in addition to establishing a special fund to provide financial support to researchers and grants for editions of manuscripts in his collection.

Árni Magnússon is primarily remembered for his contribution to the preservation and study of Icelandic manuscripts. From an early age, he interested himself in the collection of vellum and paper manuscripts, using his connections to gather a great number of them in Iceland and transport them to Copenhagen. Although 19th- and 20th-century nationalists regretted that these cultural jewels had been removed from their country of origin, there is no doubt that Árni Magnússon's work salvaged many of the Icelandic parchment manuscripts from destruction. (*See also* ÁRNI MAGNÚSSON INSTITUTE; MANUSCRIPTS, RETURN OF)

MAGNÚSSON, SKÚLI (1711–1794). The man sometimes called the "father of Reykjavík" was born on December 12, 1711, to a Lutheran minister in Þingey County. Skúli Magnússon studied in Copenhagen between 1732 and 1734, with the intention of becoming a clergyman. In 1734, the king appointed him bailiff in Skaftafell County, and he returned to Iceland the same year to take up his office. Three years later, he was promoted to the office of bailiff in Skagafjörður County where he served for the next twelve years. In 1749 Skúli Magnússon was the first Icelander to be appointed *landfógeti* (q.v.), or Royal Treasurer, in Iceland, an office he held for the remainder of his active life. Unlike most of his predecessors, he served his office with great zeal, furthering with vigor the economic development of Iceland. After moving to Viðey (q.v.), a small island just off Reykjavík's present-day harbor, he was instrumental in persuading the Danish king to establish textile workshops in Reykjavík with the intention of promoting technological innovation in the country. This venture, which was started in 1752, was not economically profitable, but it laid the foundation for the development of the town of Reykjavík. It was Skúli Magnússon's fight against the companies monopolizing Icelandic trade that has earned him the greatest praise among his countrymen, however. During years of high grain prices, merchants tried to increase their profits by importing rotten grain, a practice that the *landfógeti* tried relentlessly to put an end to. In

1793, then 81 years old, Skúli Magnússon retired from his office and died the following year.

Skúli Magnússon is rightly remembered as one of the most important persons in the history of 18th-century Iceland. With his actions as a royal official and his writings on the economy of Iceland, he was instrumental in igniting a belief in progress, which was to characterize the nationalist surge of the following century. (*See also* INNRÉTTINGAR; MONOPOLY TRADE)

MANUSCRIPTS, RETURN OF. In 1945, at the end of World War II, the new Icelandic republic requested the return of what was deemed to be its most valuable cultural treasures, the medieval Icelandic vellum manuscripts preserved in Copenhagen. Most of these manuscripts had been collected in Iceland during the 17th and 18th centuries by men such as Árni Magnússon and Bishop Brynjólfur Sveinsson (qq.v.) and were kept at the Royal Library in Copenhagen and the University Library of Copenhagen. At first, the Icelandic demands were strongly opposed by Danish scholars, as the return of such cultural objects is not a standard practice when former dependencies receive independence. A number of influential Danish politicians supported the request, however, in part because they wanted to use the issue to demonstrate how the Nordic countries could solve conflicts in a peaceful manner. In 1961, after long and difficult negotiations, the two nations came to a conclusion about the actual division of the manuscripts; about 1,700 of them were to be returned to Iceland in the space of 25 years, but about 900 were to remain in Copenhagen. On April 21, 1971, after a decade of legal debates in Denmark, the Danish minister of culture returned the first two manuscripts to his Icelandic counterpart. The return of the manuscripts is to be completed in 1997, and they are stored at the Árni Magnússon Institute (q.v.) of the University of Iceland.

MARINE RESEARCH INSTITUTE (MRI). Founded in 1965, the MRI (Hafrannsóknarstofnun) has been instrumental for the last decades in dictating the fisheries policy of the Icelandic government. The MRI's object is to conduct research on the marine environment around the country and consult the government on the utilization of various fish stocks in Icelandic waters. Recent reductions in catches, especially those of cod, have been enacted after warnings from the MRI, although the government has only recently dared to propose measures as drastic in this respect as the institute has advised. The MRI has its headquarters in Reykjavík, and its current director is Jakob Jakobsson, professor of Marine Science

at the University of Iceland (q.v.). G. J. (*See also* DIRECTOR-
ATE OF FISHERIES; FISHERIES; FISHERIES MANAGE-
MENT)

MARSHALL AID. Iceland was among the founding members of the
Organization for European Economic Cooperation (OEEC, later
Organization for European Cooperation and Development,
OECD) in 1948, set up to administer the American aid offered
under the Marshall Plan. Iceland accepted the American financial
aid in an agreement with the United States government on July 3,
1948, according to which it was to receive 38.65 million dollars,
including 29.8 million as grants and most of the rest as loans on
favorable terms. The aid was largely used to facilitate United
States imports to Iceland between 1948 and 1954, easing import restrictions, but 7.9 million dollars were invested in two water power
plants and the first fertilizer plant in the country. The most controversial aspect of the aid was the clause allowing the United States
government to set aside 5, later 10, percent of the so-called Counterpart Fund for its free disposal in Iceland, giving it direct
economic and political leverage in the country's internal affairs.
G. J.

MENNTASKÓLINN Í REYKJAVÍK (MR). The oldest secondary
school in Iceland traces its ancestry to the old Latin schools, or
gymnasia, at the two episcopal seats, Skálholt and Hólar (qq.v.).
At first, these schools, founded in the 11th and 12th centuries
respectively, were meant to educate young men for priesthood, and
this was, in fact, one of the objectives of the Latin schools until a
theological college was founded in Reykjavík (q.v.) in 1847. The
Skálholt school moved to Reykjavík in 1786, and at the beginning
of the 19th century the Hólar school merged with the Latin school
in Reykjavík. From 1805 to 1846, the school was located at
Bessastaðir (q.v.), but it was moved back to Reykjavík in 1846,
where a new house had been built specifically for the school in the
town's center.
  During the second half of the 19th century, the Latin school in
Reykjavík gradually evolved into a regular secondary school, preparing its students for university studies. This development was in
line with educational reforms in Denmark, culminating with a
change in the name of the Reykjavík school to *Menntaskóli* in
1904. Since 1937 its formal name has been *Menntaskólinn í
Reykjavík,* and it is commonly known by its acronym M.R.
  Until the late 1920s, the MR was the only school in Iceland to
have the right to give university entrance exams. As a result, al-

most all the educated elite in the country had graduated from the school, providing this group with a common identity and a sense of homogeneity. In 1928, this monopoly was broken when Jónas Jónsson (q.v.), then minister of education, granted the secondary school in Akureyri (q.v.) the same prerogative. With growing demands for university education, the number of secondary schools has increased rapidly in Iceland, and at the present over 20 different institutions prepare students for university studies. (*See also* EDUCATION)

MINISTRIES. With the establishment of home rule (q.v.) in 1904, the Ministry of Icelandic Affairs was transferred from Copenhagen to Reykjavík (q.v.). From 1904 to 1917, the government of Iceland consisted of one ministry that was divided into three offices or departments (Office of Education and Justice, Office of Economic Affairs and Transportation, and Office of Finance and Revision). When the number of ministers grew to three in 1917, each minister became a head of a separate department; the prime minister headed the Department of Justice and Ecclesiastical Affairs, the minister of economic affairs headed the Department of Economic Affairs and Transportation, and the finance minister headed the Department of Finances. In 1921, each of the three departments became independent ministries. This organization remained unchanged until 1938, when Alþingi (q.v.) established a special Ministry of Foreign Affairs, preparing for the total secession from Denmark. With the growing complexity of the Icelandic administration, the number of ministries has increased steadily. At the present there are 14 separate ministries in Iceland: Office of the Prime Minister (q.v.), Ministry of Culture and Education, Ministry of Foreign Affairs, Ministry of Agriculture, Ministry of Fisheries, Ministry of Justice and Ecclesiastical Affairs, Ministry of Social Affairs, Ministry of Health and Social Security, Ministry of Finance, Ministry of Transportation, Ministry of Industries, Ministry of Commerce, Ministry of Environment, and the Statistical Bureau of Iceland (q.v.). A permanent secretary heads each ministry, but individual ministers are often responsible for more than one portfolio; thus, there are ten ministers in Davíð Oddsson's (q.v.) cabinet formed in the spring of 1995. (*See also* ACT OF UNION; CABINET; PRIME MINISTER; REPUBLIC OF ICELAND)

MODERNIZATION GOVERNMENT, THE. In October 1944, close to the end of World War II (q.v.), the two parties at the opposite poles of the political spectrum, the conservative Independence Party

(IP, q.v.) and the radical Socialist Unity Party (SUP, q.v.) formed a coalition government with the participation of the Social Democratic Party (SDP, q.v.). Each of the three parties had two ministers in the government, with Ólafur Thors (q.v.) of the IP serving as prime minister (q.v.). The main objective of the government, which was known as Nýsköpunarstjórnin (the Modernization Government) was to secure the economic basis of the new republic and use the large foreign exchange reserves collected during the war to modernize economic infrastructures. For the next two years, the government spent liberally on various projects, especially on the modernization of the fishing fleet and of the fishing industry in general. In addition to these economic measures, the government introduced extensive educational and social reforms, including new legislation for Icelandic primary education, a new standardized entrance exam for secondary schools, and expanded welfare legislation. In the summer of 1946, the coalition parties won a decisive victory in parliamentary elections, but in October of the same year, the socialist ministers resigned from the government because of their opposition to the airport agreement made between the governments of Iceland and the United States. In February of the following year, a coalition government of the Progressive Party (q.v.), the IP, and the SDP replaced the Modernization Government. (*See also* KEFLAVÍK)

MONOPOLY TRADE. The monopoly trade, which became the most hated aspect of Danish rule in Iceland, was formally introduced in 1602, when the king decided to give only Danish merchants licenses to trade with Iceland. In the preceding century, the royal government had sold such monopoly rights over certain regions to individual Danish or German merchants, but now this system was to cover the whole country. The king wanted to increase the royal revenues from his dependency and boost the business of the Danish merchant class. Strict monopoly regulations were in full effect in Iceland until 1786–88, when a royal edict opened the Icelandic trade to all Danish subjects. The Danish government abolished the last vestiges of this economic policy as late as 1855.

The monopoly trade had very adverse effects on the Icelandic economy. Its inflexibility and exclusion of all competition stifled economic initiative, because the regulations made it more or less impossible for merchants to invest their earnings in Iceland. Therefore, all profit went out of the country. Moreover, some merchants became very unpopular for their unscrupulous trading practices; the quality of their imports was sometimes suspect, and their supplies insufficient. In part, this was the result of strict price regulations on most imports to Iceland, which could lead to great losses for the Danish merchants in times of scarcity. In the 19th century, Icelandic nationalists viewed the monopoly trade as an example of Danish oppression, but recent studies have emphasized that it was a widespread economic practice at the time in the neighboring countries and, to a certain extent at least, that it served the interests of a part of the Icelandic elite. (*See also* MAGNÚSSON, SKÚLI; TRADE, FOREIGN)

MORGUNBLAÐIÐ. The largest and most influential newspaper in Iceland was founded in 1913. Although *Morgunblaðið* prides itself on being the newspaper of all Icelanders, its editorial policy has leaned to the right in politics since its foundation, and it has had strong links with the Independence Party (IP, q.v.) from the establishment of that party in 1929. *Morgunblaðið* has, however, never had formal ties with the IP, and in recent years it has become more independent of the party than before; at the same time as the political parties in Iceland are losing their influence over the press. At the present, *Morgunblaðið* is published six times a week, and each issue sells over 50,000 copies—or almost one copy for every five inhabitants.

- N -

NATIONAL AND UNIVERSITY LIBRARY OF ICELAND. The National Library of Iceland in Reykjavík was established as Íslands Stiftis Bókasafn in 1818, changing its name to Landsbókasafn Íslands in 1881. The library was opened to the public in 1848, moving to its own building in 1909. In 1994, with the opening of a new library building on the University campus in Reykjavík, the Icelandic National Library merged with the University Library, making it by far the largest library in Iceland. The National Library is a depository for all printed material in Iceland, and a great number of private archives and manuscripts from the early modern and modern periods are stored in its manuscript section. The holdings of the National and University Library of Iceland are, therefore, of crucial importance in the study of Icelandic history and culture.

NATIONAL ARCHIVES OF ICELAND (NAI). The National Archives of Iceland trace their history to a proclamation, made by the governor of Iceland in 1882, announcing that the archives of a few of the highest government offices in Iceland should be stored under one roof in Reykjavík. The National Archives were formally established, however, on August 10, 1900, under the name of Landsskjalasafn Íslands. They were given their current name, Þjóðskjalasafn Íslands, in 1915. With the home rule (q.v.) of 1904, the documents of the Icelandic Bureau in Copenhagen were moved to Iceland and stored in the NAI, and in 1928, a large number of documents pertaining to Icelandic history were transported from Copenhagen to be placed in the NAI.

Today, the NAI are bound by law to collect and preserve public records (that are over 30 years old) from all government institutions in Iceland, including the state church, in addition to serving as a depository of private documents that are placed in their care. Moreover, they oversee the management of public records in the various government agencies and supervise the preservation of documents in local archives.

NATIONAL BANK OF ICELAND (NBI). The National Bank of Iceland (Landsbanki Íslands) was established with an act passed in Alþingi (q.v.) in 1885 and started operations in the following year. Since that time, the NBI has been the leading banking institution in Iceland, and at the time of its foundation the NBI was actually the only bank in Iceland. The scale of its operations was initially limited, but its activities increased considerably at the turn of the century, in response to growing demand for capital from the burgeoning fishing industry. Originally, the NBI had the right to issue a limited quantity of treasury notes, but in 1904, Alþingi granted a private bank by the name Íslandsbanki (Bank of Iceland) the right to print bank notes, in addition to the treasury notes of the NBI. In 1928, this permission was revoked, and the NBI received the sole right to issue currency in Iceland. For the next decades the NBI remained a commercial bank, while it also managed the central banking (q.v.) functions of the Icelandic state; in 1961 these two functions were separated with the foundation of the Central Bank of Iceland. Today, the NBI is the largest commercial bank in Iceland and an important lender to companies in all sections of the economy. It has its headquarters in Reykjavík but operates branches around the country.

NATIONAL ECONOMIC INSTITUTE (NEI). This institute (Þjóðhagsstofnun) was founded in 1974, but its origins can be traced back to the beginning of national income accounting in Iceland during the early 1950s. The institute has a unique status, as it is placed directly under the prime minister (q.v.), rather than any particular ministry. It is now mainly responsible for economic research, national income accounting, and short-term forecasting, in addition to serving as an advisory body to the government and parliament. These different functions have placed the NEI in a somewhat complex, and even ambiguous position, as it must act as an impartial research and forecasting institution at the same time it advises the government on its economic policy. G. J.

NATIONAL POWER COMPANY OF ICELAND (NPCI). A company established in 1965 to construct and operate power plants and the main distribution lines in Iceland and to provide local utilities with electricity. The NPCI (Landsvirkjun) was formed as a joint enterprise of the Icelandic state and the city of Reykjavík. These two parties held equal shares in the NPCI until 1983, when the town of Akureyri (q.v.) became a partner. The state now owns half of the shares, Reykjavík 45 percent, and Akureyri 5 percent. The first major project of the NPCI was the construction of the Búrfell Power Plant in Árnes County, which opened in 1969; since then its activities have expanded greatly. This reflects the emphasis on energy-intensive industry (q.v.) in Iceland during the last three decades, the state having attempted to attract foreign investment to Iceland by offering inexpensive electricity. This strategy was only partly successful, however, because a severe recession in these industries in the early 1990s brought all investments to a halt. As a result, the NPCI's power plants, some of which were the largest and most complicated projects undertaken in Iceland, produced a considerable amount of surplus electricity for a number of years. Since the mid-1990s, a boom in investments, especially in the production of aluminum, has solved this problem, and the NPCI must expand its operations further in coming years to meet new demand.

At the present, the NPCI owns and operates all the largest hydroelectric power plants in Iceland, as well as the interregional power lines. The company's power supply area encompasses virtually the entire country, and its production accounts for more than 90 percent of the electricity generated in Iceland. G. J.

NATIONAL PRESERVATION PARTY OF ICELAND (NPPI). The NPPI, or Þjóðvarnarflokkur Íslands, was founded in 1953 to protest the American military presence in Keflavík (q.v.). Its platform focused primarily on this single issue, but it also advocated democratic socialism. The NPPI received 6 percent of the votes cast in the parliamentary elections of 1953, giving it two seats in Alþingi (q.v.). In 1956 and 1959 the party did not poll enough votes to have a representative elected to parliament, but in 1963 one of its leaders entered parliament through cooperation with the People's

Alliance (PA, q.v.). The same year, the NPPI ceased to exist as a political party, and most of its support went to the PA.

NATIONALISM. The idea that Icelanders had a separate identity emerged early on in their history. There is, for example, evidence in the Saga literature and the Old Icelandic law codes indicating that Icelanders perceived themselves as a separate population group from Norwegians as early as during the Commonwealth period (q.v.). The same sentiment was clearly dominant in Iceland for the next centuries, in spite of the fact that the country became a part of the Norwegian and Danish monarchies. Thus, Icelanders defended their provincial privileges, and they never abandoned the use of the Icelandic language in private or public life. It was only in the early 19th century, however, that demands for political sovereignty were voiced in Iceland. Spokesmen of this nationalist sentiment traced its origins to patriotism of earlier periods, heralding the Icelandic cultural heritage as a legitimation of their political claims. Pride in Icelandic traditions had its roots in the writings of 18th-century commentators, such as the naturalist Eggert Ólafsson (q.v.), but ideological currents of 19th-century Europe and contemporary developments in Denmark were the main sources of inspiration for the political agenda of the Icelandic nationalist movement (q.v.).

During most of the 19th century, and well into the 20th, nationalism remained the dominant political ideology in Iceland. Thus, opinions on Iceland's position in the Danish monarchy and the future status of the country dictated political allegiances in this period. With the Act of Union (q.v.) in 1918, which granted Iceland full sovereignty and the status of a free state, this chapter in Icelandic political history came to an end. This did not mean the end of nationalism in Iceland, however, as the preservation of national culture and independence are still extremely important. For this reason, opposition to the NATO base in Keflavík (q.v.) was very strong during the cold war, and most Icelanders take great pride in the preservation of their culture and the political independence of the nation. Icelandic authorities have also been very hesitant about entering the EU (q.v.), because of fear that membership in the Union could compromise Icelandic sovereignty. (*See also* FJÖLNIR; SIGURÐSSON, JÓN)

NJÁLS SAGA. The "Saga of the Burning of Njáll" *(Brennu-Njáls saga),* or *Njáls Saga,* is the longest and probably best-known of the Icelandic family sagas (q.v.). In essence, it is a tragic story of two friends, Gunnar and Njáll, living in the southern part of Iceland in the late 10th and early 11th centuries. Gunnar was a heroic figure, tall, handsome, and brave, while Njáll was renowned for his cunning and wisdom. The two men met similar destinies, however, as both were killed by their adversaries—Gunnar by the weapons of his enemies, Njáll by fire. *Njáls Saga* is a complex story, presenting a diverse set of characters in an elaborate narrative structure. It is clearly written as a literary work, although the writer was well-versed in the oral traditions of his time. The saga is also interesting for its detailed description of the legal procedures at Alþingi (q.v.). The author demonstrates a strong longing for peace and harmony in society; he is a firm believer in the importance of Christianity, but he is also a protagonist of the values of the old society that had vanished during the violent Age of the Sturlungs (q.v.). This author is unknown, as are those of all the family sagas, but scholars have dated its composition with relative certainty to the period from around 1275 to 1290. The great number of manuscripts of *Njáls Saga* that are preserved, both from the Middle Ages and from later periods, is a clear testimony to its popularity throughout the centuries. (*See also* LITERATURE)

NORDAL, JÓHANNES (1924–). Former director of the Central Bank of Iceland (CBI) and a leading authority on Iceland's economic policy. Jóhannes Nordal, the son of the literary scholar Sigurður Nordal (q.v.), was born in Reykjavík on May 11, 1924. After graduating from Menntaskólinn í Reykjavík (q.v.) in 1943, he entered the London School of Economics, where he completed a B.S. degree in 1950 and a Ph.D. degree in 1953. He worked as economic advisor at the National Bank of Iceland (q.v.) from 1954 to 1959, when he was appointed director of the bank. At the time of the foundation of the CBI in 1961, he became one of its directors, and chairman of its Board of Directors in 1964. He served both of these functions until his retirement in 1993.

Jóhannes Nordal was one of the most influential persons in Icelandic economic life for over three decades. As director of the CBI, he played a crucial role in the formation of Icelandic monetary policy, and as chairman of numerous steering committees and governing bodies of diverse institutions and companies, such as the Icelandic Science Fund and the National Power Company of Iceland (q.v.), he has wielded a strong influence in various fields of Icelandic society. (*See also* CENTRAL BANKING)

NORDAL, SIGURÐUR (1886–1874). Professor of Icelandic literature and one of the founders of what has been called the Icelandic School in Old Norse studies. He was born on September 14, 1886, the illegitimate son of a farmservant and a maid in northern Iceland. Raised by his uncle, Sigurður Nordal was to enjoy the privilege secondary school education in Reykjavík, completing a university entrance exam in 1906. In the fall of the same year, he enrolled in the department of Old Norse studies at the University of Copenhagen. He finished a master's degree in 1912 and defended his doctoral dissertation on the *Saga of St. Ólafur* two years later. After studying philosophy at Oxford University for one year, Sigurður Nordal returned to Iceland in 1918, becoming professor of literature in the recently founded University of Iceland (q.v.). In this position, he established himself as a leading scholar on Old Norse literature, shaping generations of Icelandic students in this field. Throughout his career, he was a firm spokesman of a scholarly tradition called "bookprose theory," which considers the Icelandic sagas more or less pure fiction rather than historical accounts based on oral traditions. Because of his reputation as a scholar of international stature, the Icelandic government appointed him ambassador to Denmark in 1951. His role was primarily to negotiate a solution of a dispute between the new republic and its old mother country concerning the return of Icelandic manuscripts preserved in Danish libraries. After returning to Iceland in 1957, he resumed his former post as a professor at the University of Iceland.

For decades, Sigurður Nordal was a towering figure in the field of Old Norse studies. His research shattered the old beliefs in the historical veracity of the sagas, although in later years his approach has been criticized for ignoring their oral sources as well as their social and political message. Although modern scholars have abandoned his strict bookprose theory, Sigurður Nordal's works continue to offer valuable insights into the interpretation of saga literature. In 1986, a special institute, carrying his name, was founded at the University of Iceland with the purpose of supporting research in Icelandic culture, both in Iceland and abroad. (*See also* MANUSCRIPTS, RETURN OF; SAGAS)

NORDIC COUNCIL. The Nordic Council serves as a forum for inter-parliamentary and intergovernmental cooperation between the five Nordic countries (Denmark, Finland, Iceland, Norway, and Sweden) and three provinces (Åland, Faeroe Islands, and Greenland). Established in 1953, from the non governmental Nordic Associations, the Nordic Council has served as the basis for cultural, social, and economic cooperation among the Nordic countries. The Council has furthered a strong sense of common identity, although there is some doubt that it will survive the entrance of Denmark, Sweden, and Finland into the European Union (q.v.). The Nordic Council runs a cultural center, the Nordic House, and a research institute in volcanology in Reykjavík.

NORTH ATLANTIC TREATY ORGANIZATION (NATO). Iceland is one of the twelve founding states of NATO, which served as a military union of the western bloc during the cold war. Iceland has always been an active member of NATO, although the fact that the country maintains no armed forces has limited its direct participation mainly to nonmilitary functions. Since the defense agreement with the United States in 1951, Iceland has, however, contributed to the military operations of NATO by allowing the United States to maintain a military base in Keflavík (q.v.) on the southwest coast. In this way, the American military has undertaken the defense of Iceland on behalf of NATO, while the Keflavík base has served as an important link in NATO's surveillance of the North Atlantic, both in air and at sea.

The presence of a foreign army on Icelandic soil has been among the most divisive issues in Icelandic politics for decades, which has led many to oppose NATO membership as well. Nationalistic sentiments have fueled these views, because many have perceived the United States military presence as a compromise of Icelandic sovereignty. Hostility toward American foreign policy, especially during the war in Vietnam, has also motivated objections from the leftist parties to the base in Keflavík. Thus, the Left-Wing Government (q.v.) of Ólafur Jóhannesson (q.v.), formed in 1971, vowed to revise the defense agreement with the United States, aiming at the United States' withdrawal from Keflavík. In response, a group of Icelandic NATO supporters collected a massive number of signatures on a petition protesting the planned withdrawal. The government resigned in the summer of 1974 without acting upon its promise. Since then, the withdrawal of the NATO forces from Iceland has never been seriously discussed. The waning of the cold war has also helped to diffuse the issue, and the opposition to NATO membership is no longer a cornerstone in the platform of any political party in Iceland. Therefore, the future of the military base seems to depend more on the willingness of the United States to keep it open than on the policies of Icelandic authorities.

NORWAY (RELATIONS WITH). Because the first permanent settlers in Iceland were of Norwegian origin, Iceland's relations with Norway are as old as Icelandic history. From the beginning, ties between the two countries were formed and maintained through extensive personal and institutional contacts. Thus, it was in Norway that Icelanders sought the model for their first law codes, and it was through Norwegian initiative that Icelanders converted to Christianity around the year 1000. Moreover, when the archbishopric in Trondheim was established in 1153, the two dioceses in Iceland came under the jurisdiction of the Norwegian archbishop. It was not surprising, therefore, that the Norwegian king sought to augment his formal authority in Iceland during the last decades of the Commonwealth period (q.v.). In the early 13th century, many Icelandic chieftains had become courtiers in the service of the Norwegian king, some of them actively promoting his authority. Between 1262 and 1264, after decades of violent upheavals, Icelanders approved a treaty with the king, promising him allegiance and tributes in return for his pacification of the country. In 1380, Iceland accompanied Norway into a union with Denmark, although it continued to be regarded as a part of the Norwegian realm.

During the last century of the Middle Ages, relations with Norway decreased in importance for Icelanders. This happened as the administrative center moved to Copenhagen in the late 14th century and as foreign trade with Iceland ceased to go through Norwegian harbors in the 15th century. In the 19th century, Icelanders began, however, to look to Norway for political support and economic contacts. Norway's status as one of the most progressive democracies in northwestern Europe, and the historical ties between the two countries, served as an incentive for this development.

Relations between the two countries have been extensive, and usually amicable, in recent decades. Common interests in issues like fisheries (q.v.) have often led to close cooperation, a situation that has been further enhanced through both countries' membership in institutions such as EFTA, NATO, and the Nordic Council (qq.v.). But similar economic interests have also been a source of friction between the two countries. Bitter conflicts over fishing rights in the North Atlantic and the Barents Sea are obvious manifestations of this antagonism, but the debates have been fueled by declining fish stocks in the northern waters. The two nations have, therefore, competed intensely over fishing rights in these regions, both attempting to get as much as possible from a limited economic source. (*See also* ALÞINGI; CONVERSION TO CHRISTIANITY; OLD COVENANT)

NÝ FÉLAGSRIT. An Icelandic periodical published in Copenhagen from 1841 to 1873. Its editor and main contributor was Jón Sigurðsson (q.v.), the leader of the Icelandic nationalist movement (q.v.). The journal closely reflected the views and interests of its founder, publishing a mixture of political essays and practical treatises on economic issues. The style of *Ný félagsrit* was often thought to be rather abstruse, and, despite the high quality of its articles, it was never a great financial success. But because of the prestige and political importance of its editor, *Ný félagsrit* occupies a central place in the history of Icelandic journalism. (*See also ÁRMANN Á ALÞINGI; FJÖLNIR*)

- O -

ODDSSON, DAVÍÐ (1948–   ). One of the most prominent politicians in Iceland since the early 1980s. Davíð Oddsson was born on January 17, 1948, in Reykjavík. After completing a university entrance exam from Menntaskólinn í Reykjavík (q.v.), he studied law at the University of Iceland (q.v.), receiving his degree in 1976. He worked for the Reykjavík Health Insurance Fund from 1976 to 1978, serving as its director from 1978 to 1982.

Davíð Oddsson became active in politics at an early age, and in 1974 he was elected to Reykjavík's city council for the Independence Party (IP, q.v.). In 1982, he led the party to an overwhelm-ing victory in elections to the city council, regaining a majority in the council for the IP after a short interlude of left-wing control. In the same year, he became mayor of Reykjavík. Under his undis-puted leadership, the IP gained a dominant position in Reykjavík's city council, and his influence in the party grew with his success in governing the capital. Davíð Oddsson took his first step toward the leadership of the IP when he became its vice-chairman in 1989. Two years later he defeated Þorsteinn Pálsson (q.v.), the sitting chairman of the IP, in elections for leadership of the party. The same year, Davíð Oddsson was elected to Alþingi (q.v.) for the first time. After the elections of 1991, he was given the mandate to form a new government, as he and his party were the unques-tioned victors of the elections. From 1991 to 1995, he served as prime minister (q.v.) in a coalition government of the IP and the Social Democratic Party (q.v.), and since 1995 he has held the same office in a coalition government of the IP and the Progressive Party (q.v.).

Davíð Oddsson earned respect in his party for the effective government of Reykjavík, although his forceful political style made him controversial, at least among his adversaries. On a na-tional level, Davíð Oddsson has united the IP after a decade of internal disputes, and under his leadership the party seems to have regained its former cohesion after serious dissension during most of the 1980s.

ÓLAFSSON, EGGERT (1726–1768). Vice-lawman, poet, and naturalist. Born to a prosperous farmer in Barðaströnd County in western Iceland, Eggert Ólafsson completed the university entry exam from Skálholt (q.v.) in 1746. He enrolled in the University of Copenhagen the same year, and studied natural sciences for a few years. From 1752 to 1757, he travelled with Bjarni Pálsson around Iceland, collecting information on its nature and society. This research led to publication of a two-volume treatise in 1772, which was later translated into a number of languages. Like other enlightened intellectuals of his time, Eggert Ólafsson attempted to dissipate what he saw as superstitious beliefs clouding people's understanding of Icelandic natural phenomena. When appointed vice-lawman in 1767, he returned to Iceland but died the following year, only 41 years old.

Although Eggert Ólafsson was a loyal subject of the Danish king and looked to him as the most likely source of economic and social progress in Iceland, he became an important inspiration for nationalists in the 19th century. It was primarily his fervent patriotism and emphasis on the preservation of the Icelandic language that earned him their respect. Thus Eggert Ólafsson's ideas bridged the gap between 18th-century Enlightenment (q.v.) and romanticism of the following century.

OLD COVENANT. In the years 1262–64, Icelanders accepted a treaty with the king of Norway in Alþingi (q.v.). They agreed to pay tribute to the king in return for protection and a guarantee of a minimum amount of trade between the two countries. The treaty, which later was known as the Old Covenant (Gamli sáttmáli), was passed after one of the most turbulent periods in Icelandic history—the Age of the Sturlungs (q.v.)—in order to establish internal peace and secure the provision of foreign goods. At the same time it introduced the state as an institution in Iceland, bringing the chaos of the late Commonwealth period (q.v.) to an end.

The Old Covenant formed the basis for the relationship between Iceland and the Norwegian monarchy, and later between the Danish king and his Icelandic subjects. In itself, the treaty did not change much in the government of Iceland, as it allowed Icelanders to retain most of their institutions intact. Gradually, however, royal power in Iceland increased, and the Old Covenant was effectively abrogated in 1662 with the introduction of absolutism (q.v.). (*See also* KÓPAVOGUR'S MEETING, THE)

OLD NORSE. *See* ICELANDIC LANGUAGE.

OLGEIRSSON, EINAR (1902–1993). One of the most eloquent spokesmen of the Communist Party of Iceland (CPI) and Socialist Unity Party (SUP) (qq.v.) from the late 1920s until the early 1960s was born in Akureyri (q.v.) on August 14, 1902. After graduating from the secondary school in Reykjavík in 1921, Einar Olgeirsson studied German and English at Friedrich-Wilhelm Universität in Berlin for three years. During his student years in Berlin, he became a convinced Marxist, and upon returning to Iceland in 1924 he joined the left wing of the Social Democratic Party (SDP, q.v.). From 1924 to 1928 he taught at the secondary school in Akureyri, but in 1928–31 he served as director of the state-owned Icelandic Herring Exportation Company, working primarily on trade with the Soviet Union. From 1931 to 1935 he was the director of the Icelandic-Russian Trading Company.

With the foundation of the CPI in 1930, Einar Olgeirsson became one of its most gifted agitators. He edited various communist and socialist newspapers from 1935 to 1946, and in 1937 he was elected to parliament as one of CPI's first three representatives. In 1939, shortly after the formation of the SUP, he became its chairman, a position he held until the party was formally dissolved in 1968. He sat in parliament for 30 years, for the CPI and SUP, and for the People's Alliance (PA, q.v.) from its foundation in 1956. With the formal dissolution of the SUP and the change of the PA into a political party in 1968, Einar Olgeirsson retired from political life. He left politics at the time when the Icelandic socialist movement began to distance itself from its Marxist legacy and severed its ties with the Soviet Union.

- P -

PÁLSSON, ÞORSTEINN (1947–). Minister of justice and fisheries and a former prime minister (q.v.), born in Selfoss, a town in southern Iceland, on October 29, 1947. He was educated in Reykjavík and graduated with a law degree from the University of Iceland (q.v.) in 1974. From 1970 to 1975 he worked as a reporter for *Morgunblaðið* (q.v.), and 1975–79 as an editor for the afternoon daily, *Vísir*. In 1979, he was appointed director of the Confederation of Icelandic Employers (q.v.), a position he held until he was

He served his first ministerial post as minister of finance from 1985 to 1987 in a coalition government of the IP and the Progressive Party (q.v.). Since then, he has served as minister of industries (1987), prime minister (1987–88), and minister of justice, ecclesiastical affairs, and fisheries since 1991.

Þorsteinn Pálsson became involved in politics at a very young age. During his student days, he was the president of the conservative student union, and in 1975–77 he sat on the steering committee of the youth organization of the IP. He was selected for the IP's central committee in 1981, and in 1983 he was elected chairman of the IP. In 1991, Davíð Oddsson (q.v.) challenged and defeated him in an election for the chairmanship, being the rising star in the party at the time. Þorsteinn Pálsson retains a powerful position in the party, however, as he has administered two of the most influential ministries in Iceland in two successive governments. (*See also* DAGBLAÐIÐ VÍSIR)

PAPAR. A name given to Irish hermits who allegedly strayed to Iceland in the seventh and eighth centuries. The Irish scholar Dicuil mentions in his geographical treatise *De mensura orbis terrae,* written in the early ninth century, that he had spoken with men that had visited the island of *Thule* around the year 795. Early Icelandic sources, such as the *Book of Settlement* and the *Book of Icelanders* (qq.v.), also mention the *papar.* According to these sources, the *papar* left Iceland at the beginning of the Settlement period (q.v.) because they did not want to live among pagans. The only traces of these first settlers of Iceland are to be found in place names, but no certain physical evidence of their existence has been discovered.

PARLIAMENT. See ALÞINGI.

PEOPLE'S ALLIANCE (PA). Alþýðubandalag, or the People's Alliance, was formed in 1956 as an alliance of the Socialist Unity Party (SUP, q.v.) and a group of former members of the Social Democratic Party (SDP, q.v.) under the leadership of Hannibal Valdimarsson (q.v.). Originally the PA was to be an election coalition only, but in 1968 it was transformed into a regular political party.

The basic tenets of the PA were socialism, mixed with a strong opposition to Iceland's participation in NATO (q.v.). In recent years, the socialism has moderated considerably, and the party has dropped all references to Marxism from its platforms. Opposition to NATO, the American base in Keflavík (q.v.), foreign investments in Iceland, and membership in European organizations like

EFTA (q.v.) and the EU (q.v.) has, however, made the PA one of the most nationalistic of today's political parties. The attempts of Ólafur Ragnar Grímsson (q.v.), who was chairman of the PA from 1987 to 1995, to change the party's position toward NATO after the conclusion of the cold war met strong resistance.

The PA inherited most of the traditional supporters of the SUP—workers and intellectuals. From the late 1950s to the early 1980s, it polled from 15 to 22 percent of the popular vote in parliamentary elections, putting it into third place in Alþingi (q.v.) throughout most of the period. Because of its strength in parliament, the party has served in a number of coalition governments, without causing any radical social change. Since the late 1980s, the PA has suffered internal frictions, which have caused a marked decline in its popular support—down to 13 to14 percent in the last three elections (1987, 1991, and 1995). This has, in part, been the effect of a challenge from the Women's Alliance (q.v.), but the decline has also been caused by general changes in the political atmosphere in Iceland since the end of the cold war. (*See also* NATIONAL PRESERVATION PARTY)

PÉTURSSON, HALLGRÍMUR (circa 1614–1674). The poet and clergyman Hallgrímur Pétursson was born around 1614, at Hólar (q.v.) in Hjaltadalur, the old episcopal seat in northern Iceland, to the bellringer of the cathedral. He attended the Latin school at Hólar, but did not complete his studies. After leaving school, he went abroad, most likely to Glückstadt in modern Germany and to Copenhagen. According to legend, it was in Copenhagen that Brynjólfur Sveinsson (q.v.), later bishop in Skálholt (q.v.), found him working as a blacksmith in 1632. Brynjólfur Sveinsson encouraged him to enter school in Copenhagen, but he left without a final degree in 1637. The same year, he returned to Iceland, and in 1644 he was appointed pastor in a poor parish in southwest Iceland. Seven years later, he transferred to a more prosperous parish in western Iceland. In his last years, he suffered from leprosy, and he died in 1674.

Hallgrímur Pétursson is commonly viewed as Iceland's greatest religious poet. To posteriority, he is primarily known for his *Passíusálmar* (*Hymns of the Passion*), which is a set of fifty hymns describing the passion and death of Christ.

PIETISM IN ICELAND. A Lutheran religious movement that spread to Iceland from Denmark in the early 18th century. Pietism never became a popular movement in Iceland, but it had a strong influence among the clergy because of its emphasis on education and moral reform. During the years 1741–45, the Danish minister Ludvig Harboe served as a special emissary from the Danish church authorities to Iceland, with the mission of examining the religious and moral state of the population. At his initiative, a number of reforms in the spirit of Pietism were instituted, affecting religious practices, the administration of the church, public morality, and instruction of the young. These efforts were certainly supported by the rising interest in education and social improvement that stemmed from the Enlightenment (q.v.). Some of these measures had a marked influence in Iceland, clearly reflected in the rising rates of literacy (q.v.) during the latter half of the 18th century. (*See also* EDUCATION; LUTHERANISM)

PÍNINGSDÓMUR. *See* LABOR BONDAGE.

PLAGUE IN ICELAND. A serious epidemic struck Iceland in 1402–04. Although it is not entirely certain, this outbreak was most likely some form of the bubonic or pneumonic plagues that ravaged Europe during the late Middle Ages. According to existing sources, the disease spread to Iceland when a sailor came from abroad in the fall of 1402, and in the following year it had affected almost the whole country. No definite account of the number of deaths exists, but scholars estimate that between 30 and 60 percent of the Icelandic population fell victim to this epidemic. The high mortality had serious effects on the economy, causing a decline in property values and rising labor costs. It also affected the structure of landed wealth in Iceland, as property was concentrated on fewer hands than ever before. This particular epidemic has commonly been called the Black Death (svarti dauði), drawing its name from Latin (mors nigra).

A second plague epidemic spread to Iceland in 1494–95. Not much is known about the mortality in this attack, which has been called the Second Plague, but it seems to have been almost as severe as the Black Death—except in the Western Fjords, which were spared this time around. These two plague epidemics, with the smallpox (q.v.) outbreak of 1707–09, are the most severe known in Icelandic history.

POPULATION. Due to its natural conditions, Iceland has always been a sparsely populated country. When the first complete census (q.v.) was taken in the year 1703, the inhabitants tallied just over 50,000. Only a scant knowledge exists of the demographic history of Iceland prior to that date, but in all likelihood its population had fluctuated somewhere between 30,000 and 70,000 from the time the country was fully settled in the 10th or 11th centuries. The 18th century was a difficult period in Iceland, when three major crises had serious effects on the demographic development of the country. As a result, the population of Iceland was at a lower level at the beginning of the 19th century than it had been a century before, just above the 47,000 mark. But, since the conclusion of a famine during the years 1783–85, caused by the Laki eruption (q.v.), the population of Iceland has grown almost incessantly. This has happened because mortality crises have totally disappeared from demographic history, infant mortality has fallen to one of the lowest levels in the world, and improvements in public healthcare have raised the life expectancy from about 38 years for women and 32 for men in 1850–60 to the present levels of 81 and 77.1 years respectively. This is clearly reflected in demographic development: according to the census of 1901, Iceland had 78,000 inhabitants, but in 1995 this number had grown to almost 268,000. Although population growth has abated somewhat in the last decades, due to declining fertility rates, it is still relatively high (with natural growth of over 1 percent p.a. in the 1980s), when compared to other industrialized countries and the Nordic countries in particular.

Population in Iceland, 1703–1995

1703	50,358	1880	72,445	1950	143,973
1785	40,623	1890	70,927	1960	175,680
1801	47,240	1901	78,470	1970	204,578
1840	57,094	1910	85,183	1980	229,187
1850	59,157	1920	94,690	1990	255,708
1860	66,987	1930	108,861	1995	267,809
1870	69,763	1940	121,474		

PRESIDENT. The highest office of the Icelandic state, founded in 1944 with the Constitution of the Republic of Iceland (q.v.). The principal prerogative of the president is to ratify laws passed in Alþingi (q.v.), but according to constitution, the legislative power is vested jointly in parliament and the president. The president does not have an absolute veto right, however, because an act he refuses to sign takes effect, subject to a popular referendum. So far, no president has used this prerogative. Other constitutional duties of the president are to convene and dissolve parliament, give prospective prime ministers (q.v.) the mandate to form governments, appoint many of the highest public officials in Iceland, and give pardons to convicted felons.

The formal power of the president is therefore extensive, but in practice he acts almost exclusively upon the decisions of the government and Alþingi. Thus, the president has been perceived as more of a symbolic figurehead than a political actor. His role is to represent the country on foreign soil and to stand above the bickering of domestic politics, although individual presidents can certainly pressure politicians through informal channels. In essence, the primary function of the office is to guarantee the democratic process in Iceland during times of crises; at the same time it is to serve as a unifying symbol for the nation.

The president is chosen in direct elections to one four-year term at a time. Any Icelandic citizen, 35 or older, who meets all the general qualifications for voting in parliamentary elections, can stand as a candidate. The constitution sets no limits on how many terms individual presidents can serve, and in cases where a sitting president runs unchallenged, no election is held. It is uncommon for political parties to play an active role in presidential elections, because there is a strong sentiment among the electorate that presidents should stand above party politics. Thus, presidential elections tend to center on personalities rather than issues, often making them fierce and emotionally charged.

So far, Iceland has had five presidents. Alþingi elected Sveinn Björnsson (q.v.) as the first president in 1944. His successor was Ásgeir Ásgeirsson (q.v.), a successful and popular politician, who defeated a candidate supported by two of the largest political parties. Ásgeir Ásgeirsson was first elected in 1952 and sat for four terms. In 1968, the director of the Icelandic National Museum, Kristján Eldjárn (q.v.), was elected president, and he was reelected without opposition in 1972 and 1976. Vigdís Finnbogadóttir (q.v.) was elected the fourth president in 1980. In 1988, she was the first president to face an opposition candidate, but she defeated her opponent by gaining almost 95 percent of the votes cast. Vigdís Finnbogadóttir ran unopposed for her fourth term in 1992, resigning in 1996. Ólafur Ragnar Grímsson (q.v.) was elected the fifth president of the Republic of Iceland in June, 1996. His election was a certain reversal of earlier trends, as he was a career politician before running for the presidency. It is unlikely, however, that this will lead to a change in the role of the president, as there seems to be no desire to make the office more political in the future than it has been in the past.

PRIME MINISTER. In 1917, with the enlargement of the cabinet (q.v.) from one to three ministers, the office of prime minister was established in Iceland. The prime minister forms governments, usually

MINISTERS OF ICELAND (1904–1917) AND PRIME MINISTERS
OF ICELAND (1917–1996)

MINISTERS OF ICELAND:

H. HAFSTEIN (HRP)	Feb. 1, 1904–March 31, 1909
B. JÓNSSON (IP)	March 31, 1909–March 14, 1911
K. JÓNSSON (Independent)	March 14, 1911–July 24, 1912
H. HAFSTEIN (Union Party)	July 25, 1912–July 21, 1914
S. EGGERZ (IP)	July 21, 1914–May 4, 1915
E. ARNÓRSSON (IP)	May 4, 1915–Jan. 4, 1917

PRIME MINISTERS OF ICELAND:

J. MAGNÚSSON (HRP)	Jan. 4, 1917–March 7, 1922
S. EGGERZ (IP)	March 7, 1922–March 22, 1924
J. MAGNÚSSON (CP)	March 22, 1924–July 8, 1926
J. ÞORLÁKSSON (CP)	July 8, 1926–Aug. 28, 1927
T. ÞÓRHALLSSON (PP)	Aug. 28, 1927–June 3, 1932
Á. ÁSGEIRSSON (PP)	June 3, 1932–July 28, 1934
H. JÓNASSON (PP)	July 29, 1934–May 16, 1942
Ó. THORS (IP)	May 16, 1942–Dec. 16, 1942
B. ÞÓRÐARSON (Independent)	Dec. 16, 1942–Oct. 21, 1944
Ó. THORS (IP)	Oct. 21, 1944–Feb. 4, 1947
S. J. STEFÁNSSON (SDP)	Feb. 4, 1947–Dec. 6, 1949
Ó. THORS (IP)	Dec. 6, 1949–March 14, 1950
S. STEINÞÓRSSON (PP)	March 14, 1950–Sept. 11, 1953
Ó. THORS (IP)	Sept. 11, 1953–July 24, 1956
H. JÓNASSON (PP)	July 24, 1956–Dec. 23, 1958
E. JÓNSSON (SDP)	Dec. 23, 1958–Nov. 20, 1959
Ó. THORS (IP)	Nov. 20, 1959–Nov. 14, 1963
B. BENEDIKTSSON (IP)	Nov. 14, 1963–July 10, 1970
J. HAFSTEIN (IP)	July 10, 1970–July 14, 1971
Ó. JÓHANNESSON (PP)	July 14, 1971–Aug. 28, 1974
G. HALLGRÍMSSON (IP)	Aug. 28, 1974–Sept. 1, 1978
Ó. JÓHANNESSON (PP)	Sept. 1, 1978–Oct. 15, 1979
B. GRÖNDAL (SDP)	Oct. 15, 1979–Feb. 8, 1980
G. THORODDSEN (IP–Idependent)	Feb. 8, 1980–May 26, 1983
S. HERMANNSSON (PP)	May 26, 1983–July 8, 1987
Þ. PÁLSSON (IP)	July 8, 1987–Sept. 28, 1988
S. HERMANNSSON (PP)	Sept. 28, 1988–April 23, 1991
D. ODDSSON (IP)	April 23, 1991–

through negotiations between the various political parties, and serves as their head. He receives his mandate from the president (q.v.) of the republic. Although the office of president is formally the highest office of the Republic of Iceland, the prime minister is *de facto* leader of the state. Since its establishment in 1917 and until—and including—the formation of Davíð Oddsson's second cabinet on April 23, 1995, 20 persons have held the office of prime minister, presiding over 31 different cabinets. (*See also* MINISTRIES)

PROGRESSIVE PARTY (PP). Eight representatives in Alþingi (q.v.) formed the PP, Framsóknarflokkur, in December 1916. In the beginning, the party was primarily a farmers' party, with roots in the cooperative movement, the Farmers' Associations, and the Youth Associations (qq.v.). The party platform has always had a populist orientation, and the PP places itself at the center of Icelandic politics.

The PP has traditionally been the second-largest political party in Iceland, and it has served as a counterbalance to the Independence Party (IP, q.v.). Its support has usually ranged from around 17–25 percent of the popular vote in parliamentary elections and, because of its strategic location in the political spectrum, it has often served as the leading party in coalition governments.

The PP has showed remarkable resilience in times of rapid social change. It has retained a strong presence in parliament since World War II (q.v.), in spite of increasing urbanization (q.v.) in recent decades. As the population of the rural areas has decreased rapidly in this period, the basis for its strongest support has eroded. Therefore, the party has had to broaden its appeal and, to a large extent, it has been successful in doing so. Under the leadership of Ólafur Jóhannesson and Steingrímur Hermannsson (qq.v.), the party held its ground, in part because it participated almost continuously in governments from 1971 to 1991. There it cooperated sometimes with the IP on the right, and sometimes with the Social Democratic Party and the People's Alliance (qq.v.) on the left. The present chairman of the PP is Halldór Ásgrímsson (q.v.). (*See also* JÓNSSON, JÓNAS)

PROHIBITION. *See* TEMPERANCE MOVEMENT.

PUBLIC SECTOR. Iceland has traditionally had a relatively small public sector and low taxes compared to other European countries. General government spending, as a percentage of Gross Domestic Product (GDP), has, nevertheless, been slowly, if irregularly, rising in the last decades. This ratio went from around 25 percent in the immediate postwar period to just under 40 percent in 1990, with the sharpest rise occurring during the 1980s. The share of government services in total employment is closer to the European norm, and in 1990 it was about 18 percent of the total work force. The relative weight of local government (q.v.) has, on the other hand, been declining, indicating a tendency toward concentration of financial responsibility in the hands of the central government. The transfer of the elementary school system from the state to the local communes in 1996 is the most significant attempt so far to reverse this development.

These indicators do not take fully into account, however, the extensive influence of the public sector in the economy. A very large portion of the annual budget was, from the turn of the 20th century until recently, devoted to a wide range of economic services, giving the government an important tool in influencing the direction of the economy. Moreover, the budget is only a part of the official apparatus of fiscal management. Government authorities were able to influence interest rates through the Central Bank, which had wide regulatory powers until the mid-1980s. The government guides borrowing in the economy through its annual credit budget that sets out targets for overall credit creation and foreign borrowing. Historically, the government has played a very prominent role in allocation of credit through its ownership of the largest part of the financial system, including commercial banks and dozens of investment credit funds. In addition, the state owns a large number of commercial enterprises in part or entirely, such as the State Monopoly of Tobacco and Alcohol, the Postal Service, the Telephone and Telegraph Services, the National Radio and Television, the State Electrical Power Works, the National Power Company (q.v.), a cement factory, a fertilizer plant, and over 300 farms. In recent years, there has been a desire among some of the political parties, the Independence Party (q.v.) in particular, to privatize public companies, and to sell the state's share in private companies. According to the belief that the state should not compete with private enterprise, the public sector is to withdraw from active participation in the market. G. J. (*See also* CENTRAL BANKING)

- R -

RASK, RASMUS CHRISTIAN (1787–1832). This Danish linguist was born on November 22, 1787, close to the town of Odense in

Denmark. As a young man, R. C. Rask learned the Icelandic language (q.v.) on his own, using published editions of Snorri Sturluson's (q.v.) *Heimskringla* as a guide. After graduating from secondary school in 1807, Rask moved to Copenhagen, where he studied linguistics without completing any final degree. He published his first scholarly work on the old Icelandic language in 1811, and two years later he had the opportunity to visit Iceland and stayed there for two years. In Iceland, he traveled extensively, both to visit historical places and to practice his Icelandic, which he mastered perfectly in these years. During this long sojourn, he became convinced that the Icelandic language was disappearing rapidly, maintaining that it would almost certainly become extinct in the following century if nothing was done for its protection. Thus, in 1815–16 he founded the Icelandic Literary Society (q.v.), to contribute to the preservation of the Icelandic language. In 1816, after returning to Copenhagen, Rask went on a long journey that took him through Russia and to India. This prevented him from working on Icelandic matters for over six years, and he was never to regain his former prestige among Icelanders—a fact that was demonstrated in 1831, the year before he died, when Icelandic students in Copenhagen ousted him from the leadership of the Copenhagen section of the Icelandic Literary Society.

RECONSTRUCTION GOVERNMENT. The most stable coalition government in Icelandic history, lasting (with a few changes of ministers) for three full terms between 1959 and 1971. The government consisted of four ministers from the Independence Party (IP, q.v.) and three from the Social Democratic Party (SDP, q.v.). Ólafur Thors (q.v.) formed the government after elections in the fall of 1959. In its platform, it vowed to strengthen and restructure the economic base of the country. In the early spring of 1960 it commenced its plan of "Reconstruction" (*viðreisn,* hence the name Viðreisnarstjórn), proposing some radical changes in economic policies. The currency was devalued by 30 percent and multiple exchange rates were abolished. At the same time the government liberalized foreign trade, introduced a 3 percent general sales tax, and made some major changes in the welfare system.

The first years of the Reconstruction Government were a period of economic growth, due in part to favorable conditions. The dramatic increase in the herring catches during the late 1950s and the early 1960s (from 50,000 tons in 1955 to 770,000 tons in 1966) was, for example, a major boost to export revenues. This period of prosperity came to an end in 1967–68 when the so-called Norwegian-Icelandic herring more or less disappeared from the

Icelandic fishing banks, leading to massive unemployment and a drastic fall in the value of exports. The economy recovered fairly quickly, however, as increased catches of other species and rising prices on the export markets made up for the loss. But the government did not reap the benefits of this recovery, loosing its majority in the parliamentary elections of 1971 to the parties at the center and to the left.

The Reconstruction Government never had the support of a large majority of representatives in parliament, but it had a great impact on social life in Iceland all the same. Under its leadership the country opened to foreign investments, with the aluminum factory in Straumsvík the most notable case. Finally, Iceland joined the European Free Trade Association (EFTA, q.v.) in 1970, during the last term of the Reconstruction Government, linking the country more closely with the emerging European economic system. (*See also* CURRENCY; INDUSTRIES, ENERGY-INTENSIVE)

REFORMATION, THE. Until the religious schism between Catholics and Lutherans began in Denmark in the early 16th century, the Catholic faith confronted no serious religious opposition in Iceland. The victory of Lutheran King Christian III in a competition for the Danish crown during the late 1530s forced the Icelandic church, however, to reconsider its position. In 1539, the first Lutheran bishop, Gissur Einarsson, took over the Skálholt (q.v.) diocese, while the Catholic bishop Jón Arason (q.v.) held on to his office at Hólar (q.v.). In the next decade, representatives of the Danish king suppressed the Catholic faction in Iceland, overcoming staunch opposition from Jón Arason and his men. On November 7, 1550, the king's representatives executed Jón Arason at Skálholt, and since then Lutheranism (q.v.) has been the dominant religious creed in Iceland.

The Reformation period was a time of intense religious activity in Iceland. An Icelandic translation of the New Testament was published in Denmark in 1540, and a translation of the Bible in its entirety was published by Guðbrandur Þorláksson (q.v.), bishop of Hólar, in 1594. The emphasis on the use of the vernacular in the Lutheran church, and the fact that Danish did not become the language of the church in Iceland, was certainly instrumental in preserving and developing the Icelandic language in the ensuing centuries. (*See also* CATHOLICISM; CONVERSION TO CHRISTIANITY)

REGIONAL POLICY. Generally, this term (*byggðastefna*) refers to policies aimed at alleviating regional inequalities and preserving habitation in rural areas and, recently, in small and remote fishing villages. In practice, this has meant adopting various regional support and development programs in order to strengthen the predominant economic activities outside the capital area. A coherent and well-defined long-term policy is, however, hard to discern in these programs.

Deliberate attempts to strengthen the rural economy vis-à-vis the urban economy have a long history in Iceland. During the 20th century, a regional policy emerged as a response to urbanization (q.v.) and migration of people from country to town. Perceived as a grave and a growing social problem, the depopulation of the countryside was countered with public financial support, beginning in the interwar period. Financial aid for farming was increased, and farmers' access to credit facilitated in order to modernize farming, expand cultivation, and aid new settlements. Rural housing was subsidized, and schools and social services improved. The regulation of milk and meat production in the mid-1930s, which included price-fixing and abolition of competition among producers, benefitted the small producer and sheltered the more remote rural areas against districts that were closer to the main markets.

The acceleration of migration from country to town during and after World War II (q.v.), and more pronounced regional imbalances in economic development, have prompted various governments to give regional policy a high priority in public spending. In order to give a more effective counterweight to the urban area around Reykjavík, towns outside the southwest corner of Iceland were included in the regional programs. From 1944 to 1947, the big investment programs of the so-called Modernization Government (q.v.) clearly reflected these considerations, especially regarding the renewal of the fishing fleet. In the early 1950s, regional planning started in conjunction with the Development Bank of Iceland (Framkvæmdabanki Íslands), which was established in 1953. Regional support continued in the 1960s through the annual government budget and funds designed for the purpose of correcting regional imbalances. In spite of these efforts, the primary economic sectors, farming and fisheries (qq.v.), have been unable to increase their employment requirements significantly, and thus the regional policy has been largely unsuccessful. The Left-Wing Government (q.v.) of 1971–74 increased regional assistance greatly, founding of State Development Institute (Framkvæmdastofnun ríkisins), designing and implementing regional plans, and creating the Regional Fund (Byggðasjóður) to finance them. The authorities did not carry out the various regional plans in any consistent manner, however, and they were only loosely integrated into the general public economic policy. Regional assistance was scaled down considerably during the 1980s, partly by the replacement in 1985 of the State Development Institute and the Regional Fund with the Institute of Regional Development (Byggðastofnun), which has maintained a much lower profile than its predecessors. G. J.

REPUBLIC OF ICELAND, FOUNDATION OF. The Republic of Iceland was founded at Þingvellir (q.v.) on June 17, 1944, when Icelanders severed all formal ties with the Danish king. This event must be seen as a logical conclusion of the long struggle for independence that began with growing nationalist sentiments during the first half of the 19th century, and it was made possible by economic transformations in the early 20th.

The foundation of the republic was based on the Act of Union (q.v.) of 1918, which gave both partners—the Danish and Icelandic parliaments respectively—the right to demand a renegotiation of the Act at the end of the year 1940. If they could not come to terms in a period of three years, either party was allowed to repeal the Act. Because of World War II (q.v.), it was impossible to follow this negotiation process to the letter, but Alþingi (q.v.) decided to repeal the Act unilaterally anyway. A motion to abrogate the Act of Union was unanimously approved in parliament in February of 1944, and a constitution for the Republic of Iceland was accepted in March of the same year. The issue was put to a referendum in May 1944, as the Act of Union required, and over 98 percent of the people who had the right to vote cast their ballot, out of which 97 percent supported the actions of Alþingi.

The method of repealing the Act of Union caused considerable bitterness in Denmark, because many felt that the Icelandic parliament should have waited until the end of the war rather than leaving the union during the German occupation of Denmark. Many Icelandic intellectuals were of the same opinion, advocating restraint in the matter, but the final outcome would certainly have been the same. (*See also* BJÖRNSSON, SVEINN; CONSTITUTION OF THE REPUBLIC OF ICELAND; PRESIDENT; RÍKISSTJÓRI)

REYKJAVÍK. The capital of Iceland, located on Iceland's southwest coast. According to the *Book of Settlements* (q.v.), Ingólfur Arnarson (q.v.), Iceland's first settler, made Reykjavík his home in the late ninth century. Through the centuries, Reykjavík was only a large farm, surrounded with small cottages on plots parceled out from its original farmland. From the 13th or 14th centuries, Reykjavík was the seat of a small parish church, but people living in the area supported themselves with a mixture of fishing on small open boats and animal husbandry (q.v.). It was only in the late 18th century that a small village formed in Reykjavík, especially after the Danish king assisted in the founding of small textile workshops in the emerging village and gave it special status as a chartered market town in 1786.

At the beginning of the 19th century, Reykjavík had only 300 inhabitants, but in the next few decades the Danish government turned this small fishing village into the center of its administration in Iceland. The 19th century was also a period of economic growth in Reykjavík, especially in commerce and fishing. In this period, it became the first real town in the country, serving as a nucleus for expanding government bureaucracy and emerging capitalist economy.

Reykjavík's development in the 20th century clearly reflects the economic, social, and political changes that have transformed the country in the last one hundred years. As other modern European societies, Iceland has developed an extensive system of private and public services, including schools, financial institutions, communication networks, and hospitals. Reykjavík serves as the hub of most of this activity, and it is also an important fishing and industrial town. Consequently, the population of the capital has grown remarkably in this century, or from 7,000 inhabitants in 1901 to over 105,000 in 1996. Moreover, the second and third largest towns in Iceland, Kópavogur and Hafnarfjörður, are in close vicinity of Reykjavík; today around 60 percent of the Icelandic population lives in the capital area. (*See also* INNRÉTTINGAR; MAGNÚSSON, SKÚLI)

REYKJAVÍK DISTRICT HEATING (RDH). The RDH (Hitaveita Reykjavíkur) is the pioneering power company in Reykjavík (q.v.), providing around 30,000 households in the Reykjavík area with geothermal water to heat their houses. Planning for the heating utility started in 1926, and the first drilling for hot water took place two years later. In the early 1930s, the first houses received geothermal water from the company, and it gradually increased its operation. By 1961, the RDH served about half of Reykjavík's residents, but since 1972 it has reached nearly the whole population of the capital.

The RDH has proven that geothermal water is an inexpensive and clean source of energy, and its example has been copied all over the country. Now, between 80 and 90 percent of Icelandic houses are heated in this way, reducing considerably the importation of fossil fuels.

RÍKISSTJÓRI. When Germany occupied Denmark in 1940, most formal relations between Copenhagen and Reykjavík were suspended. This created a constitutional dilemma in Iceland, because the Danish king was also the king of Iceland. For the first year, Alþingi (q.v.) handed over the royal power to the Icelandic government, but in May 1941, it passed an act creating the office of *ríkisstjóri*, or governor of Iceland, to substitute for the king during the war. On June 17, 1941, Sveinn Björnsson (q.v.) was elected the first, and only, person to hold this office. Exactly three years later, Alþingi selected him as the first president (q.v.) of the Republic of Iceland. (*See also* REPUBLIC OF ICELAND, FOUNDATION OF; WORLD WAR II [EFFECTS ON ICELAND])

ROYAL COMMISSIONS OF 1770 AND 1785. During the late 18th century, there was growing concern, both in Iceland and Denmark, about the economic well-being of Icelanders. This period was the apogee of enlightened absolutism in the Danish state, which led, for example, to various state-induced reforms in Danish agriculture. In the same spirit, during the 1770s and 80s, Iceland experienced the first organized attempts to formulate a coherent policy for the improvement of the economy. These efforts began with the formation of a Royal Commission in 1770, consisting of two royal officials and one merchant. The committee traveled around the country in the summer of 1770, collecting information on the economy and social practices, on the basis of which it produced detailed proposals on Icelandic economic affairs. During the next years, this led to the publication of various royal edicts, all of which had the intention of stimulating the faltering economy.

Most of these efforts came to naught, however. This was, in part, because of the great distress in the following decade caused by the Laki eruption (q.v.) in 1783–84, but also because these paternalistic measures proved to be difficult to execute. Therefore, the royal administration formed a new commission in 1785 to deal with the economic crisis in Iceland. This commission, which consisted of royal officials and directors of the royal trading company, suggested that the monopoly trade (q.v.) be abolished, coming partly in effect with a royal act in 1787. Although the second Royal Commission did not directly propose any radical changes in the administration of Iceland, increased centralization of Icelandic ecclesiastical and juridical affairs around the turn of the 19th century can be traced to its deliberations.

The two Royal Commissions had few great or lasting effects on the development of Icelandic society, but they were a clear sign of changing opinions of this distant province among the Danish and Icelandic elites. Thus, the idea that Icelandic society was destined to poverty and stagnation retreated in the late 18th century, paving the way for the belief in progress that fuelled the nationalist struggle in the 19th. (*See also* ENLIGHTENMENT, THE; INN-RÉTTINGARNAR)

- S -

SAGAS. The Icelandic sagas form a diverse group of literary works written in the period from the 12th to the 14th century. *Heilagramanna sögur* (*Stories of Saints' Lives*) and *Postulasögur* (*Apostles' Sagas*) are the oldest—the earliest of them are dated to around the mid-12th century. Most of the *Konungasögur* (*Kings' Sagas*) are from the period 1190–1230, reaching perfection with Snorri Sturluson's (q.v.) *Heimskringla* (*Orb of the World*). *Riddarasögur* (*Sagas of Knights*) are Icelandic adaptations of romances, from a tradition that began in the early 13th century with a Norse translation of the story of Tristran. Under the heading *Fornaldarsögur* (*Sagas of Ancient Times*, often called legendary sagas or mythic-heroic sagas in English), scholars group a number of sagas based on heroic legends and adventures. Most of these sagas were written in the 14th century. It is, however, with the so-called *Íslendingasögur* (*Sagas of Icelanders*), or the Icelandic family sagas, that the saga tradition reached its artistic height. There are between 35 and 40 family sagas preserved; the most notable—such as *Njáls Saga* (q.v.)—rank among the finest literary works of mediaeval Europe. All the family sagas are anonymous (although there are strong indications that Snorri Sturluson wrote *Egils Saga*), and none of them is preserved in an original manuscript. Therefore, the dating of the sagas is unclear, but the 13th century, one of the most violent periods in Icelandic history, seems to have been the time of the most creative production. The saga tradition continued into the 14th century, when the stories became more fantastic than the classical sagas of the 13th century had been, but saga writing seems not to extend beyond this point.

The scene of the family sagas is, as a rule, Icelandic society in the period stretching from the time of settlement to the mid-11th century—this is sometimes called the "Saga Age" (Söguöld). The stories describe feuds between individuals or family clans, and the preservation of honor is usually the center of the plot. They depict a society with no central government and relatively limited concentration of power. This was radically different from the time when the sagas were written, because the 13th century was a period of a constant struggle between a few clans and chieftains that dominated the rest of society.

For a long time, scholars have debated the historical value of the family sagas. It is clear that although the sagas may be based on oral legends, describing events that took place centuries before they were written, the most complex of them are, in essence, literary works. The sagas should not, therefore, be taken as accurate accounts of the history or ethics of the time they describe, and to what degree they reflect the time when they were written is also a matter of debate. The sagas do, however, give a fascinating perspective of a pre-state society, and will continue to be an invaluable source for the study of Old Norse social norms and processes. (*See also* AGE OF THE STURLUNGS; BOOK OF ICELANDERS; BOOK OF SETTLEMENTS; LITERATURE; SETTLEMENT PERIOD; STURLUNGA SAGA)

SETTLEMENT PERIOD. Iceland was first settled in a period of approximately sixty years from late ninth century to the early 10th century. The settlement started as Norwegians, some of them coming via Ireland, the Shetland Islands, the Orkney Islands, and the Hebrides, sought new land in the west. The exact date of the beginning of this population movement is unknown, but it was probably around the year 870 (the date 874 is used for official purposes). The foundation of Alþingi (q.v.) in 930 is traditionally seen as the end of the Settlement period, although immigration to Iceland continued on a smaller scale well beyond that year. The total number of settlers is unknown, but according to one estimate they were between 10 and 20 thousand.

The settlement of Iceland has to be seen as an integral part of Viking expansion from Scandinavia to Russia, the British Isles, France, the Mediterranean, Iceland, and Greenland (q.v.)—reaching temporarily as far west as the coast of North America. Limited economic resources in their countries of origins and a highly developed navigation technique were the driving forces behind this migration. According to the *Book of Settlements* (q.v.), the main reason for the immigration to Iceland was the establishment of a unified monarchy in Norway under King Harald Fairhair. Whatever the reason, the settlers found the new country attractive. The island was virginal at the time, as it had never been populated before, except, perhaps, by a few stray hermits, called *papar* (q.v.), from Ireland. For this reason, Icelandic nature was more bountiful in the Settlement period than it was in later centuries, when human exploitation had eradicated the shrubs that had covered the lowlands, leading to an extensive soil erosion.

The settlement of Iceland seems to have taken place without serious conflicts. As there was no indigenous population to suppress, the land was free to the newcomers. In order to prevent fighting, the immigrants developed elaborate rules for how to take possession of land, and in the early 10th century, the settlers adopted Norwegian law codes to regulate human interaction in the country. Thus began the so-called Commonwealth period (q.v.). (*See also* BOOK OF ICELANDERS)

SIGURÐARDÓTTIR, JÓHANNA (1942–). One of the most prominent leaders of Icelandic politics in the early 1990s. She was born on October 4, 1942, in Reykjavík as the daughter of a representative in Alþingi (q.v.) for the Social Democratic Party (SDP, q.v.). Jóhanna Sigurðardóttir holds a degree from the Commercial College in Reykjavík and worked as a stewardess from 1962 to 1971 and as a clerk from 1971 to 1978. From 1966 to 1969, she was chairwoman for the stewardess union, and from 1976 to 1983, she sat on the directing committee of the Union of Official Workers of Reykjavík and of the SDP from 1978 to 1994. She was elected deputy-chairman of the SDP in 1984, but resigned that post after a dispute with the chairman, Jón Baldvin Hannibalsson (q.v.), in 1993. In 1978, she was elected to parliament for the SDP in Reykjavík, and, from 1987 to 1994, she served as minister of social affairs in three different coalition governments.

Jóhanna Sigurðardóttir was a leading spokeswoman for the SDP's left wing during the late 1980s and early 90s, and she fought vigorously for her policies inside and outside governments. Thus, during her period in office as minister of social affairs, she forced through a reorganization of the state-guaranteed mortgage loans for residential housing, as well as of public housing funds. She earned respect among voters for her firmness, although her uncompromising political style created difficulties for the coalition governments in which she participated.

In 1994, Jóhanna Sigurðardóttir resigned from the SDP and formed a new political organization, Þjóðvaki (National Awakening, q.v.) the following year. This move evoked early strong support among voters, but the new political movement failed to sustain the early enthusiasm and seems to be headed for elimination.

SIGURÐSSON, JÓN (1811–1879). The undisputed leader of the Icelandic nationalist movement (q.v.) of the 19th century. Born on June 17, 1811, to a Lutheran minister in northwestern Iceland, Jón Sigurðsson studied at home and later completed a university entrance exam in 1829. In 1833, he sailed to Copenhagen to study at the University of Copenhagen. There, he emerged as a leading member of the Icelandic student community, which served at the time as an important intellectual link between the external world and Iceland. In 1841, he published the first issue of his *Ný félagsrit* (q.v.), a periodical that was to become a major organ for the Icelandic nationalist cause. In 1845, during Alþingi's (q.v.) first session as an elected body, Jón Sigurðsson established himself as the most influential parliamentary politician in Iceland, a role that he was to play until the early 1870s.

Jón Sigurðsson was, from the beginning, a spokesman for a liberal nationalist theory, striving for autonomy from Denmark (q.v.) as well as for the development of individual liberty in Iceland. His views were moderate and, in spite of his intransigent nationalism, the Danish government looked frequently to him to represent Icelanders in negotiations on Icelandic affairs; he was, for example, selected as one of five Icelandic members in the Danish constitutive assembly in 1848–49.

From the time Jón Sigurðsson moved to Copenhagen to study, he returned to Iceland only for brief official visits, making the Danish capital base for his political work and professional career. Besides his political activities, he was a distinguished scholar of Icelandic philology and a rigorous and productive editor of medieval and early modern texts and documents. Although he did not complete any university degree, he was respected in the academia, working for different institutions and learned societies in Copenhagen.

After his death on December 7, 1879, Jón Sigurðsson reached almost saintly status in Icelandic historical literature. He was revered for his role as a leader of the struggle for independence and as the founder of Icelandic nationalism (q.v.). It is clear, however, that Jón Sigurðsson's political liberalism was often ignored by the more conservative members of Alþingi, although they generally accepted his leadership role in negotiations with the Danish government. Today, Icelanders celebrate the legacy of Jón Sigurðsson every year on June 17, his birthday, which is the official national holiday of Iceland. (*See also* STATUS LAWS)

SKALDIC POETRY. One of the main categories of Old Norse poetry—the other being eddic poetry (q.v.). The name comes from the Old

Norse word *skáld,* meaning "poet." Skaldic poetry is differentiated from eddic poetry by the fact that its historical context and author are known. Moreover, skaldic poems are usually complex in structure and intricate in style, which is quite different from the simple meters that characterize eddic poetry. The tradition of composing skaldic poetry is older than the settlement of Iceland, and it is commonly viewed to have come to an end around 1400, although there is no agreement on this point. Most skaldic poems are preserved as parts of prose works dating from the 12th to the 14th century. (*See also* LITERATURE; SAGAS)

SKÁLHOLT. A farm, located in Árnes County, that became the first episcopal seat in Iceland. Gissur Ísleifsson, who became the second bishop of Iceland in 1082, donated Skálholt to the Catholic church on the condition that it would serve as a bishop's seat for as long as Iceland remained a Christian country. From this time until the late 18th century, Skálholt was the administrative center for a diocese that covered three-quarters of the country, and it was thus crucial for the development of religious life in Iceland. In the same period, one of the two Latin schools in Iceland was also located in Skálholt, making it also one of the most important places of learning in the country.

In 1785, following a serious earthquake that left most of its buildings in ruins, a royal decree abolished the bishop's seat in Skálholt, moving it to Reykjavík (q.v.). At the same time, the king sold the estate to the sitting bishop, Hannes Finnsson, who lived in Skálholt until his death in 1796. From that time, Skálholt gradually lost its prestige, but in recent years the church has attempted to revive its former glory. A new church was consecrated at Skálholt in 1963, and today it serves as the official residence of one of Iceland's two suffragan bishops. (*See also* CATHOLICISM; HÓLAR; LUTHERANISM; MENNTA-SKÓLINN Í REYKJAVÍK; REFORMATION, THE)

SMALLPOX. Because of Iceland's geographic isolation and sparse population, smallpox never became an endemic disease in the country. Rather, Icelanders suffered repeated, and often extremely serious, epidemic attacks, which often spread rapidly around the country. From the beginning of the 16th century to the end of the 18th, four to five such epidemics struck Iceland every century, killing primarily people born between the attacks. The epidemics varied in severity, but the worst case was the so-called "Big Pox" (*stóra bóla*) that killed around a quarter of the Icelandic population in 1707–09. From the early 19th century, the government required inoculation of all children, leading in the end to the total eradication of smallpox. Thus, the last time this dreaded guest visited Iceland (1839–40), it spread only over a limited area and deaths were minimal.

SNORRI STURLUSON. *See* STURLUSON, SNORRI.

SOCIAL DEMOCRATIC ALLIANCE (SDA). A splinter party from the Social Democratic Party (SDP, q.v.), formed in haste before the parliamentary elections of 1983 around the charismatic politician Vilmundur Gylfason (q.v.). The SDA platform supported an extensive welfare state, but its most radical ideas proposed transformation of the democratic process and a radical overhaul of the administrative structure. The SDA advocated direct elections of the prime minister (q.v.), widespread decentralization in the country, and total separation of the legislative and executive branches. The party received over 7 percent of the ballots cast in 1983. This was a remarkable accomplishment, considering the short time its leaders had to prepare for the electoral campaign. Later the same year, the early death of Vilmundur Gylfason led to a total demise of the SDA, and in 1987, it received only 0.2 percent of the votes cast. After that, the party dissolved, and most of its former leaders have since left politics.

SOCIAL DEMOCRATIC PARTY (SDP). The Alþýðuflokkur, or the Social Democratic Party, was founded in March 1916, making it the oldest existing political party in Iceland. It was formed as the political wing of the Icelandic Federation of Labor (IFL, q.v.), in order to further the interests of the working classes and advocate policies of democratic socialism. The SDP has rejected revolutionary socialism from the beginning and has often stood closer to the Independence Party (IP, q.v.) on the right than to the socialist parties on the left. In recent years, the SDP has been an ardent supporter of Iceland's participation in international bodies such as NATO (q.v.) and the European Free Trade Association (EFTA, q.v.). Jón Baldvin Hannibalsson (q.v.), the current chairman of the SDP, was also a vigorous advocate of the European Economic Area (EEA, q.v.) agreement between EFTA and the European Union (EU, q.v.), and the SDP is the only political party in Iceland openly to call for Icelandic application for membership in the EU. The traditional base for the SDP is the urban area in southwest Iceland and the fishing towns in the Western Fjords, but it has never appealed to voters in the rural areas.

In the 1916 and 1919 parliamentary elections, the SDP polled under 7 percent of the votes cast, but since the early 1920s, its support has usually been somewhere between 15 and 20 percent of the popular vote. In the early 1970s, the SDP went through a difficult period, winning only around 10 percent of the votes cast in the parliamentary elections of 1971 and 1974. In the late 1980s, the SDP seemed to have regained its former strength under the leadership of Jón Baldvin Hannibalsson (q.v.), receiving just over 15 percent of the votes cast in 1987 and 1991. The campaign for the 1995 elections was difficult for the SDP because of a split in its leadership, leading to Jóhanna Sigurðardóttir's (q.v.) resignation from the party in 1994 and the foundation of Þjóðvaki (National Awakening, q.v.) in 1995. As it turned out, the elections were a clear setback for the party, and its support fell to just over 11 percent of the votes cast. Recent polls seem to indicate, however, that the party is recovering from this last crisis. (*See also* ALÞÝÐU-BLAÐIÐ; COMMUNIST PARTY OF ICELAND; SOCIAL DEMOCRATIC ALLIANCE; SOCIALIST UNITY PARTY)

SOCIALIST UNITY PARTY (SUP). The Socialist Unity Party (Sameiningarflokkur alþýðu-sósíalistaflokkurinn) was formed in 1938 when the Communist Party of Iceland (CPI, q.v.) and a group of radical social democrats under the leadership of Héðinn Valdimarsson (q.v.) merged into one political party. The SUP espoused a Marxist ideology and sympathized obstinately with the Soviet Union, even defending the Soviet aggression in Finland during the Winter War of 1939–40. Its support was strongest among workers and intellectuals, and some of the most prominent writers and artists in Iceland were vocal adherents of the party and its ideology. In 1956, the SUP joined hands with other groups on the left to form the People's Alliance (PA, q.v.) and was formally dissolved in 1968 when the PA became an organized political party.

The impetus behind the formation of the SUP was both the growing radicalization of the working classes during the Great Depression (q.v.) and an instruction from Comintern, calling for the creation of a united front of communists and radical social democrats against fascism. Allegedly, this movement was to serve as a bulwark in the defense against fascism. The formation of the SUP continued, however, the split on the left created by the establishment of the CPI, and two parties of almost equal strength competed for popular support.

In its first parliamentary elections (1942), the SUP became the third largest party in Iceland, receiving 16.2 percent of the votes cast. It remained a strong force in parliament for the next 16 years, but, except for the years 1944–47, it was excluded from participation in governments because of its Marxist ideology. (*See also* MODERNIZATION GOVERNMENT)

SÖGUFÉLAG. *See* ICELANDIC HISTORICAL ASSOCIATION.

STATISTICAL BUREAU OF ICELAND (SBI). Since its foundation in 1914 the SBI (Hagstofa Íslands) has been the most important institution in the collection and publication of official statistics in Iceland. With the Act on the Central Government in 1969, the SBI was made a separate ministry, which means in theory that one cabinet member is responsible for the Bureau, carrying the title of the minister for the Statistical Bureau of Iceland. In practice, however, the Bureau is virtually an autonomous body that does not receive directives from the minister in question. The SBI is organized in three main sections: central administration, the statistical section, and the National Register of Persons. The statistical section is charged with the responsibility of collecting and publishing a wide range of economic and social statistics. Its main work focuses on demographic statistics and data on the labor market, prices, production and foreign trade, local government finances, health and social affairs, transport and tourism, education, and elections. It also maintains the register of enterprises. The National Register of Persons provides a uniform and centralized registration of the entire population of Iceland for administrative and statistical purposes. G. J.

STATUS LAWS. The Danish parliament passed the Status Laws (Stöðulög) in 1870, defining the status of Iceland in the Danish monarchy. The laws, which came into effect in 1871, stipulated that Iceland was an inseparable part of the Danish realm, although the country had specific prerogatives. The laws also ended a long dispute about the financial separation of Denmark and Iceland, designating considerable aid for the Icelandic budget. After enacting the Status Laws, the Danish government reorganized the administrative structure in Iceland, creating the office of *landshöfðingi* (q.v.)—governor of Iceland.

The Status Laws were immensely unpopular in Iceland, primarily because the Danish government never presented them in Alþingi (q.v.). Thus, claimed the Icelandic nationalists, the laws violated Iceland's national rights and lacked any legitimacy. Although the majority in Alþingi, under the leadership of Jón Sigurðsson (q.v.), refused to accept the laws, they formed the basis for relations between Denmark and Iceland until 1918, when Iceland became a sovereign state with the Act of Union (q.v.). *(See also* CONSTITUTIONS, 1874–1918; DRAFT, THE; GOVERNOR'S PERIOD; HOME RULE)

STEFÁNSSON, ÓLAFUR (1731–1812). The first Icelander to be appointed *stiftamtmaður* (q.v.), or governor of Iceland, was born on May 3, 1731, to a parish pastor in the northern part of the country. He graduated from the Latin school in Hólar (q.v.) in 1751, continuing his studies in Copenhagen. After completing a law degree in 1754, Ólafur Stefánsson returned to Iceland. He rose quickly to the highest ranks in the Icelandic administrative system, serving as vice-lawman from 1756 to 1764 and assisting his father-in-law, the district governor *(amtmaður,* q.v.) from 1764 to 1766. In 1766, the king appointed him district governor, which was the highest administrative post in Iceland at the time. With the reorganization of the Icelandic administrative system in 1770, when the authorities in Copenhagen divided the country into two districts and required the governor to live in Iceland, Ólafur Stefánsson became district governor in the northeastern district. Between 1783 and 1787, he held no official post, but he resumed his career as district governor in Iceland's west district in the latter year. Three years later, he was promoted to the office of *stiftamtmaður;* he held this position until he was removed temporarily from his post in 1803. He retired from official life in 1806.

Ólafur Stefánsson was both the wealthiest and the most powerful man in Iceland at the end of 18th century. His marriage in 1761 to the only child of the district governor of Iceland, one of the country's richest landowners, secured his career in the administrative system and brought him wealth that set him apart from his contemporaries. Moreover, through marriages of his children and other family connections, his relatives dominated the government of Iceland during his time. Ólafur Stefánsson's descendants, carrying the family name Stephensen, remained prominent in the Icelandic administration throughout the 19th century. *(See also* STEPHENSEN, MAGNÚS)

STEPHANSSON, STEPHAN G. (1853–1927). A poet and leading figure among the 19th-century emigrants from Iceland to America. He was born in Skagafjörður County to poor parents on October 3, 1853, emigrating to the United States (q.v.) with his parents in 1873. After living in Wisconsin for a few years, he established himself as a farmer in North Dakota in 1880. Nine years later he moved across the Canadian border to the province of Alberta, settling down in the region to the east of the Rocky Mountains. There he lived as a farmer for the remainder of his life. Stephan G. Stephansson was a self-educated man, but in North America he became a prolific poet. All his life he had to work hard to make ends meet, but he wrote poetry during the few spare moments he found. These poems are written in a realistic yet complex style, and they demonstrate a deep sympathy for working people and their conditions. Stephan G. Stephansson, or the "the poet of the Rocky Mountains" as he was often called in Iceland, was well known in Iceland during his lifetime and was considered one of the finest poets to write in the Icelandic language. (*See also* EMIGRATION)

STEPHENSEN, MAGNÚS (1762–1833). This leader of the Icelandic Enlightenment (q.v.) was born on December 27, 1762. He was the son of Ólafur Stefánsson (q.v.), one of the wealthiest and most powerful figures in late 18th-century Iceland. Magnús Stephensen enrolled in the University of Copenhagen in 1781 and graduated with a law degree in 1788. While still a young student, he was sent to Iceland to investigate the Laki eruption (q.v.) in 1783, and two years later he administrated the first sale of the lands owned by the Skálholt (q.v.) diocese. After earning his university degree, he became vice-lawman in Iceland's northwest district and lawman (q.v.) of the same district in 1789. The king appointed him the first president of the new Icelandic High Court (q.v.) in 1800, a position he held until his death in 1833.

Magnús Stephensen was one of the most influential persons in Iceland during his lifetime, although he never reached his father's status in the official hierarchy. For years he directed the only printing press in Iceland, a position that gave him a virtual monopoly over what was printed in the country. He used this situation to promote his own ideas, publishing his writings on issues ranging from legal theory to the nutritious value of seaweed. In his literary works, as well as in his office as a judge, Magnús Stephensen remained an ardent spokesman of enlightened rationalism, advocating a humane penal system, fewer strictures on foreign trade, and more effective methods in the administrative and juridical systems.

STEPHENSEN, MAGNÚS (1836–1917). The last landshöfðingi (q.v.), or governor of Iceland, was born on October 18, 1836, into one of the most prominent families of the country. In 1855, after completing a university entrance exam from the Latin school in Reykjavík, Magnús Stephensen sailed to Copenhagen to study law. Upon finishing his university studies in 1862, he was hired as clerk for the Bureau of Icelandic Affairs in Copenhagen, where he worked until 1870. That year, he was appointed Justice of the High Court (q.v.) in Reykjavík, where he served until he became governor in 1886. From 1883 to 1886, he managed the office of the district governor (*amtmaður,* q.v.) in the southwest district of Iceland, leading to his appointment as governor in 1886. For almost twenty years, Magnús Stephensen was the highest government official in Iceland. Thus, he occupied a central position during a crucial period in Icelandic political and economic history. Because of his conservative views, Magnús Stephensen was a controversial figure, but in spite of this he was generally highly respected by his countrymen. In 1904, with the introduction of home rule (q.v.), the governor's office was abolished. Therefore, Magnús Stephensen lost his post, and he was unable to find a niche in the new administrative system. He ended his distinguished career in public service as a representative in Alþingi (q.v.), where he sat from 1903 to 1907.

STIFTAMTMAÐUR. With the introduction of absolutism (q.v.) at the beginning of the 1660s, the Danish government restructured the administrative system in Iceland. In line with general practice in Denmark, Iceland was made one administrative district, *amt;* with one governor, *stiftamtmaður* (q.v.) and one district governor, *amtmaður* (q.v.). In theory, the *stiftamtmaður* was the highest official in the Icelandic administrative hierarchy, but in reality it was practically a ceremonial post until 1770, when the authorities required him to move from Copenhagen to Iceland. This happened as part of another reorganization of the Icelandic administration; now the country was divided into two districts—from 1787 into three—each administrated by a district governor. From that time, the *stiftamtmaður,* who also served as district governor in one of the districts, was the most important representative of the Danish government in Iceland. The office of *stiftamtmaður* was abolished in 1872 with the passing of the Status Laws (q.v.) and the creation of a new governor's office in Iceland, called *landshöfðingi* (q.v.).

Governors of Iceland, 1684–1873

Ulrich Christian Gyldenløve	1684–1719
Peter Raben	1719–27
Christian Gyldencrone	1728–30
Henrik Ochsen	1730–50

Otto von Rantzau	1750–68
Christian von Proeck	1768–69
Lauritz Andreas Thodal	1770–85
Hans K. D. V. von Levetzow	1785–89
Ólafur Stefánsson	1790–1806
Frederik Christopher Trampe	1806–10
Johan C. T. von Castenschiold	1813–19
E. K. L. Moltke	1819–23
Pedder F. Hoppe	1824–29
Lorenz A. Krieger	1829–36
Carl E. Bardenfleth	1837–41
Thorkil A. Hoppe	1841–47
Mathias H. Rosenørn	1847–49
Jørgen D. Trampe	1850–60
Þórður Jónassen (temporary appointment)	1860–65
Hilmar Finsen	1865–73

STÓRA BÓLA. *See* SMALLPOX.

STÓRIDÓMUR. A statute passed in Alþingi on June 30, 1564, and ratified by the king the following year. Stóridómur (the "Large" or "Long Judgment" in literal translation) redefined the penal code for moral offenses, especially in cases connected with adultery and sexual intercourse between persons related either through affinity or consanguinity. The ruling measured punishments on a fixed scale, ranging from small fines to capital punishment—decapitation for men, drowning for women. Icelandic courts enforced Stóridómur to the letter until the 18th century, but its last vestiges were eliminated from Icelandic penal codes in 1870.

STURLA ÞÓRÐARSON. *See* ÞÓRÐARSON, STURLA.

STURLUNGA SAGA. This large compilation of texts, written by various authors in the 12th and 13th centuries, is actually a historical chronicle, dealing with the period from the early 12th century to the end of the Commonwealth period (q.v.) in 1264. It belongs to a genre of sagas (q.v.) called *samtíðarsögur* (contemporary sagas); that is, a group of works written by authors many who had, for the most part, witnessed the events they described. The *Sturlunga Saga* is, therefore, one of the main sources on the history of the last decades of the Commonwealth period (q.v.), and scholars generally believe that it gives a relatively accurate account of that turbulent era.

The centerpiece of *Sturlunga Saga* is *Íslendinga Saga*, written by Sturla Þórðarson (q.v.), the nephew of the best-known Icelandic writer of the time, Snorri Sturluson (q.v.). This is a combination of family history and a general history of Iceland in a period stretching from the late 12th to the late 13th century. The account gives a remarkably balanced picture of the history of the period, considering that its author was deeply involved in the events he describes. Thus the *Sturlunga Saga* provides a unique perspective on the most violent period in Icelandic history, while it is also a testimony of the great historical interest in Iceland present at the time it was written. (*See also* AGE OF THE STURLUNGS)

STURLUSON, SNORRI (1178/9–1241). The best-known man of letters in medieval Iceland was born either in 1178 or 1179, to Sturla Þórðarson the elder in Hvammur, the man after whom the powerful Sturlung family was named. Through clever management of his financial affairs and a driving ambition, Snorri Sturluson was able to amass great wealth, becoming one of the most powerful persons in Iceland around 1220–30. Although he lived in one of the most violent periods of Icelandic history, Snorri Sturluson was not a warrior; he based his power on keen legal erudition and a shrewd sense of how to construct political alliances. In the end, however, Snorri Sturluson's enemies joined forces in their struggle against him and had him killed in September 1241. This was, in part, at the behest of the Norwegian King Hákon Hákonarson, who wanted to punish Snorri Sturluson for allying with King Hákon's rival for the Norwegian throne, Earl Skúli.

To posterity, Snorri Sturluson is better-known for his writings than for his political intrigues. He wrote some of the most superb literature of this culturally fertile period in Icelandic history and can truly be classified among the greatest literary figures of medieval Europe. Among his works are masterpieces like the *Prose-Edda*, which is a treatise on Old Norse skaldic poetry (q.v.), and *Heimskringla* (*Orb of the World*), or the history of the kings of Norway to 1177. Moreover, he has also often been credited with composing one of the best known family sagas, *Egils Saga*, but this cannot be proven conclusively. (*See also* AGE OF THE STURLUNGS; LITERATURE; SAGAS; *STURLUNGA SAGA*)

SUMMIT OF 1986. In the autumn of 1986, the leaders of the Soviet Union and the United States, Mikhail Gorbachev and Ronald Reagan, decided to hold a summit in Reykjavík (q.v.) to discuss terms of general disarmament. Gorbachev suggested Iceland as the place for this important meeting, because of its geographical location in the mid-Atlantic, right between the European continent and North America. The Icelandic government accepted the task of organizing the summit on extremely short notice, and for a few days Reykjavík (q.v.) became the center of media attention all over the globe. Although the two leaders signed no treaties at the meeting, which was held on October 11–12, 1986, the summit was a significant milestone in the waning of the cold war.

SUPREME COURT OF ICELAND. The Supreme Court of Iceland (Hæstiréttur Íslands) was founded in 1920, when the High Court in Reykjavík (qq.v.) took over the role of the Danish Supreme Court as the highest tribunal in Icelandic court cases. A two-tiered court system was established in Iceland, replacing the system that had been in use since the beginning of the 19th century. Earlier, cases could go from district courts to the High Court in Reykjavík and from there to the Supreme Court in Copenhagen. Today, appeals proceed directly from district courts to the Supreme Court in Reykjavík.

Initially, five judges sat on the Supreme Court, but at the present the bench has nine members. They are appointed for life by the president, upon the advice of the minister of justice. The judges select the president of the court from among themselves. Cases are heard by panels of either three or five judges. Almost all public and private cases can be appealed to the Supreme Court, although certain restrictions are imposed to limit the number of petty cases that can be presented to the court. In recent years, 200–300 cases have been appealed annually to the Supreme Court. (*See also* COUNTY)

SVARTI DAUÐI. *See* PLAGUE IN ICELAND.

SVEINSSON, BENEDIKT (1826–1899). A 19th-century politician and government official. Benedikt Sveinsson was born in southeast Iceland on January 20, 1826, to a country pastor. He completed a secondary school exam in 1852 and sailed to Copenhagen to continue his studies. In 1859, a year after earning a law degree from the University of Copenhagen, he was appointed a judge in the Icelandic High Court (q.v.). In 1870, he was dismissed from this post, but was appointed bailiff of Þingey County in 1874. Benedikt Sveinsson is best known for his political activities, but from 1881 until his death in 1899 he was the leader of a parliamentary faction seeking a revision of the Icelandic constitution (hence his policy was called revisionism—or *endurskoðun*). Benedikt Sveinsson was an engaging orator and a fierce opponent of Valtýr

Guðmundsson (q.v.) and his faction, because of their more conciliatory views toward the relationship with Denmark. Although Benedikt Sveinsson advocated a radical revision of Danish-Icelandic relations, his views on domestic affairs were for the most part conservative, if not reactionary. (*See also* CONSTITUTIONS, 1874–1918)

SVEINSSON, BRYNJÓLFUR (1605–1675). This bishop and theologian was born on September 14, 1605, to a Lutheran minister in Ísafjörður County in northwestern Iceland. After graduating from the Latin school at Skálholt (q.v.), he enrolled in the University of Copenhagen in 1624. Brynjólfur Sveinsson came back to Iceland in 1629 but returned to Copenhagen to resume his university studies in 1631. In 1632 he was appointed a deputy-principal of a prestigious secondary school in Roskilde, Denmark, and the following year he was awarded the title *magister* from the University of Copenhagen. In 1638, Brynjólfur Sveinsson was elected bishop of the diocese of Skálholt, a position he held from 1639 to 1674. Brynjólfur Sveinsson was highly respected as a bishop, both for his great erudition and his efficient administration. He showed much interest in literature, both as a poet and a collector of old Icelandic manuscripts.

SÝSLA. *See* COUNTY.

- T -

TEMPERANCE MOVEMENT. Improved living standards after 1820 and increased importation of foreign goods were accompanied by a rapid increase in the consumption of alcohol. Around the mid-19th century, the annual per capita consumption of alcoholic beverages amounted to an estimated three liters of pure alcohol. This situation prompted the formation of a number of societies promoting total abstinence, but it was in 1884 that they gained a permanent foothold with the foundation of the first Icelandic lodge, the International Order of Good Templars (IOGT) in Akureyri. Interest in temperance quickly spread in the following years, and a number of lodges were formed. In 1886 the Grand Lodge of Iceland was established in Reykjavík. By 1907 the number of Good Templars had risen to 6,700, or around 8 percent of the total population. The society soon wielded great influence on legislation and has received an annual state grant to promote temperance since 1893. The fight against alcohol consumption

sumption focused on high tariffs and strict licences for selling alcohol. After the turn of the 20th century the Icelandic chapter of the IOGT advocated total prohibition of the import and sale of alcohol, re-sulting in a referendum on the issue in 1908 in which 60 percent of the votes cast were in favor of prohibition. Total prohibition came into effect in 1915, but after pressure from the Spanish government, threatening to raise tariffs on salt fish, the Icelandic government was forced to allow importation of Spanish wines in 1922. The prohibition laws were abolished in 1933 after a majority (58 percent) voted against them in a referendum (the end of the prohibition came into effect in 1935). The new legislation on alcoholic drinks was very strict, however, in part as a result of the strong position of the temperance movement. The sale of beer was banned, and wine and spirits were sold at exorbitant prices in a few shops run by the State Alcohol Monopoly. Legislation has been liberalized somewhat in recent decades as the influence of the temperance movement has abated. Its greatest defeat in the postwar period came when the ban on production and sale of beer was lifted in 1989. G. J.

THORODDSEN, GUNNAR (1910–1983). A politician and legal scholar, born in Reykjavík on December 29, 1910. Gunnar Thoroddsen attended Menntaskólinn í Reykjavík (q.v.), where he finished a university entrance exam in 1929. He completed a law degree from the University of Iceland (q.v.) in 1934, continuing his studies in Denmark, Germany, and England in 1935–36. He practiced law in Reykjavík from 1936 to 1940, when he began teaching law at the University of Iceland. He was appointed professor of law at the University in 1942 and resigned his professorship in 1947 in order to devote his time to a political career.

Gunnar Thoroddsen entered politics at an early age. In 1934, he was elected to parliament for the Independence Party (IP [q.v.]) while only 24 years old, and he represented the IP intermittently until his death in 1983 (1934–37, 1942–65, and 1971–83). He sat on Reykjavík's city council from 1938 to 1962, serving as mayor of the capital from 1947 to 1959. He became a cabinet member for the first time in 1959 when he was appointed minister of finance in the so-called Reconstruction Government (q.v.). In 1965, Gunnar Thoroddsen interrupted his political career when he was appointed ambassador to Denmark. The reason for this semi-retirement was his desire to prepare for the upcoming presidential campaign and pursue his academic interests. In 1968, he defended a doctoral dissertation at the University of Iceland, but the same year he lost to Kristján Eldjárn (q.v.) in the presidential election by a wide margin. In 1970, Gunnar Thoroddsen returned to Iceland to become Justice of the Supreme Court (q.v.). He resumed his political career in the following year, when he was elected to parliament for the IP. From 1971 to 1974, Gunnar Thoroddsen served as professor of law at the University of Iceland, retiring from that post when he was appointed minister of industry and social affairs in 1974. In 1980, he led a small group of representatives who broke away from the IP to form a government with the Progressive Party (q.v.) and the People's Alliance (q.v.). He served as prime minister (q.v.) from 1980 to 1983.

Gunnar Thoroddsen's political career was both long and complex. He was vice-chairman of the IP from 1961 to 1965 and again 1974–81, and leader of its parliamentary group 1973–79, in addition to serving in numerous committees on behalf of the party. In spite of his long and distinguished service for the IP, Gunnar Thoroddsen's relationship with other members of the party leadership was strained throughout a large part of his career. In 1952 he broke the party ranks to support his father-in-law, Ásgeir Ásgeirsson (q.v.), in his bid for the presidency, a move some of his colleagues never forgave him for. His boldest defiance of party discipline came in 1980, when he formed a coalition government in open opposition to the official policy of the IP. In the spring of 1983, with the fall of his government, Gunnar Thoroddsen retired from politics, and he died in September the same year.

THORODDSEN, JÓN (1819–1868). This pioneer of modern Icelandic prose literature (q.v.) was born on October 5, 1819, in Barðaströnd County in western Iceland. He finished secondary school at Bessastaðir (q.v.) in 1840 and sailed to Copenhagen the following year to study law. In 1848, he interrupted his studies to join the Danish army in its fight against a German insurrection in the Duchies of Schleswig-Holstein. After returning to Iceland in 1850, Jón Thoroddsen was appointed bailiff in Barðaströnd County. He secured his career as a government official by completing a law degree in 1854 and served as bailiff, first in Barðaströnd County and later in Borgarfjörður County, until his death in 1868.

Jón Thoroddsen is best known for his writings, the novel *Piltur og stúlka* (*A Boy and a Girl*) in particular. He wrote this simple but charming love story, which is often called the first modern novel written in the Icelandic language, in Copenhagen during the winter of 1848–49 (published in Copenhagen in 1850). It emphasizes traditional Icelandic values, warning against the influence of Danish language and customs on Icelandic culture.

At the time of his death, Jón Thoroddsen was working on his second novel, *Maður og kona* (*A Man and a Woman*), but he died before its completion.

THORODDSEN, SKÚLI (1859–1916). A politician, state official, and journalist who became the most prominent leader of the radical independence movement in the first decade of the 20th century. Skúli Thoroddsen was born the son of Jón Thoroddsen (q.v.), a bailiff and a writer, on January 6, 1859. After completing a law degree from the University in Copenhagen in 1884, he became an attorney in Reykjavík, but late the same year he was appointed bailiff in Ísafjörður County. He resigned from this post in 1895, dedicating the rest of his life to politics. In 1886, Skúli Thoroddsen was involved in the foundation of *Þjóðviljinn*, a weekly and semi-monthly newspaper in Ísafjörður (q.v.), becoming its editor from 1887 (officially from 1892). He was elected to parliament in 1891, where he held a seat almost continuously until 1915. In 1908 he led the opposition to the so-called "Draft" (q.v.), which was a proposal for a new act regulating the union of Denmark and Iceland. After the defeat of this proposal, Skúli Thoroddsen became a prominent member of the first Independence Party (q.v.), which was formed in 1908. This was a loose federation of representatives in parliament, all of whom emphasized the fight for total independence from Denmark. In spite of his effective leadership in defeating the "Draft," which led to the resignation of his nemesis Hannes Hafstein (q.v.), Skúli Thoroddsen was unsuccessful in his bid for the post of minister of Iceland. After that, he never regained his former political stature, retiring from politics in 1915.

THORS, ÓLAFUR (1892–1964). Leader of the Independence Party (IP, q.v.) and one of the most influential politicians in Iceland during the first decades of the republic. Ólafur Thors was born in Borgarnes in Borgarfjörður County on January 19, 1892, the son of Thor Jensen (q.v.), a Danish-born merchant. After passing a university entrance exam in 1912, he studied law at the University of Copenhagen without completing the degree. From 1914 to 1939 he directed his father's trawler company, Kveldúlfur, but from the beginning of World War II (q.v.) he devoted all his time to politics. Ólafur Thors was first elected to parliament in 1925 for the Conservative Party (q.v.), and four years later he became one of the leaders of the new IP. In 1932, he served as minister of justice for a few weeks, and he was appointed minister of economic affairs in 1939. In the spring of 1942, he became prime minister for the first time, resigning later the same year.

From 1944 to 1963, Ólafur Thors led four coalition governments (1944–47, 1949–50, 1953–56, and 1959–63) and sat in the fifth as minister of economic affairs (1950–53). He was an able politician and negotiator, as is reflected in the fact that he managed to form a coalition government with the Socialist Unity Party (q.v.)—the political nemesis of the IP—at the end of the war. Moreover, as the leader of the IP for almost three decades (1934–61), he effectively directed this largest political party through times of great political upheaval, without facing any serious challenge to his leadership. (*See also* MODERNIZATION GOVERNMENT; RECONSTRUCTION GOVERNMENT)

TÍMINN. A newspaper founded in 1917 by leading members of the Progressive Party (PP, q.v.), becoming its official organ in 1938. *Tíminn* was published once a week for the first 30 years but has been a daily newspaper since 1947. From the beginning, *Tíminn* has followed the line of the PP, and its circulation has primarily been restricted to the rural areas. In recent years, *Tíminn* has faced severe financial difficulties, like all of the small party newspapers, and it is now managed by the publishers of its rival *Dagblaðið Vísir* (q.v.). In 1996, *Tíminn* merged with another former organ of the PP, *Dagur* (q.v.), and the two dailies are currently published under the name *Dagur-Tíminn.* (*See also* JÓNSSON, JÓNAS)

TOURISM. Tourism is one of the fastest-growing economic sectors in Iceland. The number of foreign visitors to Iceland has increased from just under 100,000 in 1985 to almost 190,000 in 1995, providing 11 percent of total foreign exchange revenues in 1993. This expansion has happened because of diligent efforts to promote Iceland abroad, but improved facilities and changing patterns in international tourism have also contributed to the trend. The main attraction in Iceland is its relatively untamed and rugged geography, but a harsh climate limits the main tourist season to the fairly short period of the summer months. The increase in tourism also helped the economy through a difficult period for its fisheries (q.v.), and the state has encouraged its further expansion.

TRADE, FOREIGN. Despite the distance from European markets and extreme poverty of the majority of the population in the past, foreign trade has always played an important role in the Icelandic economy. The narrow resource base and primitive division of labor called for the import of a variety of consumer and capital goods, ranging from grain and timber to machines and other manufactured goods. Moreover, the tiny home market was wholly inadequate for the most important domestic products, such as fish, wool, and even meat.

Considerable foreign trade was carried out during the Commonwealth period (q.v.). At that time, woolen textiles (so-called *vaðmál*) and, to a lesser extent, unprocessed wool and hides were the most important export articles, while grain dominated the imports. Fish exports first became significant in the 14th century in response to rising prices on the European markets. Changes in the location of the principal market places in Iceland reflect this increase in the relative importance of fish exports, as the centers of trade moved from agricultural areas in the south (Eyrar), west (Hvítárvellir), and the north (Gásar) to coastal areas near the main fishing grounds in the southern and western parts of the country (for example the Vestmanna Islands (q.v.), Hafnarfjörður, and Hvalfjörður). Between the mid-14th century and the early 19th century, dried fish (stockfish) was Iceland's principal export article, with agricultural products such as wool, hides, tallow, and salted mutton taking second place. Grain, timber, and ironware were the main imports, although Icelanders also imported luxury articles, including fine clothes, wine, wax and tar, tobacco, and spirits in later periods. Early on, Icelanders traded mainly with Norway (q.v.), with the Hanseatic merchants playing an important role, but they were pushed aside with the influx of the more advanced and powerful English fishermen and traders in the early 15th century. During the late 15th century, German merchants and the Danish king joined in excluding the English from the Icelandic trade, and in 1532 they were finally defeated in an armed conflict with merchants from the city of Hamburg.

Royal influence on Icelandic affairs, including foreign trade, greatly grew during the Reformation (q.v.) era, leading to the introduction of the monopoly trade (q.v.) in 1602. From then on, Icelandic trade became a special prerogative of the Danish king, who gave priority to his subjects in this regard. With the partial abolition of the monopoly system in 1787, trade practices became more flexible, but this did not immediately lead to any fundamental change in Iceland. The new law confined foreign trade to Danish citizens, which in practice meant that it continued to be dominated by a few Danish merchants residing in Copenhagen and channelling most trade through Denmark. With further liberalization of Icelandic trade in 1816, and the abolition of all restrictions on foreign trade in 1855, the structural impediments against free trade with the outside world were lifted. Gradually, the last vestiges of the monopoly system disappeared, and trade came increasingly into the hands of Icelandic merchants.

The export of salt fish, primarily to Spain, increased significantly around 1770, making it the most important export staple in the second quarter of the 19th century; thus, in the 1920s, this product provided up to 60 percent of all export earnings in Iceland. By 1860 Iceland ranked among the top six European countries in terms of per capita exports, and this trend continued into the 20th century. In 1990, merchandise imports and exports accounted for 27 and 28 percent respectively of the gross domestic product. Marine products are still in a dominant position, accounting for 70–80 percent of all exports, but frozen fish replaced salt fish in the 1940s as the principal export article. Manufactured products have become more significant with the introduction of energy-intensive industries (q.v.). At the present, they hold second place in the exports, around 20 percent of all in 1990, aluminum accounting for 10 percent— this percentage will increase even further in the coming years as a result of expanded foreign investment in this field. A wide range of commodities characterizes imports, however, because Icelanders depend heavily on the importation of finished consumer and investment goods, in addition to many of the most important intermediate and raw materials.

Iceland pursued a very liberal external trade policy up to the Great Depression (q.v.) of the early 1930s, when protective tariffs were set up to encourage light domestic industry and to tackle the growing unemployment problem. These protectionist policies survived longer in Iceland than in the neighboring countries, with duties first being scaled down after 1960. Since the 1960s, Iceland has been a member in various international organizations and agreements. In the 1960s the country became a contracting party to the General Agreement on Tariffs and Trade (GATT) in 1964 and a full member of European Free Trade Association (EFTA, q.v.) in 1970, followed by bilateral agreements with the EU (q.v.) and recently the European Economic Area (EEA, q.v.) agreement. This has obliged Iceland to open its markets to foreign competition. G. J. (*See also* MAGNÚSSON, SKÚLI; UNITED KINGDOM [RELATIONS WITH])

"TURKS," RAID OF. In the summer of 1627, four pirate ships from the Barbary Coast (the coast of present day Algeria and Morocco) arrived in Iceland, raiding villages on the eastern and southern coast. The pirates took around 400 Icelanders and Danes into captivity, selling them into slavery in North Africa. The most famous incident of the raid happened in the Vestmanna Islands (q.v.), just off the southern coast of Iceland. On these small islands, over 240 people were captured and 30–40 killed. Some of the captives were recovered after a ransom was paid, but the great majority of them never returned to Iceland. The raid struck great fear into the hearts of Icelanders, who had not experienced aggression of this sort before. Although the Barbary corsairs never returned, the memory of the "Turks," as the pirates were called in Iceland, lived on for centuries.

- U -

UNEMPLOYMENT. *See* EMPLOYMENT.

UNION OF LIBERALS AND LEFTISTS (ULL). Hannibal Valdimarsson (q.v.), who had left the People's Alliance (PA, q.v.) in the fall of 1968, founded the ULL (Samtök frjálslyndra og vinstri manna) in 1969. The goal of the new party was to promote a union of all social democrats and supporters of the cooperative movement (q.v.) in a single party, but in fact it only added to the friction on the left of the political spectrum. The party's platform called for an end to what it called the stagnated organization of the Icelandic political system and advocated shutting down the Ameri-can military base in Keflavík (q.v.).

The ULL was the clear victor in the 1971 election, receiving 9 percent of the popular vote. Following the election, the party participated in the second Left-Wing Government (q.v.). As the government broke up in 1974, most of the leaders of the ULL left the party, either retiring from politics or joining other parties like the Social Democratic Party (SDP, q.v.) or the PA. In 1978, the party participated in elections for the last time but failed to have a candidate elected to parliament. The ULL was formally dissolved in 1979.

UNITED KINGDOM (RELATIONS WITH). Relations with the British Isles go as far back as the settlement of Iceland, but they first became critical in the 15th century. English fishermen and traders began to visit Iceland around the end of the 14th century, filling a void left by a declining trade with Norway (q.v.). In the following decades, the English became very prominent in Iceland, often practically controlling its relations with the outer world (thus historians call the time from the early 15th to the early 16th century the English century). For the most part, Icelanders welcomed trade with England but protested their fishing, while the Danish king did what he could to control Icelandic foreign trade. In the late 15th century German merchants began to compete with the English for the Icelandic market. This often led to violent confrontations, peaking in 1532 with the killing of 15 Englishmen in Grindavík on the southwestern coast. English activities in and around Iceland declined after this, as royal grip on trade strengthened, and English fishermen shifted their attention elsewhere.

The British began to show interest in Iceland again in the late 18th and 19th centuries. The first example of this came in 1772 when the English explorer and naturalist Sir Joseph Banks visited Iceland, setting the trend for explorations of the country in the following decades. Due to Banks's influence, Iceland received favorable treatment during the Napoleonic Wars, although the British were officially at war with Denmark. It was, however, with new fishing techniques and liberalization of Icelandic foreign trade in the latter half of the 19th century that Iceland regained its former importance to the English fishing fleet. A new chapter began in British-Icelandic relations when British trawlers started to frequent Icelandic waters around 1890. Fishing very close to the coast, in the traditional grounds of the Icelandic fishermen, made the trawlers very unpopular. For this reason, Icelanders commenced a struggle to dispel the foreign fishing fleet from the Icelandic coast, causing five so-called "cod wars" (q.v.) with the British.

Due to conflicting fishing interests, diplomatic relations between Iceland and Britain have often been tense in the 20th century. Iceland's location in the mid-Atlantic put the country, however, in the British sphere of influence. This was clear in both world wars, as Britain took control over Icelandic foreign trade in the first and occupied the country early in the second. In spite of occasional confrontations, relations between the two countries remain strong, however, as is evidenced by the fact that Britain is the largest importer of Icelandic products in the world. (*See also* FISHING LIMITS; TRADE, FOREIGN; WORLD WAR I [EFFECTS ON ICELAND]; WORLD WAR II [EFFECTS ON ICELAND])

UNITED STATES OF AMERICA (RELATIONS WITH). Apart from a massive emigration (q.v.) to North America in the late 19th and the early 20th centuries, Iceland had relatively limited contacts with the United States until World War II (q.v.). During the war, Iceland's strategic location became obvious, however, as the country was crucial for securing communications between the United States and Europe. For this reason, the governments of Iceland and the United States made a treaty in 1941, the United States taking the responsibility of defending Iceland during the war and using its military installations in Iceland to facilitate transportation over the North Atlantic. After the war, the United States attempted to prolong its military presence in Iceland, but this was unequivocally rejected by Icelandic authorities. Thus, the United States handed the Keflavík (q.v.) Airport over to the Icelandic government in 1946, but the American military was given free access to the airport, which was operated for the next five years by an American civilian company at the behest of the United States government. With its entry into NATO (q.v.) in 1949, Iceland sided firmly with the United States in the cold war. This was further accentuated by a new defense treaty in 1951 and the return of the American military to Iceland the same year.

The Second World War was a watershed in military and diplomatic relations between the United States and Iceland. The American army brought with it cultural influences, which were to shape tastes in Icelandic popular culture for the next decades. During the war, the United States became one of Iceland's most important trading partners: almost half of Iceland's imports came from the United States. From the late 1940s to the late 1980s, the United States was one of the most important markets for Icelandic fish products.

During the cold war, Iceland played a crucial role in the surveillance of the North Atlantic. Recent development in international politics has changed this situation dramatically, as Russia does not pose the same military threat to the United States as the Soviet Union did before. Furthermore, Iceland's economic ties with the United States are not as strong today as they were in the postwar era, because both imports to and exports from the United States have declined in recent years. Relations between Iceland and the United States remain strong and amicable, however, and there seems to be no desire on either part to abrogate the 1951 defense treaty.

UNIVERSITY OF ICELAND. The largest institution of higher learning and scientific research in Iceland, called Háskóli Íslands. It was formally founded on June 17, 1911, commemorating the centennial of the Icelandic national hero Jón Sigurðsson (q.v.) but its history goes back to the mid-19th century. Until that time, Icelandic students had to seek all their university education abroad, studying primarily at the University of Copenhagen. In 1847, a Theological College was founded in Reykjavík, which was later to become the theological faculty of the University of Iceland. Almost three decades later, in 1876, a medical school was opened in Reykjavík, and in 1908, with the foundation of a law school in Reykjavík, the three most popular fields of university studies of the time could be pursued in Iceland. In 1911, each of these three colleges formed a separate faculty in the University of Iceland and added one new faculty, the Faculty of Arts.

The university has grown steadily since its founding, from 45 students and 11 professors in its first year to around 5,800 students and 600 teachers, administrators, and researchers in the late 1990s. Presently, the University of Iceland is divided into nine faculties (Arts, Business Administration and Economics, Dentistry, Engineering, Law, Medicine, Natural Sciences, Social Sciences, and Theology). Each of these faculties offers advanced education in its specific fields and serve as centers of research in the country. In addition, there is a number of research institutes affiliated with the University, such as the Árni Magnússon Institute (q.v.), the Sigurður Nordal Institute, and the Nordic Volcanological Institute, functioning as centers of specialized research and cooperation with other universities. As the great majority of the academic staff at the University of Iceland has earned their graduate degrees abroad, the University has always maintained strong links with foreign universities. In recent years it has also participated actively in student and teacher exchanges organized by the Nordic Council and the European Union (qq.v.).

The University of Iceland is a public university and receives most of its funding directly from the state. Formally, the University is placed under the ministry of education, but in reality the University is fairly independent in the control of its internal affairs. Thus, its president (rector) is elected by the staff and students, and the University has full authority over the appointment of its academic and professional staff. (*See also* EDUCATION; MENNTA-SKÓLINN Í REYKJAVÍK.)

URBANIZATION. Until the late 19th century Icelanders lived almost entirely in rural areas, residing on individual farmsteads spread throughout the inhabitable parts of the country. In 1901, only 16 percent of the Icelandic population lived in towns and villages with more than 500 inhabitants. At that time, Reykjavík (q.v.) was by far the largest town in Iceland with approximately 6,600 inhabitants. However, at the turn of the century, a radical transformation of demographic patterns was already under way. From the mid-19th century, population pressure in the rural areas had forced a growing number of Icelanders to seek their livelihood outside the traditional economic spheres. As a result, small fishing villages emerged around the coast, and a considerable number of Icelanders emigrated to North America. This urbanization has continued more or less continuously up to the present. In 1930, more than half of the population lived in towns and villages with over 500 inhabitants; in 1960, this number had increased to around three-quarters of the population, and in 1990 only one in ten Icelanders lived in rural areas. Today, four towns in Iceland have over 10,000 inhabitants: Reykjavík, Kópavogur and Hafnarfjörður in the southwest, and Akureyri (q.v.) in the north. Reykjavík is still by far the largest town in Iceland, and the number of its inhabitants passed the 100,000 mark in 1992.

The rapid decline of rural areas and the growth of towns began in spite of fierce opposition from most of the leading figures of Icelandic society. Social commentators in the late 19th and the early 20th centuries opined that this development would inevitably lead to moral degeneration of the Icelandic nation and a corruption of the national character. The demographic transformation went rather smoothly, however, as industrialization of the fishing industry and expansion of the service sector have provided the towns with a solid economic base. Many problems concerning population patterns are unsolved, however, because economic development seems to favor a continued concentration of the population, threatening a total social and economic breakdown in many of the less populated areas of the country. (*See also* POPULATION; REGIONAL POLICY)

- V -

VALDIMARSSON, HANNIBAL (1903–1991). The politician and labor leader Hannibal Valdimarsson was born into a farming family on January 13, 1903, in Ísafjörður County in northwest Iceland. After completing a high school exam in Akureyri (q.v.) in 1922, he studied at a Danish educational college, passing a teaching exam in 1927. Upon returning to Iceland, he served as a principal and teacher in elementary schools until the year 1931. Then he became a clerk for the Cooperative Branch in the town of Ísafjörður (q.v.), where he worked for seven years. In 1938, he was appointed principal of Ísafjörður's high school, a position he held until 1954, when he was elected president of the powerful Icelandic Federation of Labor (IFL, q.v.).

At that time, Hannibal Valdimarsson had been engaged in labor politics for a long time, beginning as the president of the labor union in Súðavík, a small village close to Ísafjörður, from 1930 to 1931.

In 1932, he was elected to the same post for the labor union of Ísafjörður, holding that office until 1939. From 1934 to 1954 he served as president of the Federation of Labor in the Western Fjords District. Work for the labor unions helped him to launch a political career. He was first elected to parliament for the Social Democratic Party (SDP, q.v.) in 1946, sitting continuously in Alþingi (q.v.) until he retired from public life in 1974. Hannibal Valdimarsson was chairman of the SDP from 1952 to 1954, but in 1956 he headed a splinter group of radical members of the SDP who had resigned from the party. This group formed an electoral alliance with the Socialist Unity Party (q.v.), called the People's Alliance (PA, q.v.). Hannibal Valdimarsson served as chairman of the PA from its foundation in 1956 to 1968, when he left to form a new political organization, the Union of Liberals and Leftists (ULL, q.v.). He led this party to a brilliant victory in the 1971 elections, putting him in a key position in forming a government (q.v.). From 1956 to 1958, he served as minister of health and social affairs for the PA. In 1971, he was appointed minister of communications and social affairs in the Left-Wing Government (q.v.) formed in that year, resigning from the cabinet (q.v.) in 1973. He retired from politics in 1974.

Hannibal Valdimarsson was a popular politician and a sincere advocate of working class interests. His professed political mission was to unite the parties on the left in one social-democratic party, but in the long run his actions only increased the confusion existing among those left of the political spectrum.

VALDIMARSSON, HÉÐINN (1892–1948). This socialist leader and economist was born on May 26, 1892, to the editor, and one of the founders of the Icelandic women's rights movement, Bríet Bjarnhéðinsdóttir (q.v.). Héðinn Valdimarsson graduated from the secondary school in Reykjavík in 1911, completing a degree in economics from the University of Copenhagen six years later. In 1917, upon returning to Iceland, he was appointed chief administrator of the Government Import Authority (GIA), a state enterprise established to organize the Icelandic import trade during World War I (q.v.). In 1926, at the time the GIA was abolished, Héðinn Valdimarsson became director of the State Tobacco Monopoly. From 1928 until his death in 1948, he served as director of the Icelandic Oil Company (Olíuverslun Íslands).

Héðinn Valdimarsson became active in the Social Democratic Party (SDP, q.v.) soon after he returned from his studies in Copenhagen. He was president of Dagsbrún, the union of unskilled laborers in Reykjavík, for 15 years between 1922 and 1942. He sat in parliament for Reykjavík from 1927 to 1942, first for the SDP and later for Socialist Unity Party (SUP, q.v.). While a member of the SDP, Héðinn Valdimarsson belonged to a radical faction of the party, and from 1937 to 1938 he advocated a merger of the SDP and the Communist Party of Iceland (CPI, q.v.). His intention was to form a united socialist front against fascism in Iceland. Most of his fellow social democrats disapproved of the idea, however, and in 1938 the SDP expelled him from its ranks. The same year, Héðinn Valdimarsson and his supporters established the SUP with the CPI, and he was elected its first chairman. At the end of the following year, he resigned from the SUP, protesting the pro-Soviet views of its communist faction. This was the end of Héðinn Valdimarsson's political career.

VATNAJÖKULL. The largest glacier in Europe is located in southeastern Iceland. It is around 8,300 sq. km (3,200 sq. mi.) in size, covering a large plateau with valleys and mountain peaks in between. The glacier is around 420 m (1,365 ft.) thick on the average, but the maximum thickness is around 1,000 m (3,300 ft.). For the most part, the glacier stands at 1,400–1,800 m (4,600–6,000 ft.) above sea level, but Hvannadalshnjúkur, the highest mountain peek in Iceland (2,119 m or 6,950 ft.), is in Öræfajökull, which extends to the south from Vatnajökull. Many volcanic outbreaks have taken place under Vatnajökull, and Grímsvötn, one of the largest geothermal areas in Iceland, is under the glacier. In former times, few people dared to venture out on the glacier, but today it has become both a tourist attraction, and a field for numerous scientific expeditions.

VESTMANNA ISLANDS, THE. An archipelago consisting of 15–18 small islands, about 12 km (7.5 mi.) off the southern coast of Iceland. Heimaey, the largest island in the group, has been inhabited since the Settlement period (q.v.), and some archaeologists have contended that its habitation preceded the Norse settlement on the Icelandic mainland. As Heimaey has an excellent natural harbor, and as the islands are close to fertile fishing grounds, the Vestmanna Islands have always been one of the most important centers for the Icelandic fisheries (q.v.).

All of the Vestmanna Islands were formed through volcanic eruptions from a fissure that extends from the southern coast of Iceland into the Atlantic. In recent decades, two major eruptions have taken place in this area; in 1963 an eruption began under the sea a few miles to the south of Heimaey, forming a new island called Surtsey. A decade later, another eruption started just to the east of the town on Heimaey. The inhabitants, 5,300 in all, were narrowly rescued in boats and evacuated to the mainland. During the next few months, portions of the town went under lava, but a substantial part of it was saved through an effort to cool down the lava. At the end of the eruption, people returned to the Vestmanna Islands, and Heimaey has regained its former status as a major fishing harbor.

VÍDALÍN, JÓN (1666–1720). A Lutheran bishop and author of religious sermons. Jón Vídalín was born to a minister in southwestern Iceland on March 21, 1666. He studied at the Skálholt (q.v.) seminary from 1679 to 1682. For the next years he continued his studies under private tutors, enrolling in the University of Copenhagen in 1687. After completing a degree in theology in 1689, he enlisted in the Danish army, where he served for two years. In 1691, Jón Vídalín returned to Iceland to work for the bishop in Skálholt. From 1691 to 1697, he served as pastor in Iceland, first for Skálholt Cathedral, but later in the parish were he was born. In 1697, Jón Vídalín returned to Skálholt when the bishop named him as his assistant. The following year Jón Vídalín succeeded the bishop of Skálholt, serving the diocese until his death in 1720.

Jón Vídalín, who lost his father at an early age, was raised in relative poverty. Through his intelligence and perseverance, he was able, however, to reach the highest post in the Icelandic church hierarchy. His greatest gift was his oratory. This is clearly demonstrated in his book of sermons (*Vídalínspostilla*), for which he is best known. A thundering attack on human vices and the shortcomings of the human society, the book is written in a forceful style and was widely read in Iceland during the 18th and 19th centuries, shaping to a considerable extent the religious ideas in Iceland in the period. (*See also* LITERATURE)

VIÐEY. A small island in Kollafjörður, just off Reykjavík's (q.v.) coast. In the late Middle Ages, it was home to the wealthiest monastery in Iceland, founded in 1226 but abolished with the Lutheran Reformation (q.v.) in the mid-16th century. After the Reformation, the Danish king appropriated Viðey with the property of other religious houses in Iceland. This led to its decline, but it regained some of its former prestige when Skúli Magnússon (q.v.), royal treasurer in Iceland, made it his home in the mid-18th century. At Skúli Magnússon's request, the royal authorities had one of the first stone houses in Iceland built on the island in 1753–55, designed by a Danish architect in the style of a Danish manor house. Later in the 18th century, Ólafur Stefánsson (q.v.), the governor of Iceland, moved to the island, and after him, his son Magnús Stephensen (q.v.), Chief Justice of the High Court (q.v.) in Reykjavík. For a short period during Magnús Stephensen's time, Viðey became a cultural center, as he operated a printing press on the island, publishing literature on various subjects. In the early 20th century, Viðey played a new role, as one of the first trawler companies in Iceland had its headquarters there from 1907 to 1914, but from 1913, with construction of new harbor in Reykjavík, the fishing port of Viðey gradually declined. Today, Viðey is mostly deserted, but it remains a popular tourist attraction, especially since the town of Reykjavík restored the 18th-century stone house and turned it into a restaurant.

VINLAND. In the late 10th century, or around the year 986, Viking expansion continued west from Iceland, first to Greenland (q.v.), where people of Norse extraction lived at least until the early 15th century. After living for only a few years in the new place, the settlers of Greenland came upon a land further to the west, that is, the North American mainland. Around the year 1000, the son of the first settler in Greenland, a man by the name of Leifur Eiríksson (q.v.), explored the coast of a land he named Vinland (the name means either "Vine Land" or "Meadow Land"). After spending the winter in this new land, he returned home to Greenland. In the following decades, Greenlanders made a few attempts to settle the "new world," but these ventures were all abandoned, leaving no permanent Norse settlement in present day Canada and the United States.

The explorations of Vinland are described in two Icelandic sagas, *Grænlendinga saga* (*The Saga of Greenlanders*) and *Eiríks saga rauða* (*The Saga of Eiríkur the Red*), both of which were indited in Iceland in the 13th century. Based on oral legends, these stories give neither a consistent account of the events, nor a certain location for Vinland. Archaeologists have, however, excavated a Norse settlement on the northern tip of the Great Northern Peninsula in Newfoundland, and there are clear indications from the findings there that its inhabitants had at least some contacts with regions further south in the St. Lawrence valley.

- W -

WELFARE STATE. Through most of Icelandic history, the state took almost no part in supporting the poor. The family or kin-group had the responsibility to maintain all of its members, but when they were unable to do so, the local commune (q.v.) where the pauper had legal residence took over. With increased urbanization and a growing working class in the towns, there was mounting pressure on the state to secure minimum health insurance for its citizens. The first step in this direction was the foundation of state-guaranteed insurance funds for victims of industrial accidents in 1903, but the first comprehensive social insurance legislation was not passed until 1936. This happened in accordance with the demands of the Social Democratic Party (q.v.) set as conditions for its participation in the so-called "Government of the Laboring Classes" (q.v.) with the Progressive Party (q.v.). With this legislation, about half of the Icelandic population was covered by a state organized healthcare plan, and the foundations for a general retirement and disability compensation plan were laid, as well as other welfare schemes.

The development of the Icelandic welfare state has been rapid since World War II (q.v.). The general trend has been to expand the system into new areas of health and educational services, including all Icelanders regardless of their financial means. Today, the welfare system is similar to those in other Nordic countries, although Iceland's welfare expenditures are lower than those of its neighbors (18.9 percent of the Icelandic GNP in 1992 compared to between 30.8 percent [Norway] and 38.7 percent [Sweden] in the other Nordic countries). The peculiar age structure in Iceland explains this difference to a certain extent, as high birth rates since World War II lower the ratio of elderly people in the total population. As in the other Nordic countries, the basic premises of the system are that the state provides all Icelanders with healthcare services for a minimum fee; it provides all of its citizens with a pension insurance; and most of the educational institutions are either free of charge or demand only a fairly low fee.

Increasing unemployment and a crisis in state finances have put a strain on the welfare system in recent years. All the Icelandic political parties have played a part in its construction, however, and voters have grown accustomed to its benefits. Therefore, there seems to be no general desire to dismantle the welfare state at the present time.

WHALING. At the end of the 16th century, Basque whalers from northern Spain and the southwest coast of France began to frequent Icelandic waters. Until then, only limited whaling had been pursued around the coast, because Icelanders did not possess the techniques to hunt whales. Modern, industrialized whaling began in Iceland in the latter half of the 19th century, especially after the first Norwegian whaling station began operations in Iceland in 1883. From that year, until a whaling moratorium in the Icelandic waters came into effect in 1916, it is estimated that Norwegian whalers processed over 17,000 whales in its Icelandic factories, or over 500 whales p.a. on average. The whaling ban, which had originally been passed in Alþingi (q.v.) in 1913, was lifted in 1928, but whaling began in earnest after World War II (q.v.), with the foundation of the first Icelandic whaling company, Hvalur h.f., in 1949. From 1949 to 1985, over 14,000 whales of larger species (primarily finback, sperm whale, and sei whale) were brought to land in Iceland, in addition to up to around 200 minke whales a year. In 1982, the International Whaling Commission (IWC) suspended all commercial whaling in the world, effective from the beginning of 1986. This decision was very unpopular in Iceland, because there was not much scientific evidence to support a total ban on whaling. In spite of the general opposition to the whaling ban, a one-vote majority in Alþingi agreed not to oppose IWC's moratorium, passing instead a resolution allowing for limited whaling for scientific purposes in the period from 1986 to 1989. This policy was virgorously protested by international environmental groups such as Greepeace, and in November 1986 members of the organization Sea Shepherd, sank two whaling boats in Reykjavík's harbor. Since the end of 1989, the moratorium on whaling has been respected in Iceland, albeit very reluctantly. It is very difficult for a nation totally dependent upon fishing to accept sentimental arguments against utilization of natural resources in the sea. For this reason, Icelanders left the IWC in 1992, and there is mounting pressure on the government to allow limited whaling again.

WOMEN'S ALLIANCE (WA). Although Icelandic women received equal political rights through two constitutional amendments in 1915 and 1920, their political influence remained fairly limited for most of the 20th century. For example, from the time that the first woman was elected to parliament in 1922 until the early 1980s, only 12 women in all had sat in Alþingi (q.v.). In the local elections of 1982, a group of women revived the idea of presenting a separate women's list, but this had been practiced in local and parliamentary elections in Iceland in the period 1908–26. In March 1983, following these local elections, a group of women formed a political organization they called the Women's Alliance (Kvennalistinn), with the expressed purpose of furthering women's issues in Icelandic politics. The WA presented candidates in three districts in the parliamentary elections of 1983, receiving 7.6 percent of the votes cast in these districts, or enough voters to give it three representatives in Alþingi. Four years later, the WA offered lists in all eight parliamentary districts, doubling its support and its number of representatives. This support declined to around 8 percent of the votes cast in 1991, but the WA remained a force to be reckoned with. At the present, the future of the WA seems uncertain, however. It polled only around 5 percent of the popular vote in the 1995 elections and barely got three women elected to parliament.

The WA has had a clear impact on Icelandic politics. The proportion of women sitting in parliament and local councils rose markedly from late 1970s to the early 1990s, or from around 5 percent to around 25 percent. This is a result of the policy of the WA to offer only women as candidates on its lists and the success of the WA has forced other political parties to seek more gender balance on their tickets.

The WA is the first political organization since the 1930s to seriously challenge the pattern of having four political parties in Iceland. Their success is based primarily on the fact that their objectives have found strong resonance among voters in general. But the WA has also challenged the foundation of the Icelandic political system, refusing to be placed into the traditional left-right spectrum and rejecting the practice of transforming their political movement into a formal institution. Unlike the other parties, the WA elects no chairman, and it has limited the time its representatives can sit in parliament to two terms in order to secure a regular renewal in its parliamentary group.

WORLD WAR I (EFFECTS ON ICELAND). Although Iceland remained at least theoretically neutral, World War I had considerable effects on Icelandic society. At its beginning, for example, Denmark was still Iceland's most important trading partner, as it had been from the days of the hated monopoly trade (q.v.) of the 17th and 18th centuries. This caused considerable annoyance in London, especially as it was suspected that Danish merchants reexported Icelandic products to Germany for high prices. Therefore, in order to strengthen its trade embargo on Germany, the British government forced Icelanders to accept British control of their foreign trade. A special treaty between the Icelandic minister and the British government, signed in London on May 16, 1916, formalized this arrangement. The treaty stipulated that all vessels leaving Iceland for countries other than the United States (q.v.) had to go through a British contraband control base. Furthermore, the treaty prohibited Icelanders from exporting products such as salt fish, fish oils, mutton, wool, and hides to all countries that shared borders with Germany or bordered on the Baltic or the North Sea—including Denmark and Sweden. At the same time, the British government agreed to supply Icelanders with necessities such as coal and salt and to purchase Icelandic products that could not be sold on the open market. To guarantee the treaty, the British government dispatched a special envoy to Iceland, who was to serve as consul in Reykjavík, overseeing all foreign trade.

During the first years of World War I, Iceland benefited considerably from rising export prices, but this trend was reversed as the war progressed. As a result of increasing German submarine warfare, it became difficult for Britain to fulfill the obligations it had agreed to earlier. Moreover, import prices in Iceland rose more rapidly than export prices, as the British government fixed the latter while the former followed general trends in international trade. For this reason, Iceland suffered a severe economic crisis at the end of the war. The war had, however, positive effects on the political situation, because it forced Icelanders to be more independent in their foreign policy and lessened economic dependency on Denmark. These factors were important in convincing Icelanders that political independence was not only feasible but also practical, a sentiment they expressed clearly in negotiations leading to the Act of Union (q.v.) in 1918. Iceland gained full sovereignty on December 1, 1918, less than a month after armistice ended the war. (*See also* UNITED KINGDOM [RELATIONS WITH])

WORLD WAR II (EFFECTS ON ICELAND). In spite of the Icelandic declaration of permanent neutrality in 1918, Iceland did not escape the effects of World War II. After the German occupation of Denmark in April 1940, the British government alerted its Icelandic counterpart of the danger that Iceland could also fall under German rule. A month later, on May 10, 1940, British Royal Marines landed at Reykjavík (q.v.) and declared the country occupied. The Icelandic government filed a formal complaint, reiterating its neutrality, but it cooperated fully with the occupying forces from the beginning.

Because of its strategic location, Iceland became an allied naval and air base, playing a crucial role in the battle for the Atlantic Ocean. It also served as an important station on the new air route between North America and the British Isles. In July 1941, or almost half a year before the United States entered the war, American forces took over the military protection of Iceland according to a defense treaty made with Icelandic authorities. The

British, however, continued air and naval operations in Iceland throughout the war.

Relations between the foreign military forces and the Icelandic population were peaceful for the most part. In fact, the war had very positive effects on the economy, as construction of military installations and the extensive services required by the soldiers ended the chronic unemployment that had plagued Iceland since the Great Depression (q.v.). As a result, towns like Reykjavík (q.v.) grew very rapidly in size, and Icelanders were generally more prosperous than ever before at the end of the war. The country was not untouched by the tragedies of the time, however. A number of Icelandic sailors perished at sea when German submarines and aircraft attacked Icelandic fishing vessels and cargo ships on the Atlantic Ocean between Iceland and Britain.

World War II entirely changed Iceland's position in the international scene. The German occupation of Denmark prompted the Icelandic parliament to entrust the government of Iceland with royal powers and later to replace the king temporarily with a special governor of Iceland (*ríkisstjóri* [q.v.]). From that time, Iceland had practically severed all of its ties with the Danish monarchy, a step that was finalized with the foundation of the republic in 1944. During the war, Iceland's military significance became obvious, and this fact greatly enhanced its status in organizations such as NATO (q.v.) during the cold war era. (*See also* KEFLAVÍK; REPUBLIC OF ICELAND, FOUNDATION OF; UNITED KINGDOM [RELATIONS WITH]; UNITED STATES [RELATIONS WITH])

- Y -

YOUTH ASSOCIATIONS. During the early 20th century a number of youth associations were established in Iceland, primarily following a Norwegian model. The goals of these associations were to cultivate patriotism in Iceland and to encourage optimism and healthy lifestyles among the young. This was very much in the nationalistic spirit of early 20th-century Iceland, where a strong connection was made between cultivation of the country and the cultural well-being of the people. The first association was founded in the town of Akureyri (q.v.) in 1906, and the Federation of Icelandic Youth Associations (FIYA, Ungmennafélag Íslands) was founded the following year. These societies flourished in the next decades, spreading all over the country. They organized sporting events, discussion groups, and planting of trees and encouraged temperance. Today, the youth associations focus primarily on sports, although they also serve as an important platform for other social activities in the rural areas of the country. Since 1940, FIYA organizes national games every third or fourth year, where representatives from the different associations compete in a wide variety of events. At the present, over 200 associations with around 25 thousand members, organized in 18 regional unions, form the FIYA.

- Þ -

ÞINGVELLIR. Þingvellir, or the Parliamentary Plains in literal translation, was the site for the general assembly called Alþingi (q.v.), meeting annually from around 930 until its abolishment at the end of the 18th century. On rocky plains at the northern tip of Iceland's largest lake, people from all over the country assembled for a few weeks in the summer to debate legal and political issues and to hold the highest court in the country. It was there that they made the most important decisions concerning the government of the country, including conversion to Christianity (q.v.) around the year 1000 and an alliance with the Norwegian king in 1262–64.

Originally, Þingvellir was chosen for its location, because it is placed at a crossing where important routes connecting Iceland's northern, western, and southern parts met. But as Þingvellir is not situated by the sea and is not well suited for agriculture of any sort, no permanent town formed at this center of Icelandic political life. Therefore, when a new, elected Alþingi was established in 1843–45, it was not placed at Þingvellir, but in the burgeoning capital, Reykjavík (q.v.). This decision evoked strong controversy at the time, but it was in line with the general policy of the Danish government to create an undisputed administrative center for the country. Þingvellir has, however, retained its symbolic value, as it still holds a sacred place in the national consciousness. This is reflected in the fact that it was designated Iceland's first national park in 1928, and it was there that Alþingi assembled on June 17, 1944, to establish the Republic of Iceland. Moreover, it has been the place for the most important national festivals of the 20th century, such as the celebration of the 1,000th anniversary of Alþingi in 1930, the 11th centenary of the Icelandic settlement in 1974, and the 50th anniversary of the Icelandic Republic in 1994.

ÞJÓÐFUNDUR. *See* CONSTITUTIVE ASSEMBLY.

ÞJÓÐVAKI. A political party established before the 1995 parliamentary elections. Þjóðvaki (National Awakening) was formed around Jóhanna Sigurðardóttir (q.v.), former minister of social affairs and vice-chairman of the Social Democratic Party (SDP, q.v.). The party platform calls for efforts to increase social equality and for unity of all so-called "socially minded" people *(félagshyggjufólk)* in one political movement. According to opinion polls, Þjóðvaki had considerable support in the weeks prior to the 1995 elections but, as it turned out, it received only 7 percent of the votes cast and had four representatives elected to Alþingi (q.v.). Since the elections, the party has consistently scored below 1 percent in opinion polls, and it seems destined soon to disappear as other similar parties of the past.

ÞJÓÐVILJINN. A daily newspaper published in Reykjavík from 1936 to 1992. It was founded by the Communist Party of Iceland (CPI, q.v.) to succeed its earlier official organ, *Verkalýðsblaðið.* Throughout its history, *Þjóðviljinn* supported the parties farthest to the left, first the CPI, later the Socialist Unity Party (q.v.), and in the end the People's Alliance (q.v.). *Þjóðviljinn* was never a great financial success and always had to rely on the loyalty of its subscribers. It ceased publication in early 1992 because of severe financial difficulties.

ÞÓRARINSSON, SIGURÐUR (1912–1983). Iceland's best-known geologist. He was born on January 8, 1912, in a farming family in Vopnafjörður in northeastern Iceland. He attended secondary school in Akureyri (q.v.), enrolling in the University of Copenhagen in 1931. The following year, Sigurður Þórarinsson moved to Stockholm, where he defended his doctoral dissertation in geology in 1944. In 1945, right before the end of the World War II (q.v.), he returned to Iceland. First he worked as a researcher for the Icelandic Science Council, but from 1947 to 1969 he served as the director of the Icelandic Natural Museum. In 1969, he was appointed the first professor of geography and geology at the University of Iceland (q.v.), a position he held until his retirement in 1982.

As was quite fitting for an Icelandic geologist, Sigurður Þórarinsson specialized in the study of glaciers and volcanoes. He was a pioneer in using layers of tephra to date archaeological findings (tephrochronology), a method that has proven invaluable for Icelandic archaeologists. For decades, Sigurður Þórarinsson was one of the leading experts of volcanology in the world, and he paved the way for the development of the scientific study of geology in Iceland.

ÞÓRÐARSON, STURLA (1214–1284). The great 13th-century historical chronicler Sturla Þórðarson was born on July 29, 1214, into one of the leading families of the 13th century, the Sturlungs. At an early age, he became involved in the complex political intrigues of the period, something he was destined to as a member of the Sturlung family. He is remembered, however, more for his literary contributions than his political deeds. He wrote a large part of the so-called *Sturlunga Saga* (q.v.) compilation, most significant part of which is *Íslendinga Saga* (*History of Icelanders*). This is a chronicle of the period from the death of Sturla Þórðarson's grandfather and namesake until the end of the Commonwealth period (q.v.) in 1264. A 17th-century copy of his version of the *Book of Settlements* (q.v.) also exists. In addition to these writings, Magnús Hákonarson, king of Norway (1263–80), hired Sturla Þórðarson to write a chronicle of his rule and of his father's life. Sturla Þórðarson's historical writings give a remarkably balanced picture of the period, especially when it is considered that he was an active participant in some of the key events he describes. During his last years, Sturla Þórðarson was known as a legal expert. He served as a lawman (q.v.) from 1277 to 1282, and he assisted with the revision of the Icelandic law codes after the country entered into union with Norway. (*See also* AGE OF THE STURLUNGS)

ÞÓRÐARSON, ÞÓRBERGUR (1888–1974). One of the leading writers of 20th-century Iceland. Þórbergur Þórðarson was born to a farmer in southeastern Iceland on March 12, 1888, but moved to Reykjavík as a young man. He worked as a laborer and a fisherman for a few years but studied at the Icelandic College of Teacher Training in Reykjavík from 1909 to 1910 and at the University of Iceland (q.v.) on an irregular basis (1913–19). He never completed a degree, but was a school teacher in Reykjavík for a number of years. Þórbergur Þórðarson published his first collection of poems in 1915, but his first major work, *Bréf til Láru* (*A Letter to Laura*), was published in Reykjavík in 1924. He was best known for his biographical essays, which give a satirical account of his own life. Þórbergur Þórðarson was, to a certain extent, a paradoxical man; he was a convinced socialist but also strongly influenced by eastern spiritualism; he was thoroughly rooted in Icelandic literary tradition and a master of the Icelandic language but was also a tireless promoter of the international language Esperanto.

ÞORGILSSON, ARI "THE LEARNED" (1067/8–1148). Not much is known about the life of this first chronicler of Icelandic history. From the age of seven, Ari Þorgilsson was fostered by Hallur Þórarinsson in Haukadalur, where he studied with men like Teitur Ísleifsson, the son of the first bishop in Skálholt (q.v.). Later, Ari Þorgilsson is believed to have served as a priest at Staður on Snæfellsnes peninsula, although this is not known for certain. During his lifetime, he was renowned for his learning—thus he was named "the learned" (*hinn fróði*)—evident in the *First Grammatical Treatise* and other medieval writings. The *Book of Icelanders* (q.v.) is the only surviving work that was certainly written by Ari Þorgilsson. There, he demonstrates a knowledge of Latin historical literature, but he chose to write his chronicle in Icelandic, thus setting the tone for historical writing in medieval Iceland.

ÞORLÁKSSON, GUÐBRANDUR (1541/2–1627). This influential bishop and religious leader was born either in 1541 or 1542 to a priest in northern Iceland. He attended the Latin school at Hólar (q.v.), completing an exam in 1559, shortly after the Lutheran Reformation (q.v.) was fully victorious in Iceland. From around 1560 to 1564, Guðbrandur Þorláksson studied at the University of Copenhagen, returning to Iceland in 1564 to become headmaster of the Latin school at Skálholt (q.v.). In 1565, he became a Lutheran minister in northern Iceland. Finally, in 1571, he was consecrated bishop over Hólar diocese. He served this post until his death in 1627.

Guðbrandur Þorláksson was a highly learned man, well versed in mathematics and geography, in addition to his knowledge of and interest in theology. He wrote extensively on religious issues and translated and published a great number of hymns and religious tracts. His greatest feat, however, was having the Bible translated into Icelandic and organizing its printing at Hólar (it was published in 1584). With this he laid the foundation for the use of Icelandic as a church language, contributing greatly to its preservation in spite of Danish rule.

ÞORLÁKSSON, JÓN (1877–1935). An engineer, politician, and businessman. Jón Þorláksson was born in Húnavatn County in northern Iceland into a well-off farming family. He studied to become an engineer in Copenhagen from 1897 to 1903, and in 1905 the minister of Iceland appointed him chief engineer for the Icelandic government (*landsverkfræðingur*). In 1921, he was elected to parliament for Reykjavík (q.v.) on a conservative ticket, and in 1924 he was instrumental in founding the Conservative Party (CP, q.v.). He became its first and only chairman, and under his leadership the party received over 40 percent of the popular votes in the parliamentary elections of 1927. When the Independence Party (IP, q.v.) was formed in 1929 he was elected its first chairman, a position he held until 1934. Jón Þorláksson was named minister of finance in 1924 and also served as prime minister from 1926 to 1927. He was elected mayor of Reykjavík in 1932, and two years later he retired from parliamentary politics.

Jón Þorláksson was one of the founders of the modern political system in Iceland. As a conservative politician, but a firm believer in free enterprise, he sought to organize the opponents of both socialism and the cooperative politics of the Progressive Party (q.v.) into one united political party. Although he was not a charismatic leader, Jón Þorláksson managed to attain that goal. Under his leadership, the CP and IP became the largest political parties in Iceland, a position which the IP has held consistently to this day.

Bibliography

Contents

INTRODUCTION

Although the bulk of the research on Iceland has always been published in Icelandic, even a bibliography emphasizing literature in English can only be partial and selective. Thus I have attempted to include books rather than articles for the sake of brevity and list only a few monographs in German and French. I have included, however, a considerable number of doctoral dissertations on Icelandic subjects, because often they provide the latest scholarship on the issues covered in this bibliography.

The best English-language bibliographies on Iceland are, without a doubt, the two editions of *Iceland* in Clio's World Bibliographic Series (John Horton, 1983, and Francis R. McBride, 1996). They provide annotated references, describing monographs and articles on Icelandic history, society and culture. Another useful bibliographic source is Jóhannes Nordal and Valdimar Kristinsson, eds., *Iceland 1986: Handbook* (Reykjavík: The Central Bank of Iceland, 1987) and a more recent edition of the same book by the same publisher, *Iceland: The Republic* (1996). In addition to survey articles on various aspects of Icelandic history, culture, society and nature, they provide a selective, classified list of books on Iceland in foreign languages (including the Scandinavian languages).

On medieval history and literature, the most recent survey work is Philip Pulsiano, ed. *Medieval Scandinavia: An Encyclopaedia* (New York: Garland, 1993), where Iceland is well represented. Each entry, written by a leading expert, includes comprehensive bibliographic information. No comparable work on the later history of Iceland exists in the English language. In general, it is striking how fragmented the literature on Iceland is in the major international languages. Thus, no comprehensive survey of Icelandic history or society has been published in English since the early 20th century (Knut Gjerset, *History of Iceland,* New York: Macmillan, 1924), and that work is, of course, thoroughly outdated. This bibliography provides a guide to the extensive academic literature on a great variety of topics for those who are interested in knowing more about Iceland.

I. GENERAL

1. *Bibliographies and Dictionaries*

Árnadóttir, Valva, ed. *Books on Iceland.* Reykjavík: Mál og menning, 1990.

Bekker-Nielsen, Hans. *Old Norse-Icelandic Studies: A Select Bibliography.* Toronto: U of Toronto P, 1967.

Bergsveinsson, Bergsveinn. *Isländisch Wörterbuch—Íslenzk-þýzk orðabók.* Leipzig: Verlag Enzyklopädie, 1967.

Bibliography of Old Norse-Icelandic Studies. (Copenhagen, 1963–).

Bogason, Sigurður Örn. *Ensk-íslensk orðabók. English-Icelandic Dictionary.* Reykjavík: Ísafoldarprentsmiðja, 1976.

Boots, Gerard. *Íslensk-frönsk orðabók. Dictionnaire Islandais-Français.* Reykjavík: Ísafoldarprentsmiðja, 1950.

Boots, Gerard, and Þórhallur Þorgilsson. *Frönsk-íslensk orðabók. Dictionnaire Français-Islandais.* Reykjavík: Ísafoldarprentsmiðja, 1953.

Brehdal-Petersen, Fredrik E. "A Bibliography for Ethnographic Research on Iceland." *Behaviour Science Research* 1 (1979): 1–35.

Brynjólfsson, Ingvar. *Isländisch-Deutsch. Deutsch-Isländisch.*

Langenscheits Universal Wörterbuch.   Berlin: Langenscheit
1964.

Cleasby, Richard, and Guðbrandur Vigfússon. *An Icelandic-English Dictionary.* 2nd ed. Supplement by W. A. Craigie. Oxford: Clarendon, 1969.

Egilsson, Sveinbjörn, and Finnur Jónsson. *Lexicon poeticum antiquæ linguæ septentrionalis. Ordbog over det norsk-islandske Skjaldesprog.* 2nd ed. Copenhagen: Kongelige nordiske Oldskrift-Selskab, 1966.

Ellertsson, Björn. *Íslensk-þýsk orðabók.   Isländisch-Deutsch Wörterbuch.* Reykjavík: Iðunn, 1993.

Fry, Donald K. *Norse Sagas Translated into English: A Bibliography.* AMS Studies in the Middle Ages 3. New York: AMS Press, 1980.

Guðjónsson, Elsa E. *Bibliography of Icelandic Historical Textiles and Costumes.* Reykjavík: National Museum of Iceland, 1977.

Hannesson, Jóhann S. *Bibliography of the Eddas: A Supplement to Islandica XIII.* Islandica 37. Ithaca, N.Y.: Cornell UP, 1955.

_____. *The Sagas of Icelanders (Íslendinga sögur): A Supplement to Islandica I and XXIV.* Islandica 38. Ithaca, N.Y.: Cornell UP, 1957.

Hermannsson, Halldór. *A Bibliography of the Eddas.* Islandica 13. Ithaca, N.Y.: Cornell U Library, 1920.

_____. *Bibliography of the Icelandic Sagas and Minor Tales.* Islandica 1. Ithaca, N.Y.: Cornell U Library, 1908.

_____. *Bibliography of the Sagas of the Kings of Norway and Related Sagas and Tales.* Islandica 3. Ithaca, N.Y.: Cornell U Library, 1910.

_____. *Catalogue of the Icelandic Collection Bequeathed by Williard Fiske.* Ithaca, N.Y.: Cornell U Library, 1914.

_____. *Catalogue of the Icelandic Collection Bequeathed by Williard Fiske. Addition 1913–26.* Ithaca, N.Y.: Cornell U Library, 1927.

_____. *Catalogue of the Icelandic Collection Bequeathed by Williard Fiske. Addition 1927–42.* Ithaca, N.Y.: Cornell U Library, 1943.

_____. *Icelandic Books of the Seventeenth Century.* Islandica 14. Ithaca, N.Y.: Cornell U Library, 1922.

_____. *Icelandic Books of the Sixteenth Century.* Islandica 9. Ithaca, N.Y.: Cornell U Library, 1916.

_____. *Old Icelandic Literature: A Bibliographic Essay.* Islandica 23. Ithaca, N.Y.: Cornell UP, 1933.

_____. *The Periodical Literature of Iceland Down to the Year 1874: An Historical Sketch.* Islandica 11. Ithaca, N.Y.: Cornell U Library, 1918.

_____. *The Sagas of Icelanders (Íslendingasögur): A Supplement to Bibliography of the Icelandic Sagas and Minor Tales.* Islandica 24. Ithaca, N.Y.: Cornell UP, 1935.

Hollander, Lee Milton. *A Bibliography of Scaldic Studies.* Copenhagen: Ejnar Munksgaard, 1958.

Hólmarsson, Sverrir, Christopher Sanders, and John Tucker. *Concise Icelandic-English Dictionary.* Reykjavík: Iðunn, 1989.

Holthausen, Ferdinand. *Vergleichendes und etymologisches Wörterbuch des Altwestnordischen.* Göttingen: Vandenhoeck & Ruprecht, 1948.

Horton, John J. *Iceland.* World Bibliographic Series 37. Oxford: Clio P, 1983.

Íslensk bókaskrá/Icelandic National Bibliography. 1974– . Reykjavík: Landsbókasafn Íslands-Háskólabókasafn, 1975– .

Jóhannesson, Alexander. *Isländisches etymologisches Wörterbuch.* 2 vols. Bern: Francke, 1951–1956.

Kalinke, Marianne E. *Bibliography of Old-Icelandic Romances.* Islandica 44. Ithaca, N.Y.: Cornell UP, 1985.

Kvaran, Böðvar, and Einar Sigurðsson. *Íslensk tímarit í 200 ár/200 Years of Icelandic Periodicals: A Bibliography of Periodicals,*

Newspapers, and Other Serial Publications 1773–1973. Reykjavík: Landsbókasafn Íslands, 1991.

McBride, Francis R. *Iceland.* Rev. ed. World Bibliographic Series 37. Oxford: Clio P, 1996.

Mitchell, P.M., and Kenneth H. Ober. *Bibliography of Modern Icelandic Literature in Translation, including Works Written by Icelanders in Other Languages.* Islandica 40. Ithaca, N.Y.: Cornell UP, 1975.

Nordal, Jóhannes, and Valdimar Kristinsson, eds. *Iceland 1986: Handbook.* Reykjavík: Central Bank of Iceland, 1987.

_____. *Iceland. The Republic.* Reykjavík: Central Bank of Iceland, 1996.

Ober, Kenneth. *Bibliography of Modern Icelandic Literature in Translation (Supplement).* Islandica 47. Ithaca, N.Y.: Cornell UP, 1990.

Ófeigsson, Jón. *Þýzk-íslensk orðabók. Deutsch-isländisches Wörterbuch.* 3rd ed. Reykjavík: Ísafoldarprentsmiðja, 1982.

Pulsiano, Philip, ed. *Medieval Scandinavia. An Encyclopaedia.* New York: Garland, 1993.

Sigurðardóttir, Þórunn. *Manuscript Material, Correspondence, and Graphic Material in the Fiske Icelandic Collection. A Descriptive Catalogue.* Islandica 48. Ithaca, N.Y.: Cornell UP, 1994.

Sigurðsson, Arngrímur. *Icelandic-English Dictionary.* 3rd ed. Reykjavík: Prentsmiðjan Leiftur, 1980.

Sigurmundsson, Sigurður. *Spænsk-íslensk orðabók.* Reykjavík: Ísafold, 1976.

Sörensson, Sören. *Ensk-íslensk orðabók með alfræðilegu ívafi. (English-Icelandic Dictionary).* Reykjavík: Örn og Örlygur, 1984.

Turchi, Paolo Maria. *Íslensk-ítölsk orðabók—Dizionaria islandese-italiano.* Reykjavík: Iðunn, 1994.

Vries, Jan de. *Altnordisches etymologisches Wörterbuch.* Leiden: E.J. Brill, 1962.

_____. *Altnordische Literaturgeschichte.* 2nd ed. Berlin: Walter de Gruyter, 1964–67.

Zoëga, G. T. *A Concise Dictionary of Old Icelandic.* Oxford: Clarendon, 1910.

_____. *Ensk-íslenzk orðabók. English-Icelandic Dictionary.* 3rd ed. Reykjavík: Sigurður Kristjánsson, 1932.

_____. *Íslensk-ensk orðabók. Icelandic English Dictionary.* 2nd ed. Reykjavík: Sigurður Kristjánsson, 1922.

2. General Information and Interdisciplinary Studies

Biays, Pierre. *L'Islande. Que sais-je?* Paris: PUF, 1983.

Iceland Review (1963–). A quarterly magazine on Icelandic affairs.

News from Iceland. (1975–). A monthly periodical with highlights from Icelndic news.

Nordal, Jóhannes, and Valdimar Kristinsson, eds. *Iceland 1874–1974. Handbook Published by the Central Bank of Iceland on the Occasion of the Eleventh Centenary of the Settlement of Iceland.* Reykjavík: Central Bank of Iceland, 1975.

_____. *Iceland 1986.* Reykjavík: Central Bank of Iceland, 1987.

_____. *Iceland. The Republic.* Reykjavík: Central Bank of Iceland, 1996.

3. Guides and Yearbooks

Höfer, Hans. *Iceland.* Singapore: APA, 1992.

Kidson, Peter. *Iceland in a Nutshell. Complete Reference Guide.* 4th ed. Reykjavík: Örn og Örlygur, 1974.

4. Statistical Abstracts

Alþingiskosningar. Elections to the Althing. Reykjavík: Statistical Bureau of Iceland, 1991– .

Hagtölur án landamæra. Statistics Unlimited. CD-Rom. Reykjavík: Statistical Bureau of Iceland, 1992– .

Icelandic Agricultural Statistics 1994. Reykjavík: Icelandic Agricultural Information Service, 1994.

Icelandic Foreign Trade. Reykjavík: Statistical Bureau of Iceland, 1993.

Landshagir. Statistical Abstract of Iceland. Reykjavík: Statistical Bureau of Iceland, 1991– .

Mannfjöldaskýrslur árin 1971–80. Population and Vital Statistics 1971–1980. Reykjavík: Icelandic Statistical Bureau, 1988.

Neyslukönnun 1990. Household Expenditure Survey. Reykjavík: Icelandic Statistical Bureau, 1990.

Sveitarstjórnarkosningar. Local Elections. Reykjavík: Statistical Bureau of Iceland, 1990– .

Tölfræðihandbók 1984. Statistical Abstract of Iceland 1984. Reykjavík: Statistical Bureau of Iceland, 1984.

Verslurnarksýrslur. External Trade. Reykjavík: Statistical Bureau of Iceland, 1988– .

Vinnumarkaðskannanir 1991–1993. Labour Force Surveys 1991–1993. Reykjavík: Statistical Bureau of Iceland, 1991– .

Women and Men in Iceland 1994. Reykjavík: Statistical Bureau of Iceland, 1994.

5. Travel and Description

Auden, W.H., and Louis MacNeice. *Letters from Iceland.* New York: Random House, 1937.

Boucher, Alan. *The Iceland Traveller: A Hundred Years of Adventure.* Reykjavík: Iceland Review, 1989.

Bárðarson, Hjálmar R. *Ice and Fire. Contrasts of Icelandic Nature.* 4th ed. Reykjavík: Hjálmar R. Bárðarson, 1991.

Carwardine, Mark. *Iceland: Nature's Meeting Place: A Wildlife Guide.* Reykjavík: Iceland Review, 1986.

Collingwood, W.G., and Jón Stefánsson. *A Pilgrimage to the Saga-Steads of Iceland.* Ulverston: W. Holmes, 1899.

Escritt, Tony. *Iceland: The Traveller's Guide.* London: Iceland Information Centre, 1990.

Gaimard, Paul. *Voyage en Islande et au Groënland exécuté pendant les années 1835 et 1836 ....* 12 vols. Paris: A. Bertrand, 1838–52.

Hálfdanarson, Örlygur, and Steindór Steindórsson. *Iceland Road Guide.* 4th ed. Reykjavík: Örn og Örlygur, 1988.

Holland, Henry. *The Iceland Journal of Henry Holland 1810.* Edited by A. Wawn. London: Hakluyt Society, 1987.

Magnússon, Sigurður A. *The Icelanders.* Reykjavík: Forskot, 1990.

Ólafsson, Eggert. *Travels in Iceland by Eggert Ólafsson and Bjarni Pálsson: Performed 1752–1757 by Order of His Danish Majesty....* 2nd ed. Reykjavík: Örn og Örlygur, 1975.

Philpott, Don. *The Visitor's Guide to Iceland.* 2nd ed. Ashborne, Derbyshire: Moorland, 1989.

Wawn, Andrew. "John Thomas Stanley and Iceland: The Sense and Sensibility of an Eighteenth-Century Explorer." *Scandinavian Studies* 53 (1981): 52–76.

West, John F., ed. *The Journals of the Stanley Expedition to the Faroe Islands and Iceland in 1789.* 3 vols. Tórshavn: Føroya Fróðskaparfélag, 1970–76.

Williams, David. *Essential Iceland.* Basingstoke: AA Publishing, 1992.

_____. *Iceland: The Visitor's Guide.* London: Stacey, 1985.

II. CULTURE

1. *Art and Music*

The Arts in Iceland. A special issue of *Iceland Review* 1 (1988).

Augé, Marc. *Erró, Mythical Painter.* Paris: Lit du Vent, 1994.

Bergendal, Göran. *New Music in Iceland.* Reykjavík: Icelandic Music Information Center, 1991.

Bløndal, Torsten, et al., eds. *Northern Poles: Breakaways and Breakthroughs in Nordic Painting and Sculpture of the 1970's and 1980's.* Copenhagen: Bløndal, 1986.

Cowie, Peter. *Icelandic Films.* Reykjavík: Kvikmyndasjóður Íslands, 1995.

Eldjárn, Kristján. *Ancient Icelandic Art.* München: Hans Reich, 1957.

Freeman, Julian, ed. *Landscapes from a High Latitude. Icelandic Art 1909–1989.* London: Lund, Humphries, 1989.

Ingólfsson, Aðalsteinn, *Naive and Fantastic Art in Iceland.* Reykjavík: Iceland Review, 1989.

Ingólfsson, Aðalsteinn, and Matthías Johannessen. *Kjarval: A Painter of Iceland.* Reykjavík: Iceland Review, 1981.

Ingólfsson, Guðmundur. "Photography in Iceland: Two Pioneers." In *The Frozen Image: Scandinavian Photography*, 60–65. New York: Abbeville Press, 1982.

Kristjánsson, Gunnar. *Churches of Iceland. Religious Art and Architecture.* Reykjavík: Iceland Review, 1988.

Kvaran, Ólafur. "Einar Jonsson's Sculpture, Development of Form and Sphere of Meaning." Diss., U of Lund, 1987.

Magnússon, Sigurður A. *Iceland Crucible. A Modern Artistic Renaissance.* Reykjavík: Vaka, 1985.

Magnússon, Þór. *A Showcase of Icelandic National Treasures.* Reykjavík: Iceland Review, 1987.

Nordal, Bera, et al., eds. *Arts and Culture in Iceland: Theatre, Films and Ballet.* Reykjavík: Ministry of Culture and Education, 1990.

_____. *Arts and Culture in Iceland: The Visual Arts.* Reykjavík: Ministry of Culture and Education, 1990.

Schram, Hrafnhildur, and Halldór Laxness. *Nína Tryggvadóttir: Serenity and Power.* Reykjavík: Iceland Review, 1982.

Sigurbjörnsson, Þorkell. *Arts and Culture in Iceland: Music.* Reykjavík: Ministry of Culture and Education, 1990.

Varnedoe, Kirk. *Northern Light: Nordic Art at the Turn of the Century.* New Haven: Yale UP, 1988.

2. *Language and Literature*

a. Language

Árnason, Kristján. *Quantity in Historical Phonology: Iceland and Relating Cases.* Cambridge: Cambridge UP, 1980.

_____. *The Rhythms of Drottkvætt and other Old Icelandic Metres.* Reykjavík: Institute of Linguistics, U of Iceland, 1991.

Benediktsson, Hreinn. *Early Icelandic Scripts as Illustrated in Vernacular Texts from the Twelfth and Thirteenth Centuries.* Íslenzk handrit 2. Reykjavík: Handritastofnun Íslands, 1965.

_____. "Icelandic Dialectology: Methods and Results." *Lingua Islandica* 3 (1961–62): 72–112.

_____. "The Vowel System of Icelandic: A Survey of its History." *Word* 15 (1959): 282–312.

Benediktsson, Hreinn, ed. *The First Grammatical Treatise.* University of Iceland Publications in Linguistics 1. Reykjavík: Institute of Nordic Linguistics, 1972.

Buckhurst, H. M. *Elementary Grammar of Old Icelandic.* London: Methuen, 1925.

Einarsson, Stefán. *Icelandic Grammar, Texts, Glossary.* 2nd ed. Baltimore, Md.: Johns Hopkins UP, 1949.

Friðjónsson, Jón. *A Course in Modern Icelandic. 1–2: Texts, Vocabulary, Grammar, Exercises, Translations.* Reykjavík: Skák, 1978.

Gordon, E.V. *An Introduction to Old Norse.* 2nd ed. Oxford: Oxford UP, 1957.

Groenke, Ulrich. "On Standard, Substandard, and Slang in Icelandic." *Scandinavian Studies* 38 (1966): 217–230.

Halldórsson, Halldór. "Icelandic Purism and its History." *Word* 30 (1979): 76–86.

_____. *Old Icelandic Heiti in Modern Icelandic.* University of Iceland Publications in Linguistics 3. Reykjavík: Institute of Nordic Linguistics, 1975.

Hermannsson, Halldór. *Modern Icelandic: An Essay.* Islandica 12. Ithaca, N.Y.: Cornell U Library, 1919.

Heusler, Andreas. *Altisländisches Elementarbuch.* 7th ed. Heidelberg: C. Winter, 1967.

Jónsson, Jón Hilmar. *Das Partizip Perfekt der schwachen ja-Verben. Die Flexionsentwicklung im Isländischen.* Monographien zur Sprachwissenschaft 6. Heidelberg: Carl Winter, 1976.

Kelly, Joseph, and Helga Kress. *Icelandic Phonetics and Pronunciation.* Reykjavík: Faculty of Arts, U of Iceland, 1972.

Kress, Bruno. *Isländische Grammatik.* Leipzig: Verlag Enzyklopädie, 1982.

Kristinsson, Ari P. *The Pronounciation of Modern Icelandic: A Brief Course for Foreign Students.* 3rd ed. Reykjavík: Institute of Linguistics, U of Iceland, 1988.

Maling, Joan, and Annie Zaenen, eds. *Modern Icelandic Syntax.* Syntax and Semantics 24. San Diego: Academic Press, 1990.

Oresnik, Janez. *Studies in the Phonology and Morphology of Modern Icelandic.* Hamburg: Buske, 1985.

Ottósson, Kjartan G. "The Icelandic Middle Voice: The Morphological and Phonological Development." Diss., U of Lund, 1992.

Pálsson, Gísli. "Language and Society: The Ethnolinguistics of Icelanders." In *The Anthropology of Iceland,* edited by E. Paul Durrenberger and Gísli Pálsson, 121–139. Iowa City: U of Iowa P, 1989.

Pétursson, Magnús. *Isländisch: eine Übersicht über die moderne isländische Sprache mit einem kurzen Abriss der Geschichte und Literatur Islands.* Hamburg: Buske, 1978.

Sigurðsson, Halldór Ármann. "Verbal Syntax and Case in Icelandic." Diss., U of Lund, 1989.

Thomson, Colin D. *Íslensk Beygingafrœði. Isländische Formenlehre. Icelandic Inflections.* Hamburg: Buske, 1987.

Þráinsson, Höskuldur. *On Complementation in Icelandic.* Outstanding Dissertations in Linguistics 23. New York: Garland, 1979.

b. Literature

Anderson, Theodore M. *The Icelandic Family Saga: An Analytic Reading.* Harvard Studies in Comparative Literature 28. Cambridge, Mass.: Harvard UP, 1967.

_____. *The Problem of Icelandic Saga Origins: A Historical Survey.* Yale Germanic Studies 1. New Haven, Conn.: Yale UP, 1964.

_____, and W. I. Miller, eds. *Law and Literature in Medieval Iceland: Ljósvetninga Saga and Valla-Ljóts Saga.* Stanford, Calif.: Stanford UP, 1989.

Árnason, Vilhjálmur. "Morality and Social Structure in the Icelandic Sagas." *Journal of English and Germanic Philology* 90 (1991): 157–174.

Baetke, Walter. *Die Isländersaga.* Wege der Forschung 15. Darmstadt: Wissenschaftliche Buchgesellschaft, 1974.

_____. *Über die Entstehung der Isländersagas.* Berlin: Akademie-Verlag, 1956.

Beck, Richard. *History of Icelandic Poets 1800–1940.* Islandica 34. Ithaca, N.Y.: Cornell UP, 1950.

_____. *Icelandic Poems and Stories: Translations from Modern Icelandic Literature.* Princeton, N.J.: Princeton UP, 1943.

_____. *Jón Þorláksson. Icelandic Translator of Pope and Milton.* Studia Islandica 16. Reykjavík: Bókaútgáfa Menningarsjóðs, 1957.

Benediktsson, Einar. *Harp of the North: Poems.* Charlottesville, Va.: U of Virginia P, 1955.

Benediktsson, Jakob. *Arngrímur Jónsson and His Works.* Biblioteca Arnamagnæana 12. Copenhagen: The Arnemagneana Institute, 1957.

Benedikz, Eiríkur, ed. *An Anthology of Icelandic Poetry.* Reykjavík: The Icelandic Ministry of Education, 1969.

Bjarnason, Loftur. *An Anthology of Modern Icelandic Literature 1800–1950.* 2 vols. Berkeley, Calif.: U Extension, U of California, 1961.

Boucher, Alan, ed. *Icelandic Poems of Today: From Twenty Five Modern Icelandic Poets.* Reykjavík: Iceland Review, 1971.

Boyer, Régis. *Les sagas islandaises.* Paris: Payot, 1978.

Bragason, Úlfar. "On the Poetics of Sturlunga." Diss., U of California, Berkeley, 1986.

Carleton, Peter. "Tradition and Innovation in Twentieth-Century Icelandic Poetry." Diss., U of California, 1967.

Ciklamini, Marlene. *Snorri Sturluson.* Boston: Twayne, 1978.

Clover, Carol J. *The Medieval Saga*, Ithaca, N.Y.: Cornell UP, 1982.

Clover, Carol J., and John Lindow. *Old Norse-Icelandic Literature: A Critical Guide.* Islandica 45. Ithaca, N.Y.: Cornell UP, 1985.

Clunies Ross, Margaret. *Skáldskaparmál: Snorri Sturluson's Ars Poetica and Medieval Theories of Language.* Odense: Odense UP, 1987.

Craigie, W. A.. *The Art of Poetry in Iceland.* Oxford: Clarendon, 1937.

_____. *The Icelandic Sagas.* Cambridge: Cambridge UP, 1913.

Dronke, Ursula, ed. *Speculum norroenum: Norse Studies in Memory of Gabriel Turville-Petre.* Odense: Odense UP, 1981.

Einarsson, Stefán. *A History of Icelandic Literature.* Baltimore, Md.: Johns Hopkins UP, 1957

_____. *History of Icelandic Prose Writers 1800–1940.* Islandica 32–33. Ithaca, N.Y.: Cornell UP, 1948.

Eiríksson, Hallfreður Örn. "On Icelandic Rímur." *Arv, Scandinavian Yearbook of Folklore* 31 (1975): 139–150.

Eyrbyggja saga. Translated by Paul Schach. Introduction and verse translated by Lee M. Hollander. Lincoln, Nebr.: U of Nebraska P, 1959.

Frank, Roberta. *Old Norse Court Poetry: The Dróttkvætt Stanza.* Islandica 42. Ithaca, N.Y.: Cornell UP, 1978.

Gade, Kari Ellen. *The Structure of Old Norse Dróttkvætt Poetry.* Islandica 49. Ithaca, N.Y.: Cornell UP, 1995.

Glauser, Jürg. *Isländische Märchensagas. Studien zur Þorsaliteratur im spätmittelalterlichen Island.* Basel: Helbing & Lichtenhahn, 1983.

Hafstað, Baldur. *Die Egils Saga und ihr Verhältnis zu anderen Werken nordischen Mittelalters.* Reykjavík: The Research Institute, University College of Education, 1995.

Hallberg, Peter. *Halldór Laxness.* New York: Twayne, 1971.

_____. *The Icelandic Saga.* Translated by Paul Schach. Lincoln, Nebr.: U of Nebraska P, 1962.

_____. *Old Icelandic Poetry: Eddic Lay and Skaldic Verse.* Translated by Paul Schach and Sonja Lindgrenson. Lincoln, Nebr.: U of Nebraska P, 1975.

Hallmundsson, Hallberg, ed. *An Anthology of Scandinavian Literature. From the Viking Period to the Twentieth Century.* New York: Collier, 1965.

Hermannsson, Halldór. *Icelandic Authors of To-day.* Islandica 6. Ithaca, N.Y.: Cornell U Library, 1913.

Hollander, Lee Milton. *Old Norse Poems: The Most Important Non-Skaldic Verse not Included in the Poetic Edda.* New York: Columbia UP, 1936.

_____. *The Skalds. A Selection of Their Poems.* Ann Arbor, Mich.: U of Michigan P, 1968.

Kalinke, Marianne E. *Bridal-Quest Romance in Medieval Iceland.* Islandica 46. Ithaca, N.Y.: Cornell UP, 1990.

Keel, Aldo. *Innovation und Restauration. Der Romancier Halldór Laxness seit dem Zweiten Weltkrieg.* Basel: Helbing & Lichtenhahn, 1981.

Ker, W. P. *Epic and Romance.* New York: Dover, 1957.

Kirby, Ian J. *Bible Translations in Old Norse.* Geneva: Librairie Droz, 1986.

Koht, Halvdan. *The Old Norse Sagas.* London: George Allen & Unwin, 1931.

Kötz, Günter. *Das Problem Dichter und Gesellschaft im Werke von Halldór Kiljan Laxness: Ein Beitrag zur modernen isländischen Literatur.* Giessen: W. Schmitz, 1966.

Kress, Helga. "'You Will Find it all Rather Monotonous': On Literary Tradition and the Feminine Experience in Laxdæla Saga." In *The Nordic Mind: Current Trends in Scandinavian Literary Criticism,* edited by F. E. Andersen, and J. Weinstock, 181–196. Lanham, Md.: UP of America, 1986.

Kristjánsson, Jónas. *Eddas and Sagas: Iceland's Medieval Literature.* 2nd ed. Reykjavík: Icelandic Literary Society, 1992.

_____. *Iceland and Its Manuscripts.* Reykjavík: Stofnun Árna Magnússonar, 1989.

_____. *Icelandic Manuscripts: Sagas, History and Art.* Reykjavík: Icelandic Literary Society, 1993.

Laxness, Halldór. *The Atomstation.* Sag Harbor, N.Y.: Second Chance, 1982.

_____. *La cloche d'Islande: roman.* Paris: Flammarion, 1991.

_____. *The Fish Can Sing.* New York: Thomas Y. Crowell, 1967.

_____. *The Happy Warriors.* London: Methuen, 1958.

_____. *Independent People.* New York: Knopf, 1946.

_____. *Salka Valka.* New York: Houghton, 1936.

_____. *Under the Glacier.* Reykjavík: Vaka-Helgafell, 1990.

_____. *World Light.* Madison, Wis.: U of Wisconsin P, 1969.

Liestøl, Knut. *The Origin of the Icelandic Family Sagas.* Cambridge, Mass.: Harvard UP, 1930.

Lindow, John, Lars Lönnroth, and Gert Wolfgang Weber. *Structure and Meaning in Old Norse Literature: New Approaches to Textual Analysis and Literary Criticism.* Odense: Odense UP, 1986.

Littérature d'Islande. Paris: Europe, 1983.

Lönnroth, Lars. *Njáls Saga: A Critical Introduction.* Berkeley, Calif.: U of California P, 1976.

Loth, Agnete, ed. *Late Medieval Icelandic Romances.* Editiones Arnamagnæanæ. Series B, 20–24. 5 vols. Copenhagen, 1962–65.

Magnússon, Sigurður A. *The Postwar Poetry of Iceland.* Iowa City: U of Iowa P, 1982.

_____. "The World of Halldor Laxness." *World Literature Today* 66 (1992): 457–63.

Magnússon, Sigurður A., ed., *Icelandic Writing Today.* Reykjavík: Ministry of Education, 1982.

Manuscripta Islandica. Edited by Jón Helgason. Copenhagen: Munksgaard, 1954– .

McTurk, Rory, and Andrew Wawn, eds. *Úr Dölum til Dala: Guðbrandur Vigfússon Centenary Essays.* Leeds: Leeds Studies in English, 1989.

Modern Nordic Plays: Iceland. Oslo: Universitetsforlaget, 1973.

Njals Saga. Translated with introduction and notes by Carl F. Beyerschmidt and Lee M. Hollander. New York: American-Scandinavian Foundation, 1955.

Nordal, Sigurður. *The Historical Element in the Icelandic Family Sagas.* Glasgow: Jackson, 1957.

Ober, Kenneth H. "Modern Icelandic Literature Abroad since 1970." *Scandinavia* 27 (1988): 167–173.

Ólason, Vésteinn. *The Traditional Ballads of Iceland. Historical Studies.* Reykjavík: Stofnun Árna Magnússonar, 1982.

Pétursson, Ásgeir, and Steingrímur J. Þorsteinsson, eds. *Seven Icelandic Short Stories.* 2nd ed. New York: American Scandinavian Foundation, 1961.

The Poetic Edda. 2nd ed. Translated with an introduction and notes by Lee M. Hollander. Austin, Tex.: U of Texas P, 1986.

Poole, Russel G. *Viking Poems on War and Peace: A Study in Skaldic Narrative.* Toronto Medieval Texts and Translations 8. Toronto: U of Toronto P, 1991.

The Saga of the Jómsvíkings. Translated with introduction and notes by Lee M. Hollander. Austin, Tex.: U of Texas P, 1989.

The Saga of Þorgils and Hafliði. Edited with introduction and notes by Halldór Hermannsson. Islandica 31. Ithaca, N.Y.: Cornell UP, 1945.

Sagas islandaises. Translated by Régis Boyer. Bibliothèque de la Pléiade. Paris: Gallimard, 1987.

The Sagas of Kormák. Translated with introduction and notes by Lee M. Hollander. Princeton, N.J.: Princeton UP, 1949.

Scach, Paul. *Icelandic Sagas.* Twayne World Authors Series 717. Boston: Twayne, 1984.

Schier, Kurt. *Sagaliteratur.* Stuttgart: J.B. Metzler, 1970.

_____, ed. *Märchen aus Island.* 2nd ed. Köln: Diederichs, 1987.

See, Klaus von. *Edda, Saga, Skaldendichtung: Aufsätze zur skandinavischen Literatur des Mittelalters.* Skandinavistische Arbeiten 6. Heidelberg: Winter, 1981.

_____. *Skaldendichtung: Eine Einführung.* Munich: Artemis, 1980.

Senner, W. M. *The Reception of German Literature in Iceland.* Amsterdamer Publikationen zur Sprache und Literature 62. Amsterdam: Rodopi, 1985.

Sigurjónsson, Árni, et al., eds. *Arts and Culture in Iceland: Literature.* Reykjavík: Ministry of Culture and Education, 1989.

The Skalds: A Selection of Their Poems. Translated with introduction and notes by Lee M. Hollander. Ann Arbor, Mich.: U of Michigan P, 1968.

Sørenson, Preben Meulengracht. *The Unmanly Man: Concepts of Sexual Defamation in Early Northern Society.* Odense: Odense UP, 1983.

Stephansson, Stephan G. *Selected Translations from Andvökur.* Edmonton: Stephan G. Stephansson Homestead Restoration Committee, 1982.

Sturluson, Snorri. *L'Edda. Récits de mythologie nordique.* Translated by François Xavier-Dillmann. Paris: Gallimard, 1991.

_____. *The Prose Edda of Snorri Sturluson: Tales from Norse Mythology.* Introduction by Sigurður Nordal, selected and translated by Jean I. Young. Berkeley, Calif.: U of California P, 1964.

Sveinsson, Einar Ólafur. *Dating the Icelandic Sagas: An Essay in Method.* Viking Society for Northern Research. Text series 3. London: Viking Society, 1958.

_____. *Studies in the Manuscript Tradition of Njálssaga.* Studia Islandica 13. Reykjavík: Leiftur, 1953.

Thompson, Lawrence S., ed. *Eddukvæði. Norse Mythology: The Elder*

Edda in Prose Translation. Translated by Guðbrandur Vigfús-son and F. York Powell. Hamden, Conn.: Archon, 1974.

Tucker, John, ed. *Sagas of the Icelanders: A Book of Essays.* New York: Garland, 1989.

Tulinius, Torfi H. *La "Matière du Nord": Sagas légendaires et fiction dans la littérature islandaise en prose du XIIIe siècle.* Paris: Presses de l'Université de Paris-Sorbonne, 1995.

Turville-Petre, G. *Nine Norse Studies.* Viking Society for Northern Research. Text series 5. London: Viking Society, 1972.

_____. *Origins of Icelandic Literature.* Oxford: Oxford UP, 1953.

_____. *Scaldic Poetry.* Oxford: Oxford UP, 1978.

The Vinland Sagas. Edited with an introduction, variants, and notes by Halldór Hermannsson. Islandica 30. Ithaca, N.Y.: Cornell UP, 1944.

Whaley, Diana. *Heimskringla. An Introduction.* Viking Society for Northern Research. Text series 8. London: Viking Society, 1991.

Weinstock, John M., ed. *Saga og språk: Studies in Language and Literature.* Austin, Tex.: Jenkins, 1972.

Þórðarson, Þórbergur. *In Search for My Beloved.* New York: Twayne, 1967.

III. ECONOMY

Árnason, Ragnar. "Efficient Harvesting of Fish Stocks: The Case of the Icelandic Demersal Fisheries." Diss., U of British Columbia, 1984.

_____. *The Icelandic Fisheries: Evolution and Management of a Fishing Industry.* Oxford: Fishing News, 1995.

Blöndal, Gísli. "The Development of Public Expenditure in Relation to National Income in Iceland." Diss., London School of Economics, 1965.

Blöndal, Sveinbjörn. "Export Supply Shocks, Credit, and Macroeconomic Policy in a Small Open Economy: Iceland 1960–1980." Diss., Cambridge U, 1986.

Davis, Morris. *Iceland Extends its Fisheries Limits. A Political Analysis.* Oslo: Universitetsforlaget, 1963.

Economic Statistics Quarterly (Reykjavík: Central Bank of Iceland, 1980–).

The Economy of Iceland, May 1994. Reykjavík: Central Bank of Iceland, 1994

Einarsson, Tór. "A Supply Shock Model of a Small Open Economy Incorporating Rational Expectations, and Its Application to Iceland in the 1970s." Diss., U of Essex, 1984.

Einarsson, Tór, and Guðmundur Magnússon. *A Study in "the" Icelandic Business Cycle.* Iceland Economic Papers 2. Reykjavík: U of Iceland, 1987.

Energy Resources and Dams in Iceland. Reykjavík: Icelandic National Committee on Large Dams, 1989.

Guðmundsson, Magni. "The Danish Monopolies Legislation." Diss., U of Manitoba, 1977.

Gunnarsson, Guðmundur Örn. *The Economic Growth in Iceland 1910–1980. A Productivity Study.* Studia Oeconomica Uppsaliensia, 17. Uppsala: Almquist & Wiksell, 1990.

Gunnarsson, Gunnar Ágúst. "Industrial Policy in Iceland 1944–1974. Political Conflicts and Sectoral Interests." Diss., U of London, 1989.

Hannibalsson, Ingjaldur. "Optimal Allocation of Boats to Factories During the Capelin Fishing Season in Iceland." Diss., Ohio State U, 1979.

Iceland. OECD Economic Surveys 1991/1992. Paris: OECD, 1992.

The Icelandic Economy. Developments and Outlook. Reykjavík: National Economic Institute, 1991– . Annual.

Jónsson, Sigfús. *The Development of the Icelandic Fishing Industry 1900–1940.* Reykjavík: Economic Development Institute, 1981.

Mer, Jacques. *L'Islande: Une ouverture obligée mais prudente.* Paris: Documentation française, 1994.

Möller, Alda, ed. *Fifty Years of Fisheries Research in Iceland.* Reykjavík: Icelandic Fisheries Laboratories, 1985.

The National Economy. Developments 1974– . Reykjavík: National Economic Institute, 1975–1990.

Stefánsson, Sigurður B. "Inflation and Economic Policy in a Small Open Economy: Iceland in the Postwar Period." Diss., U of Essex, 1981.

Trade Policy Review. The Republic of Iceland. Geneva: GATT, 1994.

IV. HISTORY

1. General

Björnsson, Árni. *High Days and Holidays in Iceland.* Reykjavík: Mál og menning, 1995.

Gjerset, Knut. *History of Iceland.* New York: Macmillan, 1924.

Hitzler, Egon. *Sel. Untersuchungen zur Geschichte des isländischen Sennwesens seit der Landnahmezeit.* Oslo: Universitetsforlaget, 1979.

Hood, John C. F. *Icelandic Church Saga.* London: Society for Promoting Christian Knowledge, 1946.

Magnusson, Magnus. *Iceland Saga.* London: Bodley Head, 1987.

Magnússon, Sigurður A. *The Northern Sphinx: Iceland and the Icelanders from the Settlement to the Present.* 2nd ed. London: C. Hurst, 1984.

Rosenblad, Esbjörn, and R. Sigurðardóttir-Rosenblad. *Iceland from Past to Present.* Reykjavík: Mál og menning, 1993.

Tomasson, R. *Iceland: The First New Society.* Minneapolis, Minn.: U of Minnesota P, 1980.

Þórarinsson, Sigurður. *The Thousand Years Struggle Against Ice and Fire.* Reykjavík: Museum of Natural History, 1956.

Þorsteinsson, Björn. *Thingvellir. Iceland's National Shrine.* Reykjavík: Örn og Örlygur, 1987.

2. Archaeology and Prehistory

Einarsson, Bjarni F. "The Settlement of Iceland: Granastaðir and the Ecological Heritage." Diss., Gothenburg U, 1994.

Friðriksson, Adolf. *Sagas and Popular Antiquarianism in Icelandic Archaeology.* Aldershot: Avebury, 1994.

Guðmundsson, Barði. *The Origin of the Icelanders.* Lincoln, Nebr.: U of Nebraska P, 1967.

Nordahl, Elsa. *Reykjavík from the Archaeological Point of View.* Uppsala: Societas Archeologica Upsaliensis, 1988.

Sveinbjarnardóttir, Guðrún. *Farm Abandonment in Medieval and Postmedieval Iceland: An Interdisciplinary Study.* Oxford: Oxbow Books, 1992.

Þórarinsson, Sigurður. "Tephrochronology and Medieval Iceland." In *Scientific Methods in Medieval Archeology,* edited by Rainer Beger, 295–328. Berkeley, Calif.: U of California Press, 1970.

3. Settlement and Commonwealth Period

Aðalsteinsson, Jón Hnefill. *Under the Cloak: The Acceptance of Christianity in Iceland with Particular Reference to the Religious Attitudes Prevailing at the Time.* Studia Ethnologica Uppsaliensia 4. Stockholm: Almquist and Wiksell, 1978.

Bagge, Sverre. *Society and Politics in Snorri Sturluson's Heimskringla.* Berkeley, Calif.: U of California P, 1991.

Book of Settlements: Landnámabók. University of Manitoba Icelandic

Studies 1. Translated by Hermann Pálsson and Paul Edwards. Winnipeg: U of Manitoba P, 1972.

Byock, Jesse L. *Feud in the Icelandic Saga.* Berkeley, Calif.: U of California P, 1982.

_____. *Medieval Iceland: Society, Sagas, and Power.* Berkeley, Calif.: U of California P, 1988.

Cormack, Margaret Jean. *The Saints in Iceland: Their Veneration from the Conversion to 1400.* Subsidia hagiographia 78. Brussels: Société des Bollandistes, 1994.

Faulkner, Anthony, and Richard Perkins, eds. *Viking Revaluations. Viking Society Centenary Symposium 14–15 May 1992.* London: U College, 1993.

Foote, Peter, and David M. Wilson. *The Viking Achievement: The Society and Culture of Early Medieval Scandinavia.* London: Sidgwick & Jackson, 1970.

Gelsinger, B. E. *Icelandic Enterprise: Commerce and Economy in the Middle Ages.* Columbia, S.C.: U of South Carolina P, 1981.

Hastrup, Kirsten. *Culture and History in Medieval Iceland: An Anthropological Analysis of Structure and Change.* Oxford: Clarendon, 1985.

Hermannsson, Halldór. *The Problem of Wineland.* Islandica 26. Ithaca, N.Y.: Cornell UP, 1936.

Jochens, Jenny M. *Old Norse Images of Women.* Philadelphia: U of Pennsylvania Press, 1996.

_____. *Women in Old Norse Society.* Ithaca, N.Y.: Cornell UP, 1995.

Jóhannesson, Jón. *Íslendinga Saga: A History of the Old Icelandic Commonwealth.* Winnipeg: U of Manitoba P, 1974.

Karlsson, Gunnar. "Goðar and Höfðingjar in Medieval Iceland." *Saga Book of the Viking Society of Northern Research* 19 (1977): 358–370.

Kuhn, Hans. *Das alte Island.* Jena: Diederichs, 1971.

Miller, William Ian. *Bloodtaking and Peacemaking: Feud, Law, and Society in Saga Iceland.* Chicago: U of Chicago P, 1990.

_____. *Humiliation: and Other Essays on Honor, Social Discomfort, and Violence.* Ithaca, N.Y.: Cornell UP, 1993.

Morris, Katherine. *Sorceress or Witch? The Image of Gender in Medieval Iceland and Northern Europe.* Lanham, Md.: UP of America, 1991.

Njarðvík, Njörður P. *Birth of a Nation: The Story of the Icelandic Commonwealth.* 2nd ed. Reykjavík: Iceland Review, 1985.

Nordal, Guðrún. "Ethics and Action in Thirteenth Century Iceland. An Examination of Motivation and Social Obligation in Iceland c. 1183–1284, as Represented in Sturlunga Saga." Diss., Oxford U, 1988.

Nordal, Sigurður. *Icelandic Culture.* Ithaca, N.Y.: Cornell UP, 1990.

Pálsson, Gísli, ed. *From Sagas to Society: Comparative Approaches to Early Iceland.* Endfield Lock: Hisarlik, 1992.

Storek, Martha H. "Women in the Time of the Icelandic Family Saga." Diss., Bryn Mawr, 1946.

Sveinsson, Einar Ólafur. *The Age of the Sturlungs: Icelandic Civilization in the Thirteenth Century.* Islandica 36. Ithaca, N.Y.: Cornell UP, 1953.

Sölvason, Birgir T. R. "Ordered Anarchy, State, and Rent-Seeking: The Icelandic Commonwealth, 930–1262." Diss., George Mason U, 1991.

Þorgilsson, Ari. *The Book of Icelanders (Íslendingabók).* Translated with an introductory essay by Halldór Hermannsson. Islandica 20. Ithaca, N.Y.: Cornell U Library, 1930.

4. Late Medieval and Early Modern Period

Bjarnar, Vilhjálmur. "The Laki Eruption and the Famine of the Mist." In *Scandinavian Studies: Essays Presented to Henry Goddard*

Leach, edited by C. F. Bayersmith and E. J. Fries, 410–421. Seattle: U of Washington P, 1965.

Gunnarsson, Gísli. *Fertility and Nuptiality in Iceland's Demographic History.* Meddelande från Ekonomisk-historiska institutionen, Lunds Universitet, 12. Lund: Ekonomisk-historiska institutionen, 1980.

———. *Monopoly Trade and Economic Stagnation. Studies in the Foreign Trade of Iceland 1602–1787.* Lund: Ekonomisk-historiska föreningen, 1983.

———. *The Sex Ratio, the Infant Mortality and the Adjoining Societal Response in Pretransitional Iceland.* Meddelande från Ekonomisk-historiska institutionen, Lunds Universitet, 32. Lund: Ekonomisk-historiska institutionen, 1983.

Gustafsson, Harald. *Political Integration in the Old Regime. Central Power and Local Society in the Eighteenth-Century Nordic States.* Lund: Studentliteratur, 1994.

Hastrup, Kirsten. *Nature and Policy in Iceland 1400–1800: An Anthropology of History and Mentality.* Oxford: Clarendon, 1990.

Lárusson, Björn. *The Old Icelandic Land Registers.* Lund: Gleerup, 1967.

Wawn, Andrew. *The Anglo Man. Þorleifur Repp, Philology and Nineteenth-Century Britain.* Studia Islandica 49. Reykjavík: Menningarsjóður, 1991.

5. Nineteenth Century

Agnarsdóttir, Anna. "Great Britain and Iceland 1800–1820." Diss., London School of Economics, 1989.

Gunnlaugsson, Gísli Ágúst. *Family and Household in Iceland 1801– 1930. Studies in the Relationship Between Demographic and Socio-Economic Development, Social Legislation and Family and Household Structures.* Uppsala: Acta Universitatis Upsaliensis, 1988.

Hálfdanarson, Guðmundur. "Old Provinces, Modern Nations: Political Responses to State-Integration in Late Nineteenth and Early

Twentieth-Century Iceland and Brittany." Diss., Cornell U, 1991.

Kjartansson, Helgi Skúli. "Icelandic Emigration." In *European Expansion and Migration: Essays on the Intercontinental Migration from Africa, Asia, and Europe*, edited by P. C. Emmer and M. Mörner, 105–119. New York: St. Martin's, 1992.

Kristinsson, Júníus. *Vesturfaraskrá 1870–1914: A Record of Emigrants from Iceland to America 1870–1914.* Reykjavík: Institute of History, U of Iceland, 1983.

Óskarsdóttir, Þórkatla. "Ideas of Nationality in Icelandic Poetry 1830–1874." Diss., U of Edinburgh, 1982.

Sigurðsson, Ingi. "The Historical Works of Jón Espolín and His Contemporaries." Diss., U of Edinburgh, 1972.

6. Twentieth Century

Bittner, Donald F. *The Lion and the White Falcon: Britain and Iceland in the World War II Era.* Hamden, Conn.: Archon, 1983.

Corgan, Michael T. "Icelandic Security Policy: 1979–1986." Diss., Boston U, 1991.

Friðriksson, Þorleifur. "The Golden Fly: The Scandinavian Social Democracy's Relations to the Icelandic Labour Movement in 1916–1956: Internationalism or Intervention?" Diss., Lund U, 1990.

Gíslason, Gylfi Þ. *The Challenge of Being an Icelander.* 2nd ed. Reykjavík: Almenna bókafélagið, 1990.

Gröndal, Benedikt. *Iceland. From Neutrality to NATO Membership.* Oslo: Universitetsforlaget, 1971.

Gunnlaugsson, Gísli Ágúst. "The Historiography on Iceland in the Second World War." In *Neue Forschungen zum Zweiten Weltkrieg: Literaturberichte und Bibliographien aus 67 Ländern,* edited by J. Rohwer, and H. Müller, 210–214. Koblenz: Bernard & Graefe, 1990.

Harðarson, Sólrún B. Jensdóttir. *Anglo-Icelandic Relations during the First World War.* Outstanding Thesis from the London School of Economics and Political Science. New York: Garland, 1986.

Hart, Jeffrey A. *The Anglo-Icelandic Cod War of 1972–1973. A Case Study of a Fishery Dispute.* Research Series no. 29. Institute of International Studies. Berkeley, Calif.: U of California P, 1976.

Hunt, John Joseph. "The United States Occupation of Iceland 1941–1945." Diss., Georgetown U, 1966.

Jónsson, Guðmundur. "The State and the Icelandic Economy, 1870–1930." Diss., London School of Economics and Political Science, 1991.

Jónsson, Hannes. *Friends in Conflict: The Anglo-Icelandic Cod Wars and the Law of the Sea.* Hamden, Conn.: Archon Books, 1982.

Magnússon, Magnús S. *Iceland in Transition. Labour and Socio-Economic Change before 1940.* Lund: Lunds Ekonomisk-historiska föreningen, 1985.

Schuler, Martin. *Búsetuþróun á Íslandi 1880–1990/Settlement History of Iceland 1880–1990.* Reykjavík: Statistical Bureau of Iceland, 1994.

Valdimarsdóttir, Laufey. *A Brief History of the Woman Suffrage Movement in Iceland.* London: International Alliance of Women for Suffrage and Equal Citizenship, 1929.

Whitehead, Þór. "Iceland and the Second World War 1939–45." Diss., Oxford U, 1978.

Þór, Jón Þ. *British Trawlers in Icelandic Waters: History of British Steam Trawling off Iceland 1889–1916 and the Anglo-Icelandic Fisheries Dispute 1896–1897.* Reykjavík: Fjölvi, 1992.

V. LAW

Benediktsson, Jakob, ed. *Skarðsbók, Jónsbók and other Laws and Precepts: Ms. no. 350 fol. in the Arna-Magnæan Collection in the*

University Library of Copenhagen. Corpus codicum islandi-corum medii aevi 16. Copenhagen: E. Munksgaard, 1943.

Fisheries Jurisdiction in Iceland. Reykjavík: Ministry of Foreign Affairs, 1972.

Hermannsson, Halldór. *The Ancient Laws for Norway and Iceland.* Islandica 4. Ithaca, N.Y.: Cornell U Library, 1911.

Jónsson, Hannes, ed. *The Evolving Limit of Coastal Jurisdiction.* Reykjavík: Government of Iceland, 1974.

Laws of Early Iceland. Grágás 1. Translated by Andrew Dennis, Peter Foote, and Richard Perkins. U of Manitoba Icelandic Studies 3. Winnipeg: U of Manitoba P, 1980.

See, Klaus von. *Altnordische Rechtswörter: Philologische Studien zur Rechtsauffassung und Rechtsgesinnung der Germanen.* Tübingen: Niemeyer, 1964

Þórðarson, Gunnlaugur. *Les eaux terretoriale d'Island en ce qui concerne la pêche.* Reykjavík: Hlaðbúð, 1958.

VI. POLITICS

1. Domestic

Davis, Morris. *Iceland Extends its Fisheries Limits: A Political Analysis.* Oslo: Universitetsforlaget, 1963.

Grímsson, Ólafur Ragnar. *The Icelandic Multilevel Coalition System.* Reykjavík: U of Iceland, 1977.

Harðarson, Ólafur Þ. *Parties and Voters in Iceland: A Study of the 1983 and 1987 Althingi Elections.* Reykjavík: Social Science Research Institute, U of Iceland, 1995.

Kristinsson, Gunnar Helgi. *Farmers' Parties: A Study in Electoral Adaptation.* Reykjavík: Social Science Research Institute, U of Iceland, 1991.

Kristjánsson, Svanur. "Conflict and Consensus in Icelandic Politics 1916–1944." Diss., U of Illinois, 1977.

_____. *Corporatism in Iceland?* Reykjavík: Social Science Research Institute, U of Iceland, 1979.

Magnússon, Þorsteinn. "The Icelandic Althingi and Its Standing Committees." Diss., U of Exeter, 1987.

2. *Foreign Relations*

Fairlamb, John Robin. "The Evolution of Icelandic Defense Decision Making 1944–1981." Diss., U of South Carolina, 1981.

Gunnarsson, Gunnar. *The Keflavík Base: Plans and Projects.* Occasional Papers 3. Reykjavík: Icelandic Commission on Security and International Affairs, 1986.

Ívarsson, Jóhann Viðar. *Science, Sanctions and Cetaceans: Iceland and the Whaling Issue.* Reykjavík: Center for International Studies, U of Iceland, 1994.

Jónsson, Albert. *Iceland, NATO and the Keflavík Base.* Reykjavík: Icelandic Commission on Security and International Affairs, 1989.

Jónsson, Hannes. "Fischereiwesen und Aussenpolitik Islands. Ihr Einfluss auf das Seerecht." Diss., U of Vienna, Austria, 1980.

Nuechterlein, Donald E. *Iceland. Reluctant Ally.* Ithaca, N.Y.: Cornell UP, 1961.

VII. SCIENCE AND NATURE

1. *General*

Iceland: National Report to UNCED. Reykjavík: Ministry for the Environment, 1992.

OECD Environmental Performance Reviews: Iceland. Paris: OECD, 1993.

Reviews of National Science Policy: Iceland. Paris: OECD, 1983.

Review of National Science, Technology and Innovation Policy, Iceland
OECD, Committee for Scientific and Technological Policy. 2
vols. Paris : OECD, 1992.

2. Botany

Kristinsson, Hörður. *Flowering Plants and Ferns of Iceland.* Reykjavík:
Örn og Örlygur, 1987.

Löve, Áskell. *Flora of Iceland.* Reyjavík: Almenna bókafélagið, 1983.

Ostenfeld, C.A., and J. Grøntved. *The Flora of Iceland and the Faeroes.*
Copenhagen: Levin and Munksgaard, 1934.

Steindórsson, Steindór. *Contribution to the Plant Geography and Flora
of Iceland.* Reykjavík, 1935.

3. Geography

Ahlmann, Hans W., and Sigurður Þórarinsson. *Vatnajökull. Scientific
Results of the Swedish-Icelandic Investigations 1936–40.*
Stockholm: Geographiske annaler, 1943.

Friðriksson, Sturla. *Surtsey. Evolution of Life on a Volcanic Island.*
London: Butterworth, 1975.

Gísladóttir, Guðrún. *Geographical Analysis of Natural and Cultural
Landscape: Methodological Study in Southwestern Iceland.*
Stockholm: Stockholms U, 1993.

Preusser, Hubertus. *The Landscapes of Iceland: Types and Regions.* The
Hague: W. Junk, 1976.

Malmström, Vincent H. *A Regional Geography of Iceland.* Washington: National Academy of Sciences, National Research Council,
1958.

Roberts, Brian B. *Iceland.* London: Geographic Handbook Series, 1942.

Þorsteinsson, Björn. *Thingvellir: Iceland's National Shrine.* Reykjavík:
Örn og Örlygur, 1987.

4. *Geology*

Annels, Alwyn Ernest. "The Geology of Hornafjörður Region, Southwest Iceland." Diss., Imperial College, London, 1967.

Árnason, Bragi. *Groundwater Systems in Iceland Traced by Deuterium.* Vísindafélag Íslendinga 33. Reykjavík: Vísindafélag Íslend-inga, 1975.

Áskelsson, Jóhannes. *A Contribution to the Geology of Kerlingafjöll.* Reykjavík: Náttúrufræðistofnun Íslands, 1946.

Áskelsson, Jóhannes, G. Böðvarsson, T. Einarsson, G. Kjartansson, and Sigurður Þórarinsson. *On the Geology and Geophysics of Iceland: A Guide to Excursion no A2.* Reykjavík: Museum of Natural History, 1960.

Barth, Thomas F. W. *Volcanic Geology: Hot Springs and Geysers of Iceland.* Washington: Carnegie Institution of Washington, 1950.

Einarsson, Þorleifur. *Geology of Iceland: Rocks and Landscape.* Reykjavík: Mál og menning, 1994.

Friðriksson, Sturla. *Surtsey: Evolution of Life on a Volcanic Island.* London: Butterworth, 1975.

Guðmundsson, Ari Trausti, et al. *Guide to the Geology of Iceland.* Reykjavík: Örn og Örlygur, 1984.

Hallsdóttir, Margrét. *Pollen Analytical Studies of Human Influence on Vegetation in Relation to the Landnam Tephra Layer in Southwest Iceland (Holocene).* Lund: Lund U, 1987.

Hróarsson, Björn, and Sigurður S. Jónsson. *Geysers and Hot Springs in Iceland.* Reykjavík: Mál og menning, 1992.

Hug-Fleck, Christof. *Islands Geologie.* Kiel: Conrad Stein Verlag, 1988.

Jacoby, W., A. Björnsson, and D. Möller, eds. *Iceland: Evolution, Active Tectonics, and Structure.* Berlin: Springer, 1980.

Jóhannesson, Björn. *The Soils of Iceland.* Reykjavík: U Research Institute, 1960.

Maizels, Judith, and Chris Caseldine, eds. *Environmental Change in Iceland: Past and Present.* Dordrecht: Kluwer Academic, 1991.

Þórarinsson, Sigurður. *Hekla. A Notorious Volcano.* Reykjavík: Almenna bókafélagið, 1970.

Þórarinsson, S., Þ. Einarsson, and G. Kjartansson. "On the Geology and Geomorphology of Iceland." *Geografiska annaler* 41 (1959): 135–169.

5. Meteorology

Gunnarsson, Gísli. *A Study of Causal Relations in Climate and History with Emphasis on the Icelandic Experience.* Meddelande från Ekonomisk-historiska institutionen 17. Lund: Lund U, 1980.

Ogilvie, Astrid E. J. "Climate and Society in Iceland from the Medieval Period to the Late Eighteenth Century." Diss., U of East Anglia, 1981.

6. Zoology and Ornithology

Bárðarson, Hjálmar R. *Birds of Iceland.* Reykjavík: Hjálmar R. Bárðarson, 1986.

Breuil, Michel. *Les oiseaux d'Islande: Ecologie et biogeographie.* Paris: Lechavlier, Chabaud, 1989.

Einarsson, Þorsteinn. *Guide to the Birds of Iceland.* Reykjavík: Örn og Örlygur, 1991.

Hersteinsson, Páll. "The Behavioural Ecology of Arctic Foxes (Alopx Lagopus) in Iceland." Diss., U of Dundee, 1984.

Jónsson, Örn D., ed. *Whales and Ethics.* Reykjavík: U of Iceland, Fisheries Research Institute, 1992.

Nielsen, Ólafur Karl. "Population Ecology of the Gyrfalcon in Iceland with Comparative Notes on the Merlin and the Raven." Diss., Cornell U, 1986.

Sæmundsson, Bjarni. *Synopsis of the Fishes of Iceland.* Reykjavík: Vísindafélag Íslendinga, 1927.

The Zoology of Iceland. 1– (Cpenhagen: Munksgaard,1937–).

VIII. SOCIETY

1. *Anthropology*

Björnsdóttir, Inga Dóra. "Nationalism, Gender and the Contemporary Icelandic Women's Movement." Diss., U of California, Santa Barbara, 1992.

Björnsson, Árni. *Icelandic Feasts and Holidays: Celebrations, Past and Present.* Reykjavík: Iceland Review, 1980.

Bredahl-Petersen, Frederik E. "Family Organization in Rural Iceland." Diss., U of Edinburgh, 1973.

Durrenberger, E. Paul. *The Dynamics of Medieval Iceland: Political Economy and Literature.* Iowa City: U of Iowa P, 1992.

Durrenberger, E. Paul, and Gísli Pálsson, eds. *The Anthropology of Iceland.* Iowa City: U of Iowa P, 1989.

Hastrup, Kirsten. *Culture and History in Medieval Iceland: An Anthropological Analysis of Structure and Change.* Oxford: Oxford UP, 1985.

———. *Island of Anthropology: Studies in Past and Present Iceland.* Odense: Odense UP, 1990.

———. *Nature and Policy in Iceland 1400–1800: An Anthropological Analysis of History and Mentality.* Oxford: Oxford UP, 1990.

Koester, David C. "Historical Consciousness in Iceland." Diss., Chicago U, 1990.

Kristmundsdóttir, Sigríður Dúna. "Doing and Becoming: Women's Movements and Women's Personhood in Iceland 1870–1990." Diss., U of Rochester, 1990.

Magnússon, Finnur. *The Hidden Class: Culture and Class in a Maritime Setting, Iceland 1880–1942.* North Atlantic Monographs 1. Århus: Århus UP, 1990.

Pálsson, Gísli. *Coastal Economies, Cultural Accounts: Human Ecology and Icelandic Discourse.* Manchester: Manchester UP, 1991.

_____. *The Textual Life of Savants: Ethnography, Iceland and the Linguistic Turn.* Basel: Harwood, 1995.

Pálsson, Gísli, ed. *From Sagas to Society: Comparative Approaches to Early Iceland.* Enfield Lock: Hisarlik, 1992.

Rich, George W. "Core Values, Organizational Preferences, and Children's Games in Akureyri, Iceland." Diss., U of California, Davis, 1976.

Turner, Victor. "An Anthropological Approach to the Icelandic Saga." In *The Translation of Culture: Essays to E. E. Evans-Prithchard,* edited by T. O. Beidelman, 349–374. London: Tavistock, 1971.

2. *Education*

Classification of Educational Systems in OECD Member Countries: Iceland, New Zealand, Portugal. Paris: OECD, 1975.

Guðbjörnsdóttir, Guðný. "Cognitive Development, Gender Class and Education: A Longitudinal Study of Icelandic Early and Late Cognitive Developers." Diss., U of Leeds, 1987.

Guðmundsson, Reynir. "Media Education in the City of Reykjavík, Iceland." Diss., Boston U, 1984.

Gunnarsson, Þorsteinn V. "Controlling Curriculum Knowledge: A Documentary Study of the Icelandic Social Science Project (SSCP), 1974–1984." Diss., Ohio U, 1990.

Hansen, Börkur. "Secondary School Reorganization in Iceland: A Policy Analysis." Diss., U of Alberta, 1987.

Hanson, George. "Icelandic Education: Tradition and Modernization in a Cultural Perspective." Diss., Loyola U of Chicago, 1979.

Hilmarsson, Eiríkur. "The Role of Education in the Icelandic Labor Market." Diss., U of Wisconsin, 1989.

Jóhannesson, Ingólfur Á. "The Formation of Educational Reform as a

Social Field in Iceland and the Social Strategies of Educationists 1966–1991." Diss., U of Wisconsin, 1991.

Jósepsson, Bragi S. "Education in Iceland: Its Rise and Growth with Respect to Social, Political and Economic Determinants." Diss., George Peabody College for Teachers, 1968.

Jósepsson, Bragi S., ed. *Current Laws on Compulsory Education and School System in Iceland.* Reykjavík: Icelandic College of Education, 1986.

Óskarsdóttir, Gerður G. *Education in Iceland.* Reykjavík: Ministry of Education, 1991.

_____. *The Forgotten Half: Comparison of Dropouts and Graduates in Their Early Work Experience: The Icelandic Case.* Reykjavík: Social Science Research Institute, U of Iceland, 1995.

Pálsson, Hreinn. "Educational Saga: Doing Philosophy with Children in Iceland." Diss., Michigan State U, 1987.

Proppé, Ólafur Jóhann. "A Dialectical Perspective on Evaluation as Evolution: A Critical View of Assessment in Icelandic Schools." Diss., U of Illinois, 1982.

Sigurðsson, Jón. "Keeping Abreast of the Times: A Report of a Transformation of an Icelandic College in the Context of Educational Administration and of Instructional Methodology." Diss., Columbia Pacific U, 1990.

Trial, George T. *History of Education in Iceland.* Cambridge: Heffer, 1945.

3. *Health*

Björnsdóttir, Kristín. "Private Lives in Public Places: A Study in the Ideological Foundation of Nursing in Iceland." Diss., Columbia U, 1992.

Helgason, Lárus. *Psychiatric Services and Mental Illness in Iceland. Incidence Study (1966–1967) With 6–7 Year Follow-up.* Acta psychiatrica Scandinavica, suppl. 268. Copenhagen: Munksgaard, 1977.

Helgason, Tómas. *Epidemiology of Mental Disorders in Iceland. A Psychiatric and Demographic Investigation of 5,395 Icelanders.* Copenhagen: Munksgaard, 1964.

Jensson, Ólafur. *Studies on Four Hereditary Blood Disorders in Iceland.* Reykjavík: Landsspítalinn, 1978.

Jónsson, Vilmundur. *Health in Iceland.* Reykjavík: n.p. 1940.

Magnússon, Hallgrímur. *Mental Health of Octogenarians in Iceland. An Epidemiological Study.* Copenhagen: Munksgaard, 1989.

Samúelsson, Sigurður. *Tuberculosis in Iceland: Epidemiological Studies.* Washington, D.C.: U.S. Public Health Service, 1950.

4. Migration and Urbanization

Jónsdóttir, Salvör, and Hermannsson, Nanna. *Iceland. Reykjavík.* Scandinavian Atlas of Historical Towns 6. Reykjavík and Odense: Árbæjarsafn and Odense UP, 1988.

Reynarsson, Bjarni. "Residential Mobility, Life Cycle Stages, Housing and the Changing Social Patterns in Reykjavík 1974 to 1976." Diss., U of Illinois, 1980.

5. Religion

Aðalsteinsson, Jón Hnefill. *Under the Cloak: The Acceptance of Christianity in Iceland with Particular Reference to the Religious Attitudes Prevailing at the Time.* Studia Ethnologica Uppsaliensia 4. Uppsala: Uppsala U, 1978.

Bradshaw, Robert. *The Catholic Church Returns to Iceland. (Mid-19th Century).* Privately printed, 1991.

Björnsson, Björn. *The Lutheran Doctrine of Marriage in Modern Icelandic Society.* Oslo: Universitetsforlaget, 1971.

Kirby, Ian J. *Biblical Quotations in Old Icelandic-Norwegian Religious Literature.* 2 vols. Reykjavík: Stofnun Árna Magnússonar, 1976–1980.

212 / VIII. Society

Þórðarson, Steindór B. "A Study of Factors Related to the Numerical Growth of the Seventh-Day Adventist Church in Iceland From 1950 to 1980." Diss., Andrew U, 1985.

6. Sociology

Björnsson, Sigurjón, and Wolfgang Edelstein. *Exploration in Social Inquiry: Stratification, Dynamics and Individual Development in Iceland.* Berlin: Max Planck Institute, 1977.

Einarsson, Ingimar. *Patterns of Societal Development in Iceland.* Uppsala: Uppsala U, 1987.

Gíslason, Ingólfur V. *Enter the Bourgeoisie: Aspects of the Formation and Organization of Icelandic Employers 1894–1934.* Lund: Lund U, 1990.

Kristinsdóttir, Guðrún. *Child Welfare and Professionalization.* Umeå Social Work Studies, 15. Umeå: Umeå U, 1991.

Ólafsson, Stefán. *The Making of the Icelandic Welfare State: A Scandinavian Comparison.* Reykjavík: The Social Science Research Institute, U of Iceland, 1989.

_____. "Modernization and Social Stratification in Iceland." Diss., Oxford U, 1982.

Pétursson, Pétur. *Church and Social Change. A Study of the Secularization Process in Iceland 1830–1930.* Lund: Plus Ultra, 1983.

Tomasson, R., *Iceland: The First New Society.* Minneapolis, Minn.: U of Minnesota P, 1980.

Þórlindsson, Þórólfur. "Social Organization, Role-Taking, Elaborated Language, and Moral Judgment in an Icelandic Setting." Diss., U of Iowa, 1977.

About the Author

GUÐMUNDUR HÁLFDANARSON (B.A. University of Iceland and Lund University, Sweden; Cand.Mag. University of Iceland; Ph.D. Cornell University) is an Associate Professor of History in the Department of History at the University of Iceland, and chairman of the International Relations Committee of the University. He is an expert in European social history, specializing in theories and practices of nationalism. His doctoral dissertation, "Old Provinces, Modern Nations: Political Responses to State-Integration in Late Nineteenth and Early Twentieth-Century Brittany," is a comparative study on two European regions in a period of state formation. He has written extensively on his fields of expertise in Icelandic and international journals.